macromedia®
FLASH®MX
2004

certified designer
study guide

What every Flash designer needs
to know to pass the Certified Flash MX
Designer Exam

James English

macromedia®
CERTIFIED
PROFESSIONAL PROGRAM

Macromedia Flash MX 2004 Certified Designer Study Guide
James English

Published by Macromedia Press, in association with Peachpit Press,
a division of Pearson Education.

Macromedia Press
1249 Eighth Street
Berkeley, CA 94710
510/524-2178
510/524-2221 (fax)
Find us on the World Wide Web at:
www.peachpit.com   www.macromedia.com

To report errors, please send a note to errata@peachpit.com

Copyright © 2005 by James English

Macromedia Press Editor: Angela C. Kozlowski
Technical Editor: Mike Lyda
Production Coordinator: Myrna Vladic
Copy Editor: Barb Terry
Index: Rebecca Plunkett
Cover and Interior Design: Maureen Forys, Happenstance Type-O-Rama
Page Layout: David Van Ness

ISBN 0-321-22366-7

9 8 7 6 5 4 3 2 1

Printed and bound in the United States of America

ACKNOWLEDGEMENTS

I would like to take a moment to thank the people who helped in the production of this book; so much enthusiasm surrounded this project from so many sources that it made it a pleasure to write.

First, my thanks to the folks at Macromedia, who recommended me to Peachpit. I was rather flabbergasted, I have to admit, and it has been my goal to live up to the confidence that you showed in me by that much appreciated suggestion.

Second, I would like to thank Nilson Neuschotz, the owner of Motion Over Time, and my employer. It's not very often that you have an employer that not only allows you to work on a personal project during office hours, and rarer yet is the employer who is actually enthusiastic about it. He is a joy to work with, and something of a kindred soul.

Special thanks to James Talbot, Sue Hove, Robert Crooks, Jeanette Stallons, and Matt Boles for the wonderful courseware they've all produced. As in science, we build from the work of others, and without their work, this book would have been lacking.

Thank you to ML, my tech editor, who kept me honest.

Finally, my thanks to Angela, a patient editor to say the least. I've never actually met Angela in person, but after having spoken on the phone, and corresponded by email, I'd be willing to bet that she smiles a lot. And any editor that can smile is a blessing to any author, especially moody authors used to writing fiction.

Again, my thanks to all of the above people, and those of you I didn't mention, and who would want to remain nameless at that. Thank you for reminding me about priorities. You're in my thoughts, lest you feel otherwise, and you know who you are.

CONTENTS AT A GLANCE

Introduction   *xvii*

PART 1   The Basics of Flash MX 2004   1

    CHAPTER 1   Considerations   3

    CHAPTER 2   Content and Structure   9

    CHAPTER 3   The Interface   15

    CHAPTER 4   The Structure of Flash MX 2004   21

    CHAPTER 5   Flash MX 2004 Tools   29

    CHAPTER 6   Panels   41

    CHAPTER 7   The Flash Player   53

PART 2   Artwork, Text, and Organization   61

    CHAPTER 8   Laying Out Your Project   63

    CHAPTER 9   Organizational Tools and Where to Find Them   71

    CHAPTER 10   Layers and the Timeline   79

    CHAPTER 11   Bitmap and Vector Artwork   87

    CHAPTER 12   Using Artwork Created Elsewhere   95

    CHAPTER 13   Working with Vector Art   101

    CHAPTER 14   Using Text   109

    CHAPTER 15   Breaking Up a Project   121

PART 3   Symbols in Depth   131

    CHAPTER 16   Graphic and Font Symbols   133

    CHAPTER 17   Button Symbols   141

    CHAPTER 18   The Movie Clip Symbol   151

    CHAPTER 19   Components   163

PART 4 Animation   **173**

    CHAPTER 20 Animation Basics   175

    CHAPTER 21 Motion Tweening   181

    CHAPTER 22 Shape Tweening   189

    CHAPTER 23 Animating with ActionScript   195

PART 5 Sound and Video   **201**

    CHAPTER 24 Sound   203

    CHAPTER 25 Video   213

PART 6 ActionScript and Behaviors   **221**

    CHAPTER 26 The Behaviors Panel   223

    CHAPTER 27 The Actions Panel   229

    CHAPTER 28 The Basics of ActionScript   237

PART 7 Optimization and Publishing   **245**

    CHAPTER 29 Optimizing Your Flash Application 247

    CHAPTER 30 Publishing   255

PART 8 Appendix   **267**

    APPENDIX A Answers   269

    Index   *281*

CONTENTS

Introduction   *xvii*

PART 1   The Basics of Flash MX 2004   **1**

CHAPTER 1 Considerations   **3**
Flash Design Considerations   3
Making a Site Map   4
Determining Site Dimensions   5
Navigational Conventions   6
Summary   7
Sample Questions   8

CHAPTER 2 Content and Structure   **9**
Static Content   9
Dynamic Content   10
Structuring Your Application   10
Summary   13
Sample Questions   14

CHAPTER 3 The Interface   **15**
The Start Screen   15
Panels and Menus   16
The Property Inspector   17
The Timeline   17
The Layer Pane   18
The Stage   18
The Edit Bar   19
The Flash Player   19
Summary   19
Sample Questions   20

CHAPTER 4 The Structure of Flash MX 2004   **21**
Basic Documents   21
Slide Presentations   22
Form Applications   22
Templates   23
Your Own Template   24
Symbols   24
Components   25

Scenes 26
Publish Settings 26
Summary 27
Sample Questions 27

CHAPTER 5 Flash MX 2004 Tools 29
Selection Tools 29
Drawing Tools 32
Transform Tools 35
Other Tools 38
Summary 38
Sample Questions 39

CHAPTER 6 Panels 41
Design Panels 41
  The Align Panel 41
  The Color Mixer Panel 42
  The Color Swatches Panel 43
  The Info Panel 43
  The Scene Panel 44
  The Transform Panel 45
Development Panels 45
  The Actions Panel 45
  The Behaviors Panel 45
  The Components Panel 46
  The Component Inspector Panel 46
  The Debugger Panel 47
  The Output Panel 47
  The Web Services Panel 48
Other Panels 49
  The Accessibility Panel 49
  The History Panel 50
  The Movie Explorer Panel 50
  The Strings Panel 51
  Common Libraries 51
Summary 51
Sample Questions 52

CHAPTER 7 The Flash Player 53
Flash Player Settings 53
Printing 54
Quality 57
Magnification and Playback 58

Summary 58
Sample Questions 59

PART 2 Artwork, Text, and Organization 61

CHAPTER 8 Laying Out Your Project 63
Creating a Template 63
Rulers 65
Using Guides 66
Using Guide Layers 66
Using and Editing the Grid 67
Summary 68
Sample Questions 68

CHAPTER 9 Organizational Tools and Where to Find Them 71
The Library 71
Shared Libraries and Symbols 72
The Layer Pane in Brief 74
The Timeline in Brief 75
The Movie Explorer 76
The Info Panel 76
Summary 77
Sample Questions 77

CHAPTER 10 Layers and the Timeline 79
Adding and Removing Layers 79
Organizing Layers 81
Layer Types 81
The Timeline 83
The Playhead 83
Frames and Keyframes 83
Nested Timelines 85
Summary 85
Sample Questions 85

CHAPTER 11 Bitmap and Vector Artwork 87
Bitmap Art 87
Vector Artwork 88
Using Trace Bitmap 89
Roundtrip Editing 90
Swapping Bitmaps 90
Runtime JPGs 91
Summary 93
Sample Questions 93

CHAPTER 12 Using Artwork Created Elsewhere ... 95
What Can Be Imported? ... 95
Import Options ... 96
Importing and Editing Bitmap Artwork ... 97
Importing and Editing Vector Artwork ... 98
Importing Fireworks PNGs ... 98
Importing PDF and EPS Files ... 99
Summary ... 99
Sample Questions ... 99

CHAPTER 13 Working with Vector Art ... 101
Drawing in Flash ... 101
Manipulating Your Graphics ... 102
Using the Color Mixer ... 104
Using the Fill Transform Tool ... 105
Making Your Own Color Swatches ... 106
Summary ... 107
Sample Questions ... 108

CHAPTER 14 Using Text ... 109
The Different Types of Text ... 109
Adding Static Text ... 109
Breaking Text Apart ... 111
Using Input Text ... 112
Using Dynamic Text ... 114
Text Components ... 116
TextArea ... 116
TextInput ... 117
Label ... 117
Font Issues ... 118
Summary ... 119
Sample Questions ... 120

CHAPTER 15 Breaking Up a Project ... 121
Breaking a Project into Multiple SWFs ... 121
Loading an SWF into a Movie Clip ... 122
Loading an SWF into Levels ... 125
Preloaders ... 126
Runtime Sharing ... 127
Summary ... 128
Sample Questions ... 129

PART 3 Symbols in Depth   131

    CHAPTER 16 Graphic and Font Symbols   133
    Graphic Symbols Explained   133
    Creating a Graphic Symbol   134
    Using a Graphic Symbol   135
    Editing a Graphic Symbol   136
    Graphic Symbol Capabilities and Limitations   137
    The Font Symbol   138
    Summary   139
    Sample Questions   139

    CHAPTER 17 Button Symbols   141
    Button Symbols Explained   141
    Creating Buttons   142
    Creating More Complex Buttons   144
    ActionScript and Buttons   145
        ActionScript   147
    Button Best Practices   149
    Summary   149
    Sample Questions   150

    CHAPTER 18 The Movie Clip Symbol   151
    Movie Clips Symbols Explained   151
    Creating a Movie Clip   151
    Movie Clip Timelines   153
    Movie Clip Properties   155
    Movie Clip Methods   156
    Movie Clip Events   157
    ActionScript and the Movie Clip   158
        From the Behaviors Panel   158
        Adding Actions from the Actions Panel   159
    Summary   161
    Sample Questions   161

    CHAPTER 19 Components   163
    Component Types   163
    Changing Component Parameters   165
    Adding Data to Components   168
    Changing Component Appearance   169
    Handling Events on Components   170
    Summary   171
    Sample Questions   171

PART 4 Animation　　　　　　　　　　　　　　　　　　　**173**

CHAPTER 20 Animation Basics　　　　　　　　　　　**175**
The Three Animation Types　　　　　　　　　　　　　175
Necessary Items　　　　　　　　　　　　　　　　　176
Onion Skinning　　　　　　　　　　　　　　　　　178
Summary　　　　　　　　　　　　　　　　　　　179
Sample Questions　　　　　　　　　　　　　　　　180

CHAPTER 21 Motion Tweening　　　　　　　　　　　**181**
What Can Be Motion Tweened?　　　　　　　　　　　181
Setting Up　　　　　　　　　　　　　　　　　　182
Turning On the Tween　　　　　　　　　　　　　　183
Tween Settings　　　　　　　　　　　　　　　　　185
Motion Guides　　　　　　　　　　　　　　　　　185
Mask Effects　　　　　　　　　　　　　　　　　　187
Summary　　　　　　　　　　　　　　　　　　　187
Sample Questions　　　　　　　　　　　　　　　　188

CHAPTER 22 Shape Tweening　　　　　　　　　　　**189**
What Can Be Shape Tweened?　　　　　　　　　　　189
Setting Up　　　　　　　　　　　　　　　　　　190
Shape Tween Settings　　　　　　　　　　　　　　191
Shape Hints　　　　　　　　　　　　　　　　　　192
Summary　　　　　　　　　　　　　　　　　　　193
Sample Questions　　　　　　　　　　　　　　　　193

CHAPTER 23 Animating with ActionScript　　　　　　**195**
What Can Be Animated with ActionScript?　　　　　　195
Using the onEnterFrame Event　　　　　　　　　　　196
Using the setInterval Event　　　　　　　　　　　　198
Summary　　　　　　　　　　　　　　　　　　　199
Sample Questions　　　　　　　　　　　　　　　　199

PART 5 Sound and Video　　　　　　　　　　　　　　**201**

CHAPTER 24 Sound　　　　　　　　　　　　　　　**203**
Adding Sound to Your Application　　　　　　　　　203
Sound Settings　　　　　　　　　　　　　　　　　206
Sound Events　　　　　　　　　　　　　　　　　208
The Sound Object　　　　　　　　　　　　　　　　208
Summary　　　　　　　　　　　　　　　　　　　210
Sample Questions　　　　　　　　　　　　　　　　210

CHAPTER 25 Video   **213**
Importing Video   213
Adding Video to the Timeline   215
Using Media Components   216
Embedded Video Behaviors   218
Summary   219
Sample Questions   219

PART 6   ActionScript and Behaviors   **221**

CHAPTER 26 The Behaviors Panel   **223**
Behaviors   223
Behavior Categories   224
Adding and Removing Behaviors   225
Summary   226
Sample Questions   227

CHAPTER 27 The Actions Panel   **229**
How the Panel is Organized   229
Using Panel Features   230
Using the Panel to Get Reference Information   232
Using the Panel to Set Preferences   233
Summary   234
Sample Questions   235

CHAPTER 28 The Basics of ActionScript   **237**
Object-Oriented Programming   237
Basic ActionScript Syntax   238
Variables   240
Functions   241
Attaching ActionScript to a Timeline   242
Adding ActionScript to an Object   243
Summary   243
Sample Questions   244

PART 7   Optimization and Publishing   **245**

CHAPTER 29 Optimizing Your Flash Application   **247**
The Bandwidth Profiler   247
Font Considerations   249
Sound Considerations   249
Video Considerations   251
Bitmap Images   251

Vector Shapes   252
Using Multiple SWFs   252
Using Shared Resources   252
Summary   253
Sample Questions   253

CHAPTER 30 Publishing   **255**
Publish Settings   255
Flash Considerations   257
HTML Considerations   259
HTML Code   262
Flash Player Detection   263
Publish Profiles   264
Summary   264
Sample Questions   265

PART 8   Appendix   **267**

APPENDIX A Answers   **269**
Chapter 1   269
Chapter 2   269
Chapter 3   270
Chapter 4   270
Chapter 5   270
Chapter 6   271
Chapter 7   271
Chapter 8   271
Chapter 9   272
Chapter 10   272
Chapter 11   272
Chapter 12   273
Chapter 13   273
Chapter 14   274
Chapter 15   274
Chapter 16   274
Chapter 17   275
Chapter 18   275
Chapter 19   276
Chapter 20   276

Chapter 21   276
Chapter 22   277
Chapter 23   277
Chapter 24   277
Chapter 25   278
Chapter 26   278
Chapter 27   278
Chapter 28   279
Chapter 29   279
Chapter 30   279

Index   *281*

IN THIS INTRODUCTION

What Is the Certified Flash Designer
    Exam? xvii

The Macromedia Certified Professional
    Program xvii

Reasons to Get Certified xviii

About the Exam xviii

How to Use This Book xx

Where to Go From Here xxiii

Introduction

What Is the Certified Flash Designer Exam?

The popularity of Macromedia's products continues to grow and, along with them, so has the demand for experienced designers. Once upon a time (in Internet time, that is), claiming to be a Flash designer was easy; the product was simple enough that with a minimal investment of time and energy, designers could realistically consider themselves experts.

This is not the case anymore. The Macromedia product line has grown in both breadth and complexity, and the levels of expertise and experience among designers are diverse. Claiming to be an expert isn't that easy, and recognizing legitimate expertise is even harder.

The Macromedia Certified Professional Program

This is where certification comes into play. Formal, official certification by Macromedia helps to mark a threshold that explicitly sets apart designers by their knowledge and experience, making it possible to identify the true experts.

The Certified Flash MX Designer certification is one in a series of certification tracks from Macromedia. This one is aimed at designers using Macromedia Flash MX 2004. Other exams and certification programs being developed concentrate on other products and areas of expertise.

Reasons to Get Certified

There's really only one important reason for a Flash designer to become certified: Being able to call yourself a Macromedia Certified Flash MX 2004 Designer means you can command the respect and recognition that goes along with being one of the best at what you do.

Just as has happened with other products and technologies in this space, certification is likely to become a prerequisite for employers—an additional barometer by which to measure the potential of candidates and applicants.

Whether being certified helps you find a new or better job, helps persuade your boss that the pay raise you want is justified, helps you find new clients, or gets you listed on the Macromedia Web site so you can attract new prospects—whatever the reason—it will help you stand out from the crowd.

About the Exam

Becoming a Certified Flash MX 2004 Designer requires being tested on your knowledge of Flash MX 2004 and related technologies. As far as exams go, this one isn't easy—nor should it be. In fact, more than a third of all test takers fail their first exam. This is not a bad thing; on the contrary, it means that you really have to know your stuff to pass. You don't merely receive a paper certificate; the exam and subsequent certification have real value and real significance. "Very challenging but fair" is how many examinees describe the exam itself.

How You'll Take the Exam

The exam is a set of multiple-choice and true/false questions that you answer electronically. A computer application issues the test to you, and you'll know whether you passed immediately upon test completion.

In the test you're presented with each question and the possible answers. Some questions have a single correct answer, while others have two or more (you'll be told how many answers to provide). If a question stumps you, you can skip it and come back to it later.

After you have answered all the questions, you can review them to check your answers. After you're done, or after the 70-minute time limit is up, you get your results. You need to have at least 75 percent correct to pass and achieve certification. If you don't pass, you need to wait at least 30 days before you can try taking the test again. You may take the test no more than three times in a single year, starting from the date of your first test.

You will be required to pay the full exam fee each time you take the certification exam.

What You'll Be Tested On

Being a Flash MX 2004 expert requires knowing more than just how to use all the menu items. As such, the exam includes questions on related technologies. You will be tested on the following subjects:

- Project architecture, page and interface layout
- Effective visual design and scripting
- Effective motion design and ActionScript
- Effective optimization and output design

Every question counts, and you can't assume that one particular topic is more or less significant than the others. You need to know it all, and you need to know it all well.

Preparing for the Exam

The most important preparation for the exam is using Flash MX 2004 itself. If you don't use it regularly or haven't done so for an extended period, you probably won't pass the exam.

Having said that, we can tell you that many experienced Flash designers still find the exam challenging. Usually, they say this is because they don't use some features and technologies, or because they learned the product but never paid attention to changing language and feature details (and thus are not using the product as effectively as they could be).

This is where this book fits in. This book is not a cheat sheet. It won't teach you Flash from scratch, nor will it give you a list of things to remember to pass the test. What it will do is help you systematically review every feature and technology in the product—everything you need to know to pass the test.

Where to Take the Exam

To offer the exams worldwide, in as many locations as possible, Macromedia has partnered with a company called VUE, which offers exams and certification programs for a wide range of companies and products, and has more than 2,500 regional testing facilities in more than 100 countries.

You can take the Macromedia Flash MX 2004 Designer exam at any VUE testing center. For a current list of locations, visit the Web site:

```
http://www.vue.com/macromedia/
```

How Much It Costs

The fee to take the exam in North America is $150 (U.S.). Pricing in other countries varies. The fee must be paid at the time you register for the exam. If you need to cancel, you must do so at least 24 hours before the exam, or the fee will not be refunded.

How to Use This Book

This book is designed to be used in two ways:

- To prepare for your exam, you should start at the beginning of the book and systematically work your way through it. The book flow, layout, and form-factor have all been designed to make reviewing content as pleasant an experience as possible. The content has been designed to be highly readable and digestible in small, bite-size chunks so that it will feel more like reading than studying.

- After you have reviewed all the content, reread the topics that you feel you need extra help brushing up on. Topics are all covered in highly focused and very manageable chapters so that you can easily drill down to the exact content you need. Extensive cross-referencing lets you read up on related topics as needed.

After the exam, you'll find that the style and design of this study guide make it an invaluable desktop reference tool as well.

Contents

The book is divided into four parts, each containing a set of highly focused chapters. Each chapter concludes with a summary and sample questions (the answers are in Appendix A).

Part I: The Basics of Flash MX 2004

This part reviews the things you need to know before you even get started. It includes chapters on:

- Identifying your audience needs
- Determining what kind of content to use
- Interface and tools

Part 2: Artwork, Text, and Organization

This part reviews the use of visual assets, and how to organize your document. It includes chapters on:

- Bitmap and vector artwork
- Text
- Navigation strategies
- Tools

Part 3: Symbols in Depth

This part reviews re-usable symbols. It includes chapters on:

- Buttons
- Graphic symbols
- Movie clips
- Components

Part 4: Animation

This part reviews what you need to produce animations. It includes chapters on:

- Motion animation
- Shape animation
- Animating with ActionScript

Part 5: Sound and Video

This part reviews the use of sound and video in Flash. It includes chapters on:

- Sound
- Video

Part 6: ActionScript and Behaviors

This part reviews the usage of ActionScript, and how to add it to your document. It includes chapters on:

- Built in ActionScript behaviors
- ActionScript syntax and concepts

Part 7: Optimization and Publishing

This part reviews techniques for keeping your published files as small as possible, and the different ways a Flash document can be published. It includes chapters on:

- Optimization strategies
- Publishing

Conventions Used in This Book

The people at Macromedia Press have spent many years developing and publishing computer books designed for ease of use and containing the most up-to-date information available. With that experience, we've learned what features help you the most. Look for these features throughout the book to help enhance your learning experience and get the most out of Flash:

- Screen messages, code listings, and command samples appear in monospace type.

- URLs used to identify pages on the Web and values for Flash attributes also appear in monospace type.

- Terms that are defined in the text appear in *italics*. Italics are sometimes used for emphasis, too.

> **TIP**
> Tips give you advice on quick or overlooked procedures, including shortcuts.

> **NOTE**
> Notes present useful or interesting information that isn't necessarily essential to the current discussion, but that might augment your understanding with background material or advice relating to the topic.

➜ Cross-references are designed to point you to other locations in this book that will provide supplemental or supporting information.

The Web Site

To further assist you in preparing for the exam, this book has an accompanying Web site. The site contains the following:

- Any updated exam information
- Links to other exam-related sites
- Any book corrections or errata
- A sample interactive test that you can use to help gauge your own exam readiness

The Web site can be found at `www.forta.com/books/0321223667`.

Where to Go From Here

Now you're ready to get started. If you think you're ready for the exam, start with the sample questions in the book or online to verify your skills. If you're not ready—or if the same questions indicate that you might not be as ready as you thought—make sure you pay attention to the topics that you need to review by reading the documentation and actually writing appropriate applications.

When you're ready, work through this book to review the content and prepare for the exam itself as described here.

And with that, we wish you good luck!

PART 1

The Basics of Flash MX 2004

1 Considerations

2 Content and Structure

3 The Interface

4 The Structure of Flash MX 2004

5 Flash MX 2004 Tools

6 Panels

7 The Flash Player

CHAPTER 1

Considerations

IN THIS CHAPTER

Flash Design Considerations   3

Making a Site Map   4

Determining Site Dimensions   5

Navigational Conventions   6

Summary   7

Sample Questions   8

Macromedia Flash MX 2004 is an interactive design tool, which makes you the interactive designer. Interactive design is quite a bit different from print design, although in some circumstances the principles for both may overlap.

This chapter will review the things you need to consider as an interactive designer before you start to construct an application in Flash. We're talking about preplanning here, which is undoubtedly nothing new to you, but it never hurts to review a little.

Flash Design Considerations

At the start of every class I teach in Flash, I always ask one question: "What is the most important consideration in building your web site or Flash application?" Almost without fail, someone will answer, "What the web site or application is going to do." That's a good answer, but it isn't the best answer, and it always surprises me how many people overlook the most important aspect of designing an application or web site.

The answer should be: "Your audience is the most important consideration." The reason this is the best answer is because your audience will drive every aspect of your web site design, from the color choices you make to what the Flash application ultimately will or won't do. If you consider functionality over end user experience, you are immediately putting yourself at a disadvantage.

> **NOTE**
> Your audience will determine the content and the context of your web site. The designer will make content choices about what the web site will have to offer based on knowing the context of the site (who it's for, what it will do, etc).

> **TIP**
>
> End-user experience and functionality are intricately entwined. However, end-user experience should be the primary consideration of an interactive designer or user interface designer. The developer will then build in the actual functionality.

Good design is subjective. However, there are some common elements of good design. You should always be sure:

- Color choice is appropriate for your user demographic

- Color use is limited and consistent

- Navigation is easy to understand and consistent from section to section

- Navigation choices are limited to what is actually needed and do not crowd the screen

- Text is legible

- Animation is used when needed, only to add value

- Sound is used prudently and doesn't overwhelm the end user

- File size of SWFs is managed as much as possible through optimizing shapes, images, sounds, and video

- Large SWF downloads are mitigated by the use of preloaders

- Content is accessible to users with visual or auditory impairments, including color vision impairments

> **TIP**
>
> Usability is a word you'll often hear thrown around in interactive design. Usability means making your application simple, intuitive, and easy to use.

Once you've determined who, what, and why, it's time to start getting things constructed. That means building a roadmap.

Making a Site Map

Perhaps the most important planning step in creating a Flash-based web site is producing a site map. A site map details where a user starts, and where they go based on what they click. It's more or less a flow chart of SWFs, and how they relate to one another.

> **TIP**
>
> Your site map is the blueprint for construction. You'll want to build it in a way that you can edit it easily if things change, either while you're brainstorming or while you're developing.

Your site map details the structure of your web site, from what's in it, what's outside of it, and where everything goes from there. Your site map also reflects a best practice of limiting the amount of options a user has to go through in order to get the information they need.

➜ See Chapter 2, "Content and Structure," and Chapter 15, "Breaking Up a Project," for more information.

Determining Site Dimensions

Knowing your audience will help you to make decisions about the physical size of your Flash application. The physical size relates to a user's viewable area within a browser, which in turn is determined by their monitor resolution. While Flash applications are scaleable in a browser, you still want your design to be optimized for a particular monitor resolution.

> **NOTE**
>
> The smallest monitor resolution in wide use is 640 x 480.

No matter what size you make your application (in terms of width and height), you need to determine a browser-safe area, which is where most of the important information you want to present will appear. You can design in such a way that content appears outside of this area for your users with better screen resolutions. Anything outside of the browser-safe area can only be accessed by scrolling to it. The browser-safe area is the visual portion of a browser when its tool bars, scroll bars, and status bars are open. Scroll bars can take up 40 to 60 pixels of space. At 640 x 480, the browser-safe area would be in a 600 x 400 block.

When you have determined what monitor resolution you want and what your browser-safe area will be, mark off in your Flash document the boundaries that you'll have to work within. Remember, the browser-safe area is only where you want critical information to display in such a way that no user will have to scroll. Your document can certainly be bigger than the specific browser-safe area, but you'll still want to mark where that area is. You can use guides or guide layers to accomplish this task.

Guides are simply lines that you drag out of a ruler and on to the Stage to help you position visual assets, such as bitmaps and text.

To use guides, the ruler must be visible. To turn on the ruler, choose View > Ruler. To make a guide, press on the horizontal or vertical ruler and drag away. As you drag out of the ruler, your guide will appear, and can be placed anywhere you want along that axis. To get rid of the guide, drag it back into the ruler. Guides do not publish in the SWF.

Guide layers are special layers that also help in placement of graphics. Like guides, they do not publish in the SWF. You can use guide layers to draw content blocks to arrange your visual assets.

➔ For more information on guide layers, see Chapter 8, "Laying Out Your Project," and Chapter 10, "Layers and the Timeline."

NOTE

Don't forget that browser toolbars, scroll bars, and status bars take up space. You'll have to account for that when you build.

Navigational Conventions

Navigation is the beating heart of usability. It's what allows a user to get from A to B to complete tasks and look up information, and generally consists of buttons, location indication, and the hierarchy of the site.

NOTE

General, or global, navigation almost always indicates the main site areas that you can visit, and as a result, shows the site hierarchy almost by default.

Good navigation is intuitive to use and constant (meaning that the main navigation options appear in all sections). Navigation options should always appear in the same areas in your site to avoid disorienting your end user. For example, global navigation bars may show at the very top of the site at all times, global navigation may contain submenus that are the same no matter where you are in the site, and different sections may have their own secondary navigation options arranged in a table off to the left of the main content area.

TIP

Name your navigation options intuitively. Ambiguity is the archenemy of navigation.

The most common navigation bars you see in Flash are drop-down menus and tabbed menus (also called tab-down menus). You also see menu bars often. Which type you use depends on what kind of navigational elements your end users are accustomed to; in any case, the navigation structure should be clearly clickable, legible, and precise.

> **TIP**
>
> One of the ways to make something clearly clickable is to give it a rollover effect. This can be done with a standard button by placing graphics in button's up, over, and down states.

➡ For more information, see Chapter 17, "Button Symbols."

Apart from creating a navigation bar, you need a navigation strategy. This has a lot to do with how you create and organize content.

In the old days, people built all their content in different scenes on the timeline, and then jumped a user from scene to scene when buttons were clicked. Each scene contained some kind of unique content that made it appear as though the user was going to a different page. That's frowned on these days, and for good reason: it makes a piece difficult to update, long to download, and only one person at a time can work on the project.

A better strategy is to break your application into multiple SWFs that are called into the interface when a user clicks a button, and not before then. This keeps initial download times low (because only your navigation and front matter needs to download), doesn't force your user to wait for content not relevant to them, makes the site easier to update, and allows multiple people to work on the same project. It's similar in idea to making multiple HTML pages that load into a frameset.

> **NOTE**
>
> The two actions that load SWFs into the Flash Player are `loadMovie()`; and `loadMovieNum()`. The `loadMovie()` action loads SWFs into target movie clips inside an SWF, and `loadMovieNum()` loads SWFs into different levels of the Flash Player.

➡ See Chapter 15, "Breaking Up a Project," for more information.

Summary

Before starting a Flash project, it's important to identify your end users and determine their needs. End user needs will determine the content of the site, as well as the general layout and design.

Site maps are essentially blueprints that visually represent different areas of your site, and how they relate to each other. They should be easy to update to reflect changes both during the brainstorming process and the development process, as needed.

Site dimensions are determined by the end-user's most common screen resolution and viewable browser area. Guides and guide layers allow you to block off browser-safe areas while you're designing, in addition to specifying a stage height and width.

Navigation structures in Flash should be clear, intuitively named, and consistent from content area to content area. Flash projects should be broken up into multiple SWFs that can be called into the interface when a user clicks a button.

Sample Questions

1. Site maps (choose 2):

   A. Reflect the structure of your application

   B. Show all Graphic assets in your site

   C. Are not part of the planning process

   D. Show how content areas relate to one another

2. Site dimensions are determined by:

   A. Operating system

   B. End user connection speed

   C. Monitor resolution

   D. Macromedia

3. Navigation systems should:

   A. Be consistent and intuitive

   B. Only be pull-down menus

   C. Be subtle and out of the way

   D. Not use visual feedback

4. Which of the following is an element of good Flash design?

   A. Use lots of colors to make sites vivid and interesting

   B. Make heavy use of animation

   C. Use sound sparingly

   D. Have as many navigation choices as possible

CHAPTER 2

Content and Structure

IN THIS CHAPTER

Static Content   9

Dynamic Content   10

Structuring Your Application   10

Summary   13

Sample Questions   14

Macromedia Flash introduced a new way of doing things on the web. Not only did it allow you to add vector graphics and animations to a web site, but it really gave designers a way to free themselves from the restrictive environment of HTML and pursue more lofty goals. With the ability to animate and add interactivity in a light-weight file format, designers quickly started creating usable interfaces that made web sites much more than look-up tools or glorified brochures.

In this chapter, we're going to review the difference between static and dynamic content, as well as discuss a way to structure your application for optimal use.

Static Content

In Flash, static content is anything inherent to the application that is not being retrieved from some external source when the piece runs in a browser, over a network, or off a CD-ROM. This content is added to the application either by importing, drawing, or writing information in and can include text, sound, video, and bitmapped images. Granted, that pretty much covers anything that can be used in Flash.

Static text is text that is added by means of the text tool, and embedded in the SWF. You add static text visually by choosing the tool, and selecting the Static text option in the Property Inspector, then clicking and typing text out on the Stage.

Images are static when they're imported into Flash. Images are imported by choosing File > Import > Import to Stage or Import to Library. In either case a physical copy of a graphic is made, whether it's a JPG, GIF, or some vector format like a

Freehand file, and embedded in the document library. Likewise, sound and video are static if they're directly imported.

Static content is tedious to update, because it requires changes to the FLA file and republishing the SWF each time something needs to be altered. Additionally, static content results in higher file sizes, and limits what you can do with your Flash application.

Essentially, static content is stuff that can't be changed when the SWF actually runs. Dynamic content, on the other hand, can be changed when the SWF runs, and when users interact with the application.

Dynamic Content

Dynamic content includes anything that sits outside of the SWF and is retrieved when it's needed, or elements that can be changed by ActionScript when the SWF is running and users are interacting with it Dynamic content can be data stored in text fields, XML files, or databases. It can be JPG images, MP3 sounds, and FLV for-matted video. Finally, it can also be other SWFs.

There are a number of distinct advantages to having dynamic content that static content simply can't match:

- **Ease of updating.** Because the content is stored outside of the SWF, changes can be made without having to republish.

- **Smaller file sizes.** If it's not actually embedded in the Flash application, it can't increase file size, right? Of course, it will still need to download when it's needed, but this breaks things up and makes things generally easier to manage in the file size realm.

- **Personalization of the user experience.** Depending on how you load data, you can create a more personalized user experience. For instance, using XML files, you can allow a user to choose their language preference, load the XML file into the interface based on that choice, and not have to worry about developing entirely different SWFs!

Structuring Your Application

In Chapter 1 we reviewed site maps and what they do for us. Site maps provide us not only navigational options, but they also give us a way to structure our applica-tion sensibly. They show us where things are and where they go.

Your site map should include:

- SWFs being loaded dynamically into movie clips or levels
- MP3 sounds and FLV formatted video being streamed with a media component
- Text files being loaded with the `LoadVars` object

You should break your Flash application down into small content-based SWFs that are loaded into the interface when called. For instance, if you are creating a site about pets, you might have your navigation SWF, and then a series of other SWFs that will load into it: `cats.swf`, `dogs.swf`, `ferrets.swf`. Each one of those content categories may load external SWFs into themselves through their secondary navigation options, such as `nutrion.swf`, `grooming.swf`, and so forth. By breaking things down into smaller SWFs, you keep your download times to a minimum.

SWFs can be loaded into movie clips in a timeline using the `loadMovie()` action. They can also be loaded into levels in the Flash player using the `loadMovieNum()` action.

➡ See Chapter 15, "Breaking Up a Project," for more information.

> **NOTE**
>
> When possible, it is a good practice to load images, sounds, and text from external sources as well.

JPG images can be dynamically loaded into a movie clip on a timeline using the `loadMovie()` action. To load a JPG image into a movie clip, use the following syntax:

```
MovieClipInstance.loadMovie("pathToJpg");
```

> **NOTE**
>
> Dynamically loaded JPGs must be in the same domain as the SWF that calls them.

> **TIP**
>
> The JPGs you load cannot be progressive scan JPGs, or this won't work. When you use this feature, if there are contents in the Movie Clip, they'll be replaced. Also, the upper left corner of the JPG will be placed at the Movie Clip's registration point, which is the center of the Movie Clip (unless it's been otherwise modified).

Alternatively, you can load a JPG into a movie clip using

```
this.loadMovie("pathToJPG","targetMovieClip");
```

where this refers to the timeline the movie clip resides in or from which the action is being called.

> **TIP**
>
> Loading JPGs dynamically not only keeps your file size down, but it also allows you to update the images when needed without affecting the SWF.

> **NOTE**
>
> Of all the bitmap formats, only JPG images can be dynamically loaded.

MP3 sounds can be dynamically loaded in one of two ways: using the Sound object, or using a Media Component. To use the Sound object, you first have to create an instance of the Sound class, and then load the file into it. Use the following syntax:

```
var mySound:Sound=new Sound();
mySound.loadSound(url,isStreaming);
```

The URL is the location of the MP3 file on the server, and isStreaming is either true or false. When isStreaming is set to true, sounds will play as they download. When set to false, the sound must completely download before it will play, making it an event sound.

> **NOTE**
>
> All sounds loaded with the Sound object are stored in the browser's cache, whether or not they're set to stream, unless the server is configured to prevent browser caching.

> **NOTE**
>
> Only MP3 sounds can be loaded dynamically.

If isStreaming is set to false, the sound has to be told when to play with a frame script or with an object script.

➡ See Chapter 24, "Sound," for details.

> **TIP**
>
> By default, MP3 files must be in the same domain as the SWF that calls them.

> **NOTE**
>
> Domain restrictions can be lifted by means of a cross domain policy, which is an XML file placed on the server that allows SWFs from other domains to retrieve assets on the server. For more information, see `http://www.macromedia.com/software/flashplayer/security/faq.html`.

To load text files (.txt), you have to use the `LoadVars` object, which, like the Sound object, has to be instantiated. The text file has to be structured in a specific way. Here, however, we'll just take a look at the script that load the data:

```
var myLoadVars:LoadVars=new LoadVars();
myLoadVars.load(url);
```

That loads the context of the text file into memory. The text file must contain name and value information.

> **NOTE**
>
> By default, text files must be in the same domain as the SWF that calls them.

Remember, it's important to reflect where these elements are coming from and where they're going in your site map, which is the roadmap for your document structure. By planning it out in advance, and using as much dynamic content as you can, you'll make simple updates much easier, while at the same time improving your end-user experience.

Summary

Static content is anything that's embedded directly into your Flash document. Changing static content requires changing the FLA file, then republishing the SWF that will reside on the server.

Dynamic content is anything stored outside of the SWF, but called into the interface when the SWF plays in the browser. Text, MP3 Sounds, JPG images, and FLV formatted video can all be loaded dynamically. SWFs can also be loaded dynamically into target movie clips in a timeline, or into levels of the Flash Player.

Sample Questions

1. Which of the following statements is true?

    A. Bitmap images cannot be dynamically loaded.

    B. Changes to external content require SWFs to be republished.

    C. Use of dynamic content can result in smaller initial download times.

    D. Dynamic content can be called from any domain without restriction.

2. Static content (choose 2):

    A. Can be any visual asset

    B. Refers to static text only

    C. Does not change when users interact with the SWF

    D. Is never needed in Flash

3. The Action that loads SWFs into movie clips is:

    A. `getURL();`

    B. `loadMovieNum();`

    C. `createTextField();`

    D. `loadMovie();`

4. The `LoadVars` Object is used to:

    A. Load text files from the server

    B. Stream MP3 sounds

    C. Load JPG images into movie clips

    D. Create text fields programmatically

CHAPTER 3

The Interface

IN THIS CHAPTER

The Start Screen   15

Panels and Menus   16

The Property Inspector   17

The Timeline   17

The Layer Pane   18

The Stage   18

The Edit Bar   19

The Flash Player   19

Summary   19

Sample Questions   20

As of Flash MX 2004, the Flash product line has been split into two different versions: Flash MX 2004 and Flash MX Professional 2004. For the most part, the two products are identical, with two notable exceptions: Flash MX Professional 2004 comes with a new development mode making use of screens, and also comes with a number of components not offered with Flash MX 2004. If you've worked with Flash MX, you'll remember components as pre-built interface elements used for rapid development. In Flash MX 2004 and Professional, components have evolved quite extensively.

➡ For more information on components, see Chapter 19, "Components."

The interface for the two products is identical until you create an application using screens or slides. The difference reflects the focus of the two products. Flash MX 2004 is geared towards designers who will spend very little time working with the programmatic tools of Flash. Flash MX Professional 2004 is geared toward programmers and application developers who need not only the design tools, but also all the ActionScript tools and capabilities needed to develop a more complex application.

The Start Screen

The Start screen is visible when Flash is first started, or when no documents are open. It is split into three main sections, and two sub-sections. The three main sections include:

- **Open Recent Item.** Allows you to open projects that you've recently been working on or other documents entirely.

- **Create New.** Allows you to create from a number of different document types.

- **Create from Template.** Allows you to build from any one of the templates that come with the install.

The subsections are split into a section that will allow you to take a tutorial or tour of the interface and a section that allows you to download updates to Flash MX 2004. Finally, at the very bottom is a checkbox that allows you to disable the Start screen entirely.

> **TIP**
>
> You can turn the Start screen on in the Preferences dialog box. On the Mac, go to Flash Professional > Preferences or on the PC go to Edit > Preferences. Select the General tab, and in the On Launch Category, you can select Show Start Screen, New Document, Last Documents Open, or No Document. These actions will execute on the next launch of Flash.

Panels and Menus

The Flash MX 2004 interface is separated into toolbars, configuration panels, a document window, a timeline, and general pull-down menus that handle a number of tasks.

The pull-down menus are Flash MX or Flash Professional on the Mac, and File, Edit, View, Insert, Modify, Text, Commands, Control, Window, and Help on both Mac and Windows.

Flash replicates very nearly all the functionality built into the pull-down menus in the panels. The panels in Flash are functional, and allow a user to modify assets, use components, create colors, and configure different items. In addition, some panels, such as the Movie Explorer, help to locate assets as well as edit them.

➔ Panels are discussed in detail in Chapter 6, "Panels."

You can retrieve all the panels in the Window pull-down menu. The out-of-the-box panels are grouped into three categories:

- **Design Panels.** Align, Color Mixer, Color Swatches, Info, Scene, and Transform

- **Development Panels.** Actions, Behaviors, Components, Component Inspector, Debugger, Output, Web Services

- **Other Panels.** Accessibility, History, Movie Explorer, Strings, and Common Libraries

> **NOTE**
>
> Common Libraries contain a number of assets that come with Flash, including buttons, classes, and learning interactions.

Panels have a title bar, an Expand/Collapse button, an Options pull-down menu at the far right of the title bar, and the Gripper tool at the far left of the title bar. Selecting and dragging the Gripper allows panels to be dragged, docked, or rearranged within a group of docked panels. Any time a black outline appears as you drag a panel, it can be docked.

After arranging a panel in the preferred layout, you can save the layout. From the Window pull-down menu, select Save Panel Layout, and then name the layout. The new layout will show in the Window > Panel Layouts category, which also contains a default layout option and several training layout options. Selecting a layout option rearranges the panels to fit that layout.

You can use keyboard shortcuts to open some panels. The shortcuts are listed next to the panel titles in the Window pull-down menu.

> **TIP**
>
> Pressing F4 will hide and show all open panels, which is great when you're working with limited screen space or a single monitor.

The Property Inspector

The Property Inspector, one of the most important panels in Flash, is a context-sensitive panel, and allows you to change properties of selected assets quickly and easily. For instance, when you click on the main document window, the Property inspector changes to allow you to set document size, quickly change your publish settings, and change both the background color and frame rate of your document.

The Property inspector will also let you change properties for text, shapes, symbols, and components.

The Timeline

The timeline is an organizational tool that allows you to arrange content over time. The timeline itself is made up of layers, keyframes, frames, and the playhead. The content itself is organized in layers using keyframes and frames.

The timeline is also where you add and organize layers, since the Layers pane is integrated with it.

➡ See Chapter 10, "Layers and the Timeline," for more details.

The Layer Pane

The Layer pane is an organizational tool that allows you to arrange content. It is part of the timeline. A layer at the top of the Layer pane is closer to the user's eye, and a layer at the bottom of the Layer pane is in the background, or farther from the user's eye.

Every visual asset in a layer stacks; a stacking order is the relationship between objects that partially obscure each other, and is determined by the order in which they're drawn or added.

➡ Stacking order inside a layer is discussed more in Chapter 10, "Layers and the Timeline."

> **TIP**
>
> To change stacking order, choose Modify > Arrange and then select Bring to Front, Bring Forward, Send Backward, or Send to Back. This is only available for grouped objects and symbols, however.

The Layer pane allows you to add or remove layers, change the properties of certain layers, or organize layers within layer folders.

The Stage

The Stage is where you build your visual content. Surrounding the Stage is the gray work area. Unlike other programs, assets located off the Stage and in the work area are still visible in the editing environment (though not when produced). This allows you to produce animations that appear to "enter" and "exit" the Stage.

How you view the Stage depends on the development mode you're using. When you are making a blank Flash document, the Stage will appear as a large canvas. When you're using screens or slides, the Stage shifts to the right, and a Screen or Slide inspector appears to the left.

➡ You'll learn more about documents, screens, and slides in Chapter 4, "The Structure of Flash MX 2004."

The Edit Bar

The Edit bar is just underneath the menus in your main document window. The Edit bar tells you whether you're using edit in place mode for groups or symbols, allows you to switch to different scenes, and enables you to edit specific symbols.

➡ See Chapter 16, "Graphic and Font Symbols," Chapter 17, "Button Symbols," and Chapter 18, "The Movie Clip Symbol," for more on symbols.

At the far right of the Edit bar is a Zoom control that allows you to zoom in or out of the Stage. In addition to the preset numbers (25%, and so on), the control offers three other options:

- **Fit In Window.** Fits your entire Stage in the viewable window space.

- **Show Frame.** Displays the entire Stage.

- **Show All.** Shows the content of the current frame. If there is nothing in the frame, the entire Stage is shown.

> **NOTE**
> You can also use the Zoom tools, or select View > Zoom In, View > Zoom Out, or their keyboard shortcut equivalents.

The Flash Player

The Flash Player is the software that allows an end user to see the SWF files you produce. The Flash Player must be installed on an end user's computer for an SWF file to be read. SWF files not viewed through a web page are visible as long as the Flash Player is installed somewhere.

The current Flash Player is Version 7, which supports all the new features of Flash MX 2004. SWF files produced for earlier versions of the Flash Player will run in Flash Player 7.

You can access the Flash Player settings by right- or Control-clicking a running Flash application in a web page, or through the Flash Player's display menu.

You can download the Flash Player from the Macromedia web site for free.

➡ The Flash Player is detailed in Chapter 7, "The Flash Player."

Summary

The Flash MX 2004 authoring environment contains tools, panels, a document window, and pull-down menus. Tools allow you to add and modify assets. Panels allow you to change asset properties as well as organize content. Pull-down menus allow you to access panels as well as use additional configuration options.

The Flash Player is the software that allows an end user to see an SWF file. The player is currently in Version 7.

Sample Questions

1. How do you change the stacking order of graphics that are all within the same layer?

   A. Choose Edit, then Bring to Front, Bring Forward, Send Backward, or Send to Back.

   B. Select an asset and change its Z index on the Property Inspector.

   C. Choose Modify > Arrange, then Bring to Front, Bring Forward, Send Backward, or Send to Back.

   D. Stacking order inside a layer cannot be changed.

2. The context-sensitive panel that is used to change asset properties is:

   A. The Transform panel

   B. The Align panel

   C. The Document Title bar

   D. The Property inspector

3. The Gripper:

   A. Allows you to dock and undock panels

   B. Is the tool used to move the Stage and its contents around

   C. Is used to select objects

   D. None of the above

4. Which of the following Zoom choices fits the entire stage in the viewable window space (choose 2)?

   A. Window > Fit in Window

   B. Fit in Window from the Edit bar's Zoom menu

   C. Show All

   D. View > Magnification > Fit in Window

CHAPTER 4

The Structure of Flash MX 2004

IN THIS CHAPTER

Basic Documents   21

Slide Presentations   22

Form Applications   22

Templates   23

Your Own Template   24

Symbols   24

Components   25

Scenes   26

Publish Settings   26

Summary   27

Sample Questions   27

As of Flash MX 2004 and Flash MX Professional 2004, you have numerous options as to the type of Flash document you can create. Apart from the normal, run-of-the-mill Flash document, you can now create slide and form applications, external ActionScript files, ActionScript Communication files, Flash JavaScript files, and the Flash Project, discussed in a later project. This chapter focuses on basic documents, slides, and screen applications. This chapter also covers the critical building blocks of Flash. Documents are covered first, because they are the cornerstone of your application.

Basic Documents

As with all document types, you can create a new, basic Flash document directly from the Start screen by clicking the Flash Document button. In addition, you can create the new document by selecting File > New from the pull-down menus. The new document will open at a default size of 550 x 400 pixels the first time Flash is launched.

You can change default document properties after you open a document. To access the Document Properties dialog box, use one of these methods: Click the Size button on the Property inspector, right- or Control-click the document background, or select Modify > Properties from the pull-down menus.

The Document Properties dialog box allows you to change the dimensions of the Stage, the background color, the frame rate, and the units of measurement. You can make any settings you specify the default settings by clicking the Make Default button so that every new blank document you create will have those settings.

Slide Presentations

To create a new slide presentation, use the Start screen, or select File > New, and select Slide Presentation from the New Document dialog box. The slide presentation will divide your document window into two sections. The slides themselves are instances of a special component called a screen.

The Stage will now appear to the right. To the left is the Screen inspector, which allows you to add, remove, reorder, and rename slides. To add a new slide, click the Add Screen (+) button at the upper right corner of the Screen inspector. To remove a slide, select the slide, then click the Delete Screen (–) button next to the Add Screen (+) button. To reorder slides, select and drag them to their new positions.

The first slide in the Screen inspector is the master slide, and will determine the background color and dimensions of all the slides that follow it. To change the properties of the master slide, select the master slide first, and then select the Stage. From there, you can change properties the same as you would change them for a basic document.

> **NOTE**
> Slides other than the master slide can have their own nested or "child" slides. Slides are nested by dragging one slide to the right of another. Nested slides can also be added by right- or Control-clicking a screen, and selecting Insert Nested Screen from the dialog box.

A slide must have a name. Flash specifies default names when you add slides (slide1, slide2, and so on). You can change the name either by double-clicking it in the Screen inspector, or by selecting the slide and changing the name in the Property inspector.

> **IMPORTANT**
> Slide names must begin with a letter and cannot contain spaces or special characters.

Form Applications

To create a new form application, use the Start screen, or select File > New, and select Form Application from the New Document dialog box. As it does with the slide presentation, Flash divides your main document window into a Screen inspector on the left and the Stage to the right.

Form applications, like slides, are built using the screen component. To add screens, click the Add Screens (+) button in the Screen inspector. To remove screens, click the Delete Screen (–) button. As with positioning slides, you can select and drag screens to new positions, thereby rearranging their order.

The first screen is the master screen and determines the properties of all the other screens after it. To change the properties of the master screen, select the master screen, and then select the Stage. From there, you can change properties the same way as you change them for a basic document.

> **NOTE**
> To nest screens, drag them to the right of another screen or right- or Control-click a screen and select Insert Nested Screen.

To change screen names, double-click the name in the Screen inspector, or select the screen and rename it in the Property inspector.

> **IMPORTANT**
> Screen names must begin with a letter and cannot contain spaces or special characters.

Templates

Flash MX 2004 comes with a number of templates (see Table 4.1) that you can use as launching points for applications that you want to build.

Table 4.1   Built-In Flash Templates by Categories

TEMPLATE	USE
Advertising	Used to build Flash-based web ads
Form Applications	Used to construct query-response or windowed applications
Mobile Devices	Used to publish Flash content for hand-held devices and Internet-capable phones
Photo Slideshows	Creates Web photo galleries
Presentations	Builds PowerPoint-style presentations with included assets
Quiz	Creates AICC or SCORM compliant quizzes for e-learning apps
Slide Presentations	Builds PowerPoint-style presentations, without included assets
Video	Builds video-driven presentations and interfaces that allow users to select bandwidth settings

To start a new document from one of the many Flash templates, use the Templates category of the Start screen, or select File > New, and from the New Document dialog box, switch to the Template tab. Select the template you want.

The templates in Flash are not locked down, and documents built from them are readily modifiable.

Your Own Template

You can save any Flash document that you're working on as a template, whether it's a basic document, a slide presentation, or a form application. To save a document as a template, select File > Save as Template.

The Save as Template dialog box will appear. You will be prompted to name your template, select a category from the Category pull-down menu (or type a category title in the textbox to create your own category), and type a description. When your template has a visual element on the Stage, Flash generates a preview.

After you save the template, you can build new documents from it.

➜ We'll go over this again in Chapter 8, "Laying Out your Project."

Templates are stored in two different places, the first in the Install directory, and the second in a user-specific directory whose location is different depending on which platform you happen to be using. Flash does not have a button or menu option to open and edit a template you've already created. In OS X, user-created templates are stored in yourUserName/Library/Application Support/Macromedia/FlashMX2004/en/Configuration/Templates. In Windows, it is in C:\Documents and Settings\yourUserName\Local Settings\Application Data\Macromedia\Flash MX 2004\en\Configuration\Templates. Local Settings is hidden by Windows by default, so you'll need to unhide folders and files.

Symbols

If the document is the cornerstone of your Flash Document, then symbols are the bricks and stones that build the house. While we'll be treating symbols in detail on their own in Part 3, we'll introduce them here, because they are a vital part of the Flash anatomy. The three main symbols of Flash are:

- The Button symbol
- The Graphic symbol
- The Movie Clip symbol

Of the three, Movie Clip symbols and Button symbols have the ability to be used with ActionScript. All three symbols are reusable, which means that the original graphic is stored in a single location for every symbol, and each use of the symbol (a symbol instance), has a negligible, if any, impact on the file size of our document.

Additionally, the Movie Clip symbol is the basis of many elements in Flash, including your main document.

> **NOTE**
>
> All symbols are stored in the document library, which can be retrieved through the Window pull-down menu.

> **TIP**
>
> There is a fourth symbol, the Font symbol, which is used to share fonts between SWFs and FLAs. It's not a symbol like the main three, but it's useful because you can embed it in an SWF, and then share it across other SWFs to prevent the same outline from being embedded in every document that uses the font. It can be used for author time sharing as well. See Chapter 9, "Organizational Tools and Where to Find Them," for information on sharing symbols.

Components

Components are special pre-built movie clips, and have a number of editable parameters and properties. Components speed up development, and at the same time provide shareable resources, such as code and interface graphics, in a neat little package.

➜ For more details on components, see Chapter 19, "Components."

The components that come with Flash fall into three categories:

- Data components
- Media components
- User Interface components

Data components allow you to connect to outside resources such as web services, databases, and XML files to create a flexible, data-driven Flash application. Data components are not visual; that is to say, they do not appear as a graphic in the published piece. Media Components are designed to work with MP3 audio files and Flash Live Video (FLV) video files. User Interface components are just that: user interface items such as pull-down menus, text areas, calendars, and menu bars, that allow you to quickly develop a user driven interface.

You can find these components in the Component panel. To add a component to your Flash piece, select and drag the component from the Component panel and drop it anywhere on the Stage.

Scenes

Scenes are a way to organize your document by theme or concept. Scenes are essentially timelines placed one in front of the other, like the cars of a train, and they play in order from start to finish.

To add scenes from the Insert pull-down menu, select Insert > Scene. To add scenes from the Scene panel, select Window > Design Panels > Scenes. Then you can add or remove scenes, duplicate scenes, rename them, and change their order of appearance by selecting and dragging the scene to its new position. The first scene to play in a document will be the scene at the very top of the Scene panel.

> **NOTE**
> If you are building an application using screens (form applications or slides), you cannot use scenes.

Publish Settings

A discussion of Publish Settings may seem out of place here, but in reality, it's part of the anatomy. Setting your Publish Settings before you start to heavy work on an application may save you some headaches later on, especially if you are authoring for an earlier version of the Flash Player.

➔ Publish settings are detailed in Chapter 30, "Publishing."

The Publish Settings dialog box permits you to determine the format you want to publish a document in, the version of the Flash Player you're going to build for, the version of ActionScript you're going to use (if you're going to publish in Flash Player 6 or 7 format), and the HTML template you're going to use.

> **NOTE**
> The HTML templates, discussed later in the book, alter how the OJBECT and EMBED tags are written so that SWF files can be used over the web.

To open the Publish Settings dialog box, select File > Publish Settings, or click once on the background and select the Settings button on the Property Inspector.

Summary

Flash MX 2004 can create basic documents, slide presentations, or form applications. Slide presentations and form applications make use of a special development mode and a component called a Screen. Screens can be added, deleted, rearranged, and nested.

All documents can be saved as a template. Additionally, you can start from a number of pre-built templates that come with Flash MX 2004.

Flash documents can be organized using symbols, which are reusable elements, scenes, and components. Button symbols, Movie Clip symbols, and components can also be used to add interactivity and functionality to a site. Scenes are an organizational method the chunks the timeline up into logical content groupings. Scenes play in order.

Publish settings specify the format that you will output when you publish, the most common of which are the SWF and HTML formats. SWF is needed to view your application over the web, and the HTML option produces the HTML tags that embed the SWF in a web document.

Sample Questions

1. Document properties can be set using (choose 2):

   A. Edit > Document Properties

   B. The Settings button on the Property Inspector

   C. Modify > Document

   D. File > Publish Settings

2. The four symbols used in Flash are:

   A. Scenes, Movie Clips, Text, Button

   B. Buttons, Screen, Scenes, Font

   C. Components, Graphics, Slides, Text

   D. Button, Movie Clip, Graphic, Font

3. Which components are used to stream MP3 files?

    A. Media components

    B. Data components

    C. User Interface components

    D. Streaming components

4. Which of the following can be set in the Document Properties dialog box?

    A. Default font

    B. Sound compression

    C. Stage dimensions

    D. None of the above

CHAPTER 5

Flash MX 2004 Tools

IN THIS CHAPTER

Selection Tools   29

Drawing Tools   32

Transform Tools   35

Other Tools   38

Summary   38

Sample Questions   39

Flash MX 2004 is, at its heart, a vector animation tool. Granted, it does a lot more than that, and more and more often it's being used by clever designers and programmers to create robust interfaces and applications. Since Flash has a robust set of drawing tools, nearly all your graphic assets can be produced within Flash itself.

In this chapter, we will review the tools in Flash; what they are and what they do. We'll detail the tools that draw, select, and transform the assets that you make to create a compelling and well-designed interface.

Selection Tools

The main selection tool in Flash is the black arrow, otherwise known as the (surprise) Selection tool. Use the Selection tool to select visual assets. You can select portions of editable objects (things that aren't grouped or converted to symbols) with the Selection tool by dragging a selection box around a segment of the graphic.

You can make multiple selections with the Selection tool by holding the Shift key and clicking the objects you want to select. You can also drag a selection box around multiple objects.

The Selection tool options in the Options panel are Snap to Objects, Straighten, and Smooth. Snap to Objects allows you to snap objects together when dragging them around on the Stage, regardless of the layer those objects are in (the option doesn't move the objects across layers though). When you are dragging an object around on the Stage and Snap to Objects is turned on, you'll see a small black ring under the cursor; this is the snap ring. As you approach an object, the snap ring will get bigger to indicate that you're now within snapping distance of that object. If you let go of the mouse at that point, the object you are dragging will snap to the object you were approaching.

> **NOTE**
>
> You can also turn on Snap to Objects by selecting View > Snapping > Snap to Objects.

> **TIP**
>
> It's easier to control snapping if you drag an object from either the center or one of its edges.

> **TIP**
>
> Snap tolerance can be adjusted in Preferences. Select Edit > Preferences on PC, or Flash MX 2004 > Preferences on Mac, and choose the Editing Tab in the dialog box. Tolerance is adjusted in the Connect Lines menu, and has three choices: Must be Close, Normal, and Can Be Distant.

To use Straighten or Smooth, an editable object like a Stroke must be selected. Clicking either of these buttons can straighten out jagged line segments, or smooth them to make more curved lines.

The Subselection tool is the white arrow, and it allows you to modify shapes by adjusting anchor points. Anchor points can be curve or corner points. When you select an object with the Subselection tool, its anchor points and tangent handles will appear. To change the shape, select one of the anchor points or tangent handles, and drag them about to make the new shape.

The Subselection tool also allows you to delete anchor points by selecting them, then pressing delete on your keyboard.

> **TIP**
>
> To convert a corner point to a curve point, select the point with the Subselection tool, then Alt-drag (Option-drag on the Mac) to add the tangent handles.

> **NOTE**
>
> The Subselection tool allows you to change the shapes of strokes and fills.

The Lasso tool allows you to select portions of an editable object by dragging a selection area around or within the object. The selection area can be freeform, so that you can select irregular shapes.

> **NOTE**
> Unlike other editing tools, the Lasso tool selects vector artwork only. Bitmaps must be broken apart before any portion of them can be selected with the Lasso tool.

The Lasso tool options in the Options panel are: Polygon Lasso, Magic Wand, and Magic Wand Tolerance. The Polygon Lasso allows you to click and release to add points in a selection area. This gives you more control over the selection. The Magic Wand option allows you select pixel regions in bitmapped artwork based on color. The colors included in the selection are set in the Magic Wand Tolerance.

> **NOTE**
> To use the Magic Wand tool, you must first break apart the bitmap image. To break apart an image, select Modify > Break Apart.

The Eyedropper tool is also a selection tool in that it allows you to select colors used from an editable or broken apart graphic for stroke or fill settings. To use the Eyedropper tool, select it, hover over an area of color, and click. When you click an area of fill, the Eyedropper tool will switch over to the Paint Bucket tool. When you select a color from a stroke, it switches to the Ink Bottle tool.

> **NOTE**
> The Eyedropper tool from the Tools panel will select colors only from editable objects.

> **TIP**
> To select colors from bitmaps, break them apart.

The Eyedropper tool is built into any panel that allows you to select color, such as the Colors portion of the Tools panel, or the Stroke color chip on the Property Inspector. When you click a color chip, the cursor changes to an eyedropper, allowing you to mouse over any object in Flash, editable or otherwise, and select a color from it.

Drawing Tools

The drawing tools in Flash are the Oval, Rectangle, Polystar, Pen, Line, Brush, and Pencil tools. In Flash, lines are referred to as strokes.

To draw a straight line, select the Line tool, and drag to draw a line on the Stage. Pressing and holding the Shift key while drawing constrains your strokes to 45-degree angles.

When you have the Line tool selected and want to change its settings before you draw, you can change the color, line style, and line height on the Property inspector. You also can change the stroke color in the Colors section of the Tools panel, the Color Mixer, or with the system Color Picker Changing stroke settings after drawing is covered later in this chapter.

> **TIP**
>
> The Color Picker is not a panel that can be opened with the Window pull-down menu. To open it, you have to Alt-double-click or Option-double-click on the Mac on top of either a stroke or fill color option on the Colors section of the Tools panel, the Color Mixer, or the Property inspector.

To draw a stroke freehand, select the Pencil tool. The Pencil tool has three options in the Options panel: Straighten, Smooth, and Ink. As you draw a stroke with Straighten mode selected, Flash straightens out the line when you have finished drawing it. Likewise, Smooth smoothes the line out. Ink simply draws the lines as is, neither straightening nor smoothing the stroke.

When you have the Pencil tool selected and want to change stroke settings before drawing, you can change the stroke settings on the Property inspector, or stroke color alone in the Colors section of the Tools panel or the Color Mixer.

The Pen tool in Flash is another vector drawing tool, and it allows you to draw lines with a higher degree of precision and flexibility. It mirrors the Pen tool in other applications, such as Freehand.

To use the Pen tool, select it from the Tools panel. To draw straight line segments, click and release to add anchor points. Anchor points for straight line segments are called corner points. As you add points, Flash connects the line segments. To draw curved lines, press and drag. This adds curve points and tangent handles. You can control and refine line curvature by using the tangent handles that the Pen tool adds. Curved line segments are called Bezier Curves.

> **NOTE**
> After you draw a line, you can add additional corner or anchor points to it by selecting the Pen tool and then selecting a line segment. Clicking an anchor point that already exists deletes it.

> **TIP**
> To convert a curve point to a corner point, click it with the Pen tool.

You change the stroke settings of the Pen tool before drawing the same way you change those of the Line and Pencil tools.

To draw ovals and circles, select the Oval tool, and then, press and drag on the Stage to draw the object. If you hold down the Shift key, you can draw a perfect circle. If you hold down the Alt key (Option key on the Mac), you can draw your oval or circle from the center.

By default, when you draw an oval, rectangle, or polygon shape, Flash draws a stroke as well as fill. When you have the tool selected and want to draw only an area of fill and not a stroke, select the Stroke option in the Color section of the Tools panel, click the color chip, and select the white rectangle with the red line. That will shut off the stroke. Likewise, you can do the same with the Fill option.

> **TIP**
> Stroke and Fill can also be shut off in the Property inspector and the Color Mixer.

To draw a rectangle, select the Rectangle tool, and drag on the Stage. To draw perfect squares, press and hold the Shift key while dragging. Holding the Alt key (Option key on Mac) will allow you to draw from the center when creating your rectangles and squares.

When you have the Rectangle tool selected and want to draw a rectangle with rounded corners, click the Rounded Rectangle Radius button in the Options panel before you draw, and specify a rounding radius. Do this before drawing.

> **NOTE**
> You can also round corners of a rectangle while drawing. Before releasing the mouse button while drawing, use the Up and Down Arrow keys on the keyboard to round and sharpen corners. The Down Arrow key rounds, the Up Arrow key sharpens.

The Polystar tool is a hidden option in the Rectangle tool. To select it, click and hold the mouse button down over top of the down arrow on the Rectangle tool, and select the Polystar tool from the menu when it appears.

The Polystar tool can draw polygon shapes or star shapes. When you have the Polystar tool selected and want to change the shape and number of sides, click the Options button on the Property inspector. To draw the shape, press and drag on the Stage.

> **TIP**
>
> You can draw between 3 and 32 sides, and can have star point sizes between 0 and 1.

> **TIP**
>
> If you press and hold down the Control key while you draw (Command key on Mac), your polygon will snap to rotation points of 90 degrees.

The Brush tool draws areas of fill, unlike the Pen, Line, or Pencil tools. The Brush Tool options are Brush Mode, Brush Size, and Brush Style. Brush Size is really intended to mimic the pressure one puts on brush when painting, and the Brush Style determines the kind of fill swath drawn. Table 5.1 lists the Brush modes.

Table 5.1 Brush Modes

MODE	ACTION
Paint Normal	Paints anywhere, including over lines and fills
Paint Fills	Paints only fills, or empty areas on the Stage
Paint Behind	Paints behind objects when you are painting on the same layer
Paint Selection	Paints fill areas of selected objects only
Paint Inside	Paints only the fill area that you start painting in, and never paints over strokes

> **TIP**
>
> For those of you using a Wacom tablet or other kind of pressure-sensitive input device, varying the pressure on the stylus will produce strokes of different width, which can be rather interesting when you use the Tilt modifiers in the Brush tool's options.

Transform Tools

The transform tools are the Free Transform, Fill Transform, Paint Bucket, Ink Bottle, and Eraser tools. These tools change the scale, rotation, and general appearance of assets so that you can adjust their overall shape, color, and style settings.

The Free Transform tool allows you to change the scale, rotation, and center of rotation of a selected graphic, stroke, or fill. If the object is editable, you can skew and distort it. When you have the Free Transform tool selected, the Options panel has an Envelope option, which further allows you to alter the shape and appearance of editable graphics.

To use the tool, select an asset with the Selection tool, then switch to the Free Transform tool.

> **TIP**
> You can also select with Free Transform tool, but be careful. If you select an object that has both stroke and fill, it will only select what you've actually clicked on. You can select an entire object by double-clicking on it with the Free Transform tool.

To move the graphic, position the mouse cursor anywhere inside the bounding box of the graphic and drag it about. Be careful not to select the white dot in the center. That's the transformation point, and when you move it, it changes the center of rotation and scale.

To rotate a graphic, click and drag outside one of the control handles. The graphic will rotate around the transformation point, which can be moved by dragging it to a new position inside or outside of the graphic's bounding box. Holding down the shift key while you rotate constrains the rotation to 45-degree angles. Alt- or Option-dragging will rotate the graphic around the corner opposite from your mouse cursor.

In order to scale, you must drag one of the control handles. If you want to maintain the graphic's proportions, you can Shift-drag, or you can select the Scale option and drag from a corner handle.

> **TIP**
> You can also transform with the Transform panel, the Property inspector, and the Info panel. The Info panel, however, doesn't let you constrain your proportions.

You can skew a selection by pressing on the bounding box between two control handles and dragging, or by choosing the Skew and Rotate option from the Tools panel. To distort, Control or Command-drag a corner or side handle. If you want to taper objects, you can Shift-Control- or Shift-Command-drag a corner handle. You can also use the Distort option in the Tools panel to distort and taper objects, but you still need the keyboard modifiers to taper.

The Envelope option is another way of skewing and distorting graphics. You can choose it from the Tools panel with the Free Transform tool selected, or you can select Modify > Transform > Envelope with a graphic selected. The graphic will be encased in bounding box with control points and tangent handles that you can drag to reshape the graphic.

TIP

The Free Transform tool can only distort editable objects. Envelope and Distort options will not be available for symbols, grouped objects, text, or bitmaps, although all of those objects can be scaled, rotated, and skewed.

The Fill Transform tool allows you to change the angle, position, rotation, and length of gradient and bitmapped fills. To use the tool, select it and then click an area of gradient or bitmapped fill. Control handles will appear to allow you to change the center point of the fill, and control handles. When you mouse over a control handle, your cursor will change to reflect what that control handle does.

➡ See Chapter 6, "Panels," and Chapter 11, "Bitmap and Vector Artwork," for more on bitmap fills.

For gradients, you can change the center point, scale the gradient, and rotate it. The square control handle changes the scale when you drag it, and the center circle changes the center point of the gradient. When you're working with a circular gradient, you can also change the gradient's radius by dragging the middle control handle.

Bitmap fills are a little different. When a bitmap fill is applied, it automatically tiles through the shape to which it's been applied. The Fill Transform tool will allow you to change the scale, rotation, and skew of the bitmaps filling the object.

➡ See the Color Mixer Entry in Chapter 6, "Panels."

When you select an object with a bitmap fill using the Free Transform tool, the tiled bitmap that you clicked on will appear with three square control handles in its lower left corner, three circular control handles in its upper right corner, and a center point. Dragging the center point changes the position of the tile. Dragging the square control handles changes the scale of the tile; the corner square will maintain the proportions, while the two side squares change width and height. The corner circle control handle changes the rotation of the tiled fill, and the side circles skew and slant.

The Paint Bucket tool allows you to change the fill color or fill type of any enclosed object. You can select fill color in the Colors section on the main toolbar, on the Property inspector, or in the Color Mixer. Fill type (gradients and bitmapped fills) are set in the Color Mixer. To use the Paint Bucket tool, select it, change the color or type settings, and then click an enclosed object.

The Inkbottle tool has much the same functionality of the Paint Bucket tool, with one marked difference: it changes stroke settings. You can change stroke color on the Colors panel, the Property inspector, and the Color Mixer. You can change the Line style on the Property inspector. To use the Inkbottle tool, select it, change the stroke settings, and then click a stroke. To add a stroke to an enclosed object that hasn't got one, click the edge of the object, and a stroke will be added.

The Eraser tool may not be a transform tool proper, but it sure changes shapes! The eraser tool is used with editable objects, and, strangely enough, erases things. In the options for the eraser tool, you can change the eraser size and shape, from different sized ovals to different sized rectangles. You can also change the eraser setting (see Table 5.2).

Table 5.2   Erase Setting

SETTING	FUNCTION
Normal	Erases any portion of an editable object that the eraser passes over
Fills	Erases only portions of fill areas that the eraser passes over, and doesn't affect strokes
Lines	Erases only areas of stroke that the eraser passes over without affecting fills
Selected Fills	Erases areas of selected fill selected by the user
Erase Inside	Erases only fills that the erase begins in, and doesn't affect anything outside that specific fill area
Faucet	Erases entire areas of fill or stroke within an object, depending on what's been clicked

To erase something, choose the tool, select an option, then press and drag over an editable object. In the case of the faucet option, simply click a stroke or a fill to remove it.

Other Tools

In the View section of the toolbar are two other tools: the Grabber tool and the Zoom tool.

The Grabber tool has no options; it's used to move the entire stage around, contents and all. To use it, select the tool, then press and drag on the stage anywhere.

The Zoom tool has two options: zoom in and zoom out, which are rather self-explanatory. To Zoom in, select the tool; zoom in is the default, but you can click the Zoom In option just to be sure. Clicking once will zoom you in 100% greater than the current setting every time you click. Pressing and dragging will zoom in proportional to the drag area you draw; the smaller the area, the greater the zoom.

To zoom out, choose the tool, and select either the Zoom Out option, or press and hold the Alt key with the zoom tool selected (the Option key on Mac). Clicking once zooms you out in 100% increments from the current setting.

> **NOTE**
> Pressing and dragging with the Zoom Out option selected does not zoom out. It always zooms to fit your selection.

> **NOTE**
> Double-clicking on the Zoom tool returns you to 100% of the Stage size.

Summary

Flash MX 2004 comes with a set of tools that allow you to modify assets in a number of ways. The selection tools allow you to not only select an asset, but in some cases change its shape. The drawing tools allow you to draw strokes and fills to make more visually compelling assets. The transformation tools allow you to alter asset properties, such as shape, scale, rotation, and fill and stroke settings. Flash also has a zoom tool that allows you to zoom in or out on the stage, and a grabber tool that moves the entire stage and its contents around.

Most of the tools in Flash have their own settings, which appear in the options section of the toolbar, and these options change how the tool works.

Sample Questions

1. Which of the following is NOT a function of the Free Transform tool?

   A. Change scale and rotation

   B. Change the center of rotation

   C. Skew and distort

   D. Transform tangent handles

2. The Subselection tool allows you to change the shape of graphics by:

   A. Dragging tangent handles

   B. Adding anchor points, then dragging them

   C. Changing scale

   D. None of the above

3. Which tool allows you to draw free form shapes to make selections?

   A. The Magic Wand tool

   B. The Lasso tool

   C. The Selection tool

   D. The Subselection tool

4. What is the maximum number of sides that the Polystar tool can draw?

   A. 22

   B. 32

   C. 12

   D. 10

CHAPTER 6

Panels

IN THIS CHAPTER

Design Panels   41

Development Panels   45

Other Panels   49

Summary   51

Sample Questions   52

Macromedia Flash MX 2004 panels are grouped under the Windows pull-down menu, and are organized into several categories: Design Panels, Development Panels, and Other Panels. We'll look at the different panels in these categories in this chapter.

Design Panels

In the Design Panel menu are the Align, Color Mixer, Color Swatches, Info, Scene, and Transform panels.

The Align Panel

The Align panel allows you to line up objects with respect to other objects, or with respect to the stage. It has four categories: Align, Distribute, Match Size, and Space. The Align category allows you to line up objects to the left, right, top, bottom, vertical, and horizontal centers of other objects, or to the Stage itself, when the To Stage button is highlighted. The Distribute category allows you to distribute objects so that they are spaced evenly across the stage, or so that their centers or edges are evenly spaced when the To Stage button is not highlighted. The Match Size category allows objects to be resized to match the height, width, or both of the largest selected object, or to match the size of the stage. Finally, the Space category allows you to evenly space graphics horizontally or vertically.

The Color Mixer Panel

The Color Mixer panel allows you to set Stroke and Fill colors. The color mode can be switched between RGB and HSB by selecting either option from the Color Mixer's Options menu.

> **NOTE**
>
> In the same context menu is an option that allows you to add a custom color to the Color Swatches panel (after it's been defined in the HSB or RGB mixers). See more about the Color Swatches panel in the next section.

To change stroke color, choose the Stroke Color icon; stroke color and opacity can be changed. To change fill color, select the Fill Color icon, then choose from solid fill, linear, or gradient fill. You can also choose a bitmap fill, but color alterations will not be affected with Bitmap selected as the fill type.

> **TIP**
>
> When you select a gradient with the Fill Transform tool, you can edit the gradient in the Color Mixer. However, no changes will actually be made on the object you're trying to edit without reapplying the fill. To see edits on-the-fly, you'll have to select your graphic with the Selection tool prior to editing the gradient.

If you choose a gradient fill, you will have a gradient editor show in the Color Mixer. By default, the gradient will be black and white. To change the gradient color, choose the color you want to change on the gradient bar, and then select the color chip in the upper left corner of the panel. Select a color, or enter a hexadecimal value in the color chip pop-up, or specify a color in the RBG or HSB mixer. Opacity can also be adjusted. To add a color to the gradient, click just underneath the gradient bar. To remove a color from the gradient, press and drag the color chip off the gradient bar.

To create your own colors, enter values in the RGB, HSB, or Hexadecimal boxes. To build from a color that already exists, select the color in the color space, and then adjust the values in RBG, HSB, or Hexadecimal boxes. To the right of the color space is a brightness bar. Adjust the brightness of the chosen color by dragging the left pointing arrow up (brighter) or down (darker). In addition, the opacity of colors can be adjusted in the Alpha box.

The Color Swatches Panel

The Color Swatches panel allows you to add to a color swatch, create your own custom color swatch, load color swatches, or use the Web 216 color swatch. You can also select colors for stroke and fill in this panel.

To select a stroke or fill color, choose the Stroke Color or Fill Color icon on the Colors section of the tool panel, and then select a color in the Color Swatches panel. The change will also be reflected in the Color Mixer panel.

The Color Swatches panel by default uses the Web 216 color swatch, and has a number of pre-created gradient fills at the very bottom of it. To create your own color set, click the Options button at the far right of the title bar, and choose Clear Colors. This will remove all the colors but the black and white chips, making it easier to add colors. Next, select the Fill Color option in either the Color Mixer, or the Colors section of your main tool bar. When the pop up menu appears, move the eyedropper over the color you want (from a photograph imported into Flash for instance) until you have the color that you want to use. Click to select the color. Finally, move the grey space in the Color Swatches panel, and when the paint bucket icon appears, click to add the color to your swatch. To delete a swatch, select it, and from the Options menu, select Delete Swatch.

> **TIP**
>
> It isn't necessary to clear colors before you add a color swatch. If you have a color set loaded already, such as the Web 216, you can add your custom colors to the end of the set using the same process.

To save a color swatch, choose Save Colors from the Options menu. Flash color swatches have a .clr extension. To import a color swatch, choose Load Colors from the Options menu. If a color swatch is already loaded into the panel, the new swatches will load at the end of the one currently open.

Color swatches can be duplicated, sorted, and the swatch set can be saved as the default swatch. All of these options are found in the Options menu.

The Info Panel

The Info Panel provides you with information about elements on the stage, and gives you the ability to modify width, height, position, and registration of an object.

To find the X and Y position of any asset on the Stage, select it with your pointer tool, and its values will change in the X and Y position in the panel. You can reposition a graphic by entering new values in those fields. Likewise, selecting an item will show you its width and height, which can also be changed by entering new values.

To change the registration point of a graphic select it, and click on one of the white boxes in the registration section of the panel. When the square turns black, the registration has changed. When you reposition the asset's X and Y position, it will change with respect to the new registration point.

To find out RGB color percentages, mouse over an asset with the Info Panel open. The color that the tip of your mouse pointer is over will be the color shown in the RGB section of the panel. Likewise, X and Y position of the mouse will show, with the X and Y points being at the very tip of the mouse pointer.

The Scene Panel

The main timeline in Flash can be organized into Scenes, which work not unlike scenes in a movie. Most of the time, Scenes are grouped as blocks of related content, and designers and developers use ActionScript to jump from one screen to the next if they're developing something like a web site, or organized different scenes in an animation. The Scene panel is one of the tools you can use to add and organize scenes.

Scenes show in the panel in order of appearance in the timeline. They play in sequence, so the scene at the top of the panel will play before the other scenes beneath it, and so on. To add scenes using the panel or by selecting Insert > Scene, Flash will assign the new scenes default names (for example, Scene 1, Scene 2, Scene 3, and so on).

To change the name of a scene, double-click on the scene name in the Scene panel, and type a new name. Name your scenes descriptively, and avoid starting scene names with numbers.

To add a scene using the Scene panel, click the Add Scene (+) button at the bottom of the panel. The scene will be added immediately below whatever scene is selected in the panel. To reorder scenes, drag them to their new positions in the panel.

Scenes can be duplicated in their entirety by clicking the Duplicate Scene button at the bottom of the panel, and they can be deleted by selecting the scene and clicking the Trash Can icon in the lower right of the panel.

TIP

Scenes can be useful for some tasks, but they are generally frowned upon since using scenes can significantly increase file size. As a best practice, make your content blocks in different SWFs and load the SWFs when needed using `loadMovie()`; or `loadMovieNum()`.

The Transform Panel

In Flash, you can change scale, rotation, and skew using a number of tools, including the Property inspector, Free Transform tool, and the menu options in Modify > Transform. The Transform panel is another tool to accomplish the basic tasks of transforming graphic's appearances.

The panel's scale option can adjust width and height numerically, and proportions can be constrained by selecting the Constrain button.

The Rotate section accepts numeric values for rotation. The Skew button accepts values for horizontal and vertical skewing.

To restore an asset to its original settings, click the Reset button at the bottom right of the Transform panel, which will remove the transform.

Finally, to take transform settings and apply it to another asset, click the Copy and Apply Transform button at the bottom of the panel.

Development Panels

The Development Panels menu includes these options: Actions, Behaviors, Components, Components Inspector, Debugger, Output, and Web Services.

The Actions Panel

The Actions panel is where you add, locate, and look up ActionScripts. The panel is divided into three sections: Categories, Code Inspector, and Script Pane. As of Flash MX 2004, Normal Mode is gone. In order to add ActionScript, you have to do some typing these days, although you can drag and drop snippets of code into the Script Pane and flesh out the rest.

You can add ActionScript to key frames or to objects. To add an ActionScript to a frame, select the frame, then add the script in the script pane. The process for adding ActionScript to an object is essentially the same; select the object first, then add the script in the script window.

➜ The basics of ActionScript and the ActionScript panel itself are covered in Chapter 27, "The ActionScript Panel," and Chapter 28, "The Basics of ActionScript."

The Behaviors Panel

The Behaviors Panel has, more or less, absorbed much of the functionality of the ActionScript Panel's Normal mode. It's broken down into the following script categories: Data, Embedded Video, Media, Movie Clip, Sound, and Web. Each of these categories contains different functionality, and can be applied to objects or keyframes depending on what it is you want to accomplish.

The panel has a Plus button and a Minus button to add and remove behaviors, and to the right of those buttons, an info bar that tells you what you're adding to the behavior. Underneath that section is the pane that shows you what scripts are attached to the object or keyframe, and the triggering event.

To add a behavior, select either a keyframe or an object. Make sure that the Behavior panel itself accurately shows what it is you're adding. Then click the Plus button, and select the behavior you want from the appropriate category. To change the event that triggers the behavior, click the event in the pane, and select the appropriate setting.

To remove a behavior, select it in the panel, and click the Minus button.

The Components Panel

The Components panel contains all of the pre-built components that come with Flash MX 2004, and any that you create yourself or download from an online resource, such as Macromedia Exchange. Out of the box, the panel is broken down into Data, Media, and User Interface Components.

> **NOTE**
>
> Data and Media components only come with Flash MX 2004 Professional, as well as a number of User Interface components.

To use a component, select the layer and keyframe that you want to display the component, then press and drag it onto the stage. This adds the component to your document library as well, making them reusable.

> **NOTE**
>
> Data components are only visually represented in the development environment, and have no visual counterpart in the published file.

The Component Inspector Panel

This panel allows you to do a number of things: bind data from one component to the next, change specific settings for the components, and change the structure of the component itself.

The Component inspector has three tabs:

- Parameters
- Bindings
- Schema

The Parameters tab allows you to change specific component settings; the changeable parameters are the same you see in the Property inspector.

The Bindings tab allows you to bind data from one component to another. To add a data binding, you have to select the component, and then click the Plus button on the data bindings section of the Component inspector. The dialog box that appears will be different from component to component. To remove a data binding, select it in the panel, and then choose the Minus button.

The Schema tab gives you information about the data structure of the selected component, depending on the component you have selected. If the component sends or receives data, the properties for the component will display in the preview pane, and what kind of data the property can accept (the data type).

When you select a property in the scheme tab, you can change it in the dialog box below the schema pane. Default values, data types, and a number of other options can be set here.

The Debugger Panel

The Debugger panel, when used with a special test mode, gives you a way to look for errors in an SWF as it plays. The panel is automatically opened when you choose Control > Debug Movie.

When the SWF loads in debug mode you can see a view of any SWF files loaded in the Flash Player. If you're familiar with debugging ActionScript or any other type of code, the Debugger panel also gives you a way to set breakpoints, which stop the SWF at critical points and allows you to step through lines of code bit by bit to try and isolate a problem. Finally, the panel allows you to change property values while the SWF is running in test mode.

The Output Panel

Another debugging tool, the Output panel will provide you with error messages when there is a problem in your ActionScript. You can check to see if you have problems with your ActionScript by either selecting Control > Test Movie, or by pressing the Check Syntax icon in the Actions panel. Any error messages will be displayed in the Output window.

In the options dialog box for the Output panel is a Filter Level option with two values: None, which gives you a minimum of information about the error, and Verbose, which gives you as much information as possible about any particular error.

In addition to error messages, the Output panel can display information that you send there using the trace() function. This gives you a way of testing functionality before you actually build it out, making the Output panel a pre-bugging tool, if you will.

The Web Services Panel

The use of dynamic data is becoming more popular in Flash, and one of the ways you can add dynamic data is through Web Services. Web Services use XML and a protocol called SOAP (Simplified Access Protocol) to transmit data between technologies. The Web Services panel allows you to add Web Services that you either subscribe to or build yourself in a single location for easy retrieval.

To add a web service to the panel, click the Globe icon on the upper left corner. When the Add Web Service dialog appears, click the Plus button, then specify the URL that points to the web service. When finished, press Enter (Return on Mac) key. To remove a web service, select the service, then press the Minus button.

When you leave the Add Web Services dialog box, Flash will attempt to communicate with the web service and retrieve its methods. If it successfully connects, then the web service will appear in the panel as an expandable/collapsible menu. When you expand the web service, all of its methods will display and show the parameters their parameters in an expandable/collapsible menu. The methods will indicate whether data is only sent out by the method, or if the method requires arguments to process data.

Right-click (Control-click on the Mac) on the method, and choose Add Method Call from the context menu to call the web service.

> **NOTE**
> The Web Services panel works in conjunction with the Web Services Connector component. When you add a method call, an instance of the component is added to your file. An instance is needed for each method call you make.

Other Panels

The Other Panels category contains the Accessibility, History, Movie Explorer, and Strings panels. It also contains a Common Libraries category, which itself allows you to launch libraries containing pre-built Buttons, Classes, and Learning Interactions.

> **TIP**
>
> If you download extensions from Macromedia Exchange that create panels, the panel's names will be stored in the Other Panels option for easy retrieval.

The Accessibility Panel

This is a unique panel in Flash, whose purpose is to provide content from your Flash movie to a screen reader, which in turn makes your Flash application accessible to users with visual impairments. The panel has three settings: Make Movie Accessible, Make Child Objects Accessible, and Auto Label.

Selecting Make Movie Accessible will instruct the Flash Player to communicate with screen readers. This option must be selected for the other options to be turned on.

Make Child Objects Accessible will allow the Flash Player to send information about Movie Clips, Buttons, Text, and other objects to a screen reader.

Auto Label does just that, automatically labels objects.

Your other options in the panel are:

- **Name**, which gives you the option of naming the object select with something descriptive of the object's purpose

- **Description**, where the object is detailed

- **Shortcut**, which specifies keyboard shortcuts to access or use the object

- **Tab Index**, which allows you to specify in which order objects should be selected when the tab key is pressed.

> **NOTE**
>
> The Tab Index option is only available in Flash MX Professional 2004.

> **NOTE**
>
> Your Flash movie can also be made accessible with ActionScript.

The History Panel

The History panel in Flash keeps track of the changes you're making as you develop your application. The panel displays History Steps in a large pane, with a drag arrow to the left. The amount of History Steps that display in the panel is the same as your number of undo levels, set in your General Preferences dialog box.

> **NOTE**
> Each change is listed in the main window. Click and drag the tab on the left of the panel to undo or redo steps. If you select a step in the panel, then click the Replay button in the lower left corner of the panel, the steps will repeat. On the lower right corner of the panel, you can copy selected steps to the clipboard. If you click the disk icon, you can save the selected steps as a repeatable command.

> **NOTE**
> When you save steps as a command, the command will show in the Commands pull-down menu. The command is saved as a JavaScript file with a JSFL extension.

> **TIP**
> To remove a command from the Commands menu, select Commands > Edit Command List, and delete it from the dialog box. If you want to change the name, go to the same dialog box, select a command, and rename it.

The Movie Explorer Panel

The Movie Explorer lists all the assets in your Flash Document, as well as in what keyframes and layers they reside. The top row of buttons determines what will show in the Movie Explorer:

- Text
- Movie Clips, Buttons, and Graphic symbols
- Action Scripts
- Video, Sounds, and Bitmaps
- Keyframes and Layers

The Movie Explorer also has a Customize Which Items to Show button which allows the designer to customize which items they want to show, and whether or not symbol assets are shown.

Below the buttons is a Find option, giving you the ability to search your application for assets.

Assets and symbol definitions show in the lower part of the window. Selecting an asset in the panel will select it on the stage (providing the layer it's in isn't locked). Text assets can be changed directly in the panel (text only, not font, size, etc). Double-clicking on a symbol puts you in symbol editing mode.

The Strings Panel

The sole purpose of the Strings panel is to allow a designer or developer to build an application that supports multiple languages. Generally speaking, you author the file in the language you speak. All the text that is to be displayed in different languages must be in dynamic or input text fields. Using the Strings panel, you select the different languages to be made available, assign each string an ID, then publish the file. When you publish, Flash will create different folders for each language you selected in the panel, and in them will be an XML file for each language.

At that point, the XML files need to be translated to their appropriate language, then re-imported through the Strings panel in order to be made available as language choices. Once that's done, you have multi-language support.

Common Libraries

The Common Libraries is a category, not a grouping of panels. The Common Libraries contain pre-created assets that can be dragged and dropped into your application. When you drag an asset from one of the libraries into your Flash document, any graphic, ActionScript, and other assets are imported directly into your library. The Libraries are: Buttons, which contain a number of interesting pre-built buttons, including arcade buttons (my favorite); Classes, which are Action Script classes for use with Components; and last but not least, Learning Interactions, for use in e-learning applications.

> **NOTE**
>
> If you're using Flash for e-learning applications, Flash can be published for AICC and SCORM compliance. AICC and SCORM have to do with score tracking largely, and are standards in e-learning.

Summary

Flash MX 2004 comes with a number of panels that facilitate development and design of any Flash application. The panels are grouped into Design panels, which contain panels that alter visual asset properties and build color swatches, Development panels, which assist in building functionality into an application, and Other panels, which contain panels that help you locate assets, undo mistakes, make accessible content, and build multi-language support.

Sample Questions

1. In which panel can you find the Web 216 color pallet?

   A. Color Mixer

   B. Color panel

   C. Color Picker

   D. Color Swatches

2. To add ActionScript to a symbol or frame, what two panels would you use?

   A. The Behaviors panel

   B. The Actions panel

   C. The Web Services panel

   D. The Strings panel

3. Which panel would you use to change the alpha of a graphic's fill color?

   A. The Info panel

   B. The Color Mixer

   C. The Color Swatches

   D. The Property inspector

4. What panel contains pre-built user interface elements, such as combo boxes and buttons that you can drag and drop into your application?

   A. The Component inspector

   B. The Web Services panel

   C. The Components panel

   D. The Movie Explorer

CHAPTER 7

The Flash Player

IN THIS CHAPTER

Flash Player Settings   53

Printing   54

Quality   57

Magnification and Playback   58

Summary   58

Sample Questions   59

The Macromedia Flash Player is a piece of software that runs the SWFs you build with Flash. It is very nearly ubiquitous, with 98 percent of Internet-enabled desktops having some version of it. That's more computers with the Flash Player than with Adobe Acrobat or Java!

In this chapter, we are going to review the Flash Player, some of the different settings it has, and printing from the Flash Player and SWFs in general.

Flash Player Settings

The current version of the Flash player is capable of using ActionScript 2.0. ActionScript 2.0 can also be used by Flash Player version 6. Both versions of the Flash Player have capabilities that can store information on the client machine in the form of Shared Objects, and both can access attached microphones and cameras, which can be used for video conferencing.

Often overlooked, the Flash Player has its own settings that can be altered on a client machine. These settings give end users greater control over what the Flash Player is doing with Flash content from web site to web site. To retrieve and change the settings, right or control click on a SWF as it's running, and from the Context menu, choose Settings.

> **NOTE**
> The Context menu or Display menu options can be disabled in the Publish Setting's HTML tab. To disable the Display/Context menu, deselect the Display Menu options. When this option is deselected, end users can only select the About Macromedia Flash Player option in either menu.

The Flash Player Settings are summarized in table 7.1.

Table 7.1   Flash Player Settings

SETTING	PURPOSE
Privacy	Allows or prevents websites from accessing cameras and microphones attached to the end-user computer
Local Storage	Allows domains to store information on the end-user computer (Shared Objects)
Microphone	Chooses audio source connected to the end-user computer
Camera	Chooses camera source connected to the end-user computer

NOTE

Information stored by an SWF is in the form of Shared Objects, which are like Flash cookies. The Local Storage determines how big shared objects can be (or how many can be stored) by domain.

Printing

There are two ways to print from an SWF. One way is to use the Print command from the Flash Player's Context menu, and the other is to use ActionScript to specify frames to print.

To print from the Context menu, right- or Control-click on the SWF, and choose Print. To print from the Flash Player's Display menu, choose File > Print. Your print dialog will appear; choose your printer and page settings, then print.

NOTE

When a user prints this way, it prints the entire viewable SWF in the first level of the Flash Player. The Flash content will be scaled to fit your page layout settings for your printer.

To use ActionScript to print from the Flash Player, you'll need to choose from one of three options: `print()`, `printasBitmap()`, or `PrintJob` class.

NOTE

The `PrintJob` class is only available for Flash Player version 7 and is an ActionScript 2.0 class.

To set up printing for Flash Player 7:

Choose what frame on the timeline you want to use for printing, and add a key-frame at that point on the timeline. To do that, select Insert > Timeline > Keyframe, or right- or Control-click the frame position, then choose Insert Keyframe from the Context menu. It's best to do this in a Movie Clip, as printing from the root timeline will print everything on the Stage, including the button that triggers the `print()` action.

Select the keyframe that you added and assign it a frame label of #p in the Property inspector.

> **TIP**
>
> #p is used to designate specific frames to print. If you omit those labels, all the frames in the timeline you want to print will print out in order.

Lay out the content on the Stage to reflect how the page should appear when printed.

> **NOTE**
>
> By default, the document's Stage size determines the print area.

In a button or movie clip event handler, issue the print command:

```
print(target,bounding box);
```

The target is the Movie Clip timeline (or specific frames in the timeline) that you want to print. The bounding box can be one of three things:

- **bmovie**: Specifies a frame in the movie to be used as the print area. The frame must be labeled with a #b, contain a graphic the size of the print area that you're going for, and be in the same timeline that you are going to print. You can only have one #b per timeline.

- **bframe**: Specifies that bounding for each printable frame should be the contents of that frame. This also changes the print area for that frame and scales objects to fit, which makes it suitable for frames that have different size objects that should be scaled to take up the whole print area.

- **bmax**: Takes all the bounding boxes of all the printable frames and combines them to make one big print area. This is good when you have printable frames that all have different sizes.

The action `printAsBitmap()` works the same as the `print()` action and takes the same arguments. The only difference is that it prints the contents of a frame as a bitmap image, which generally results in a lower quality print.

For Flash Player 7 only, you can now create a print job from the `PrintJob` class. What this ultimately allows you to do is create a queue of items to print programmatically.

First, you have to create an instance of the `PrintJob` class:

```
var myPrintJob=new PrintJob();
```

Next, start the print job so that it can accept pages:

```
myPrintJob.start();
```

> **TIP**
>
> `PrintJob.start()` opens the print dialog box that your operating system uses, and begins to spool pages to your printer. The end user can set up their print options at that point, such as setting the page to print in Landscape or Portrait, which is then detected by the `PrintJob`, allowing the designer or developer to use ActionScript to print the page properly.

Add pages to the print job using:

```
myPrintJob.addPage(target, xmin, xmax, ymin, ymax, frameNum);
```

> **TIP**
>
> The only required parameter is `target`, and that can be either a movie clip instance name or a number, which would represent a level in the Flash Player.

To send the print job to the printer:

```
myPrintJob.send();
```

And to remove the print job from memory:

```
delete myPrintJob;
```

> **TIP**
>
> Deleting the print job from memory makes things work a bit more efficiently on the client side, and is generally considered a best practice.

Quality

Quality refers to the SWF quality in Flash Player. It gives you a way of speeding up download and render times, and can be configured either in the Publish Settings HTML tab, or can be toggled in the Flash Player as the SWF is running.

To assign quality before publishing, choose File > Publish Settings. In the dialog, check the HTML option in the Formats tab, then switch to the HTML tab.

In the HTML tab, choose your quality from the Quality pull down menu option. Table 7.2 summarizes the quality settings.

Table 7.2 Quality Settings

SETTINGS	EFFECT
Low	Instructs the Flash Player not to anti-alias, speeding up playback
Auto Low	Starts off without anti-aliasing, but allows the Flash Player to decide when to improve appearance, based on whether or not the CPU can handle it
High	Always anti-aliases. If there's animation in the SWF, the Flash Player will not smooth bitmaps
Auto High	Starts off with anti-aliasing, but will sacrifice appearance when the CPU is unable to handle processing or when the actual frame rate slows down
Medium	Anti-aliases most items, but does not smooth bitmaps
Best	Everything is anti-aliased, including bitmaps, and performance is not considered

In the Flash Player's Context menu, choose Quality. You can only choose High, Medium, or Low. From the Flash Player's menu, choose View > Quality.

> **NOTE**
>
> When you set a quality setting in the Publish Settings HTML Tab, it creates a Quality parameter in the HTML code that sets the default quality for the running piece. The end user can still override that setting with the Context menu.

Magnification and Playback

The Flash Player has settings that permit an end user to increase or decrease magnification of an SWF currently playing, and also allow an end user to play, rewind, step forward, or step back in an SWF.

To zoom in or out while a SWF is running in a browser:

1. Right- or Control-click on the SWF.

2. From the Context menu, choose Zoom In or Zoom Out.

3. Choose Show All to see the entire SWF.

> **NOTE**
>
> In the Flash Player standalone, Zoom options are in the View pull-down menu.

To control playback:

1. Right- or Control-click on the SWF.

2. Choose Back, Forward, Rewind, or Play.

> **NOTE**
>
> In the Flash Player standalone, the playback options are in the Control pull-down menu. The only two options are Rewind and Play.

Summary

The Flash Player is the software that allows SWF files to be viewable over the web. It has a number of settings that give end users the capability of allowing domains to gain access to attached microphones or video cameras and to store data on the end user's computer in the form of Shared Objects.

Users can print from the Flash Player by choosing the Print command from the Context menu. The Context menu appears when a user right- or Control-clicks on an SWF playing in a browser. When the SWF is playing in the standalone Flash Player, the Print command can be retrieved from the File pull-down menu.

Users can also print from SWFs using print functionality built using ActionScript. The `print()` and `printAsBitmap()` actions can print entire timelines or frames labeled with a #p. The `PrintJob` class creates a queue of pages to print that can be sent to a printer all at once.

Quality of an SWF refers to the appearance of the SWF in the Flash Player in relation to its performance. Performance is enhanced by toggling anti-aliasing on or off, depending on which setting you use. Quality can be set at Publish > Char > Time, or can be controlled by the end user with the Flash Player Context menu.

Sample Questions

1. If you want to make a single frame printable from an SWF, what label should you use on that frame?

   A. `bmax`

   B. #p

   C. `bframe`

   D. `#bframe`

2. Which versions of the Flash Player support ActionScript 2.0?

   A. Versions 5 and 6

   B. Version 7 only

   C. Versions 6 and 7

   D. Versions 5, 6, and 7

3. What Quality setting shuts off anti-aliasing when the playback of a SWF drops below the set frame rate?

   A. Auto Low

   B. Auto High

   C. Medium

   D. Best

4. When using `print()` on the main timeline, the print area can be determined by (choose 2):

   A. The document Stage size

   B. Setting the `xmin`, `xmax`, `ymin`, and `ymax` parameters to the appropriate size

   C. A graphic in a frame labeled #b

   D. The target's `xscale` and `yscale` properties

PART 2

Artwork, Text, and Organization

8 Laying Out Your Project

9 Organizational Tools and Where to Find Them

10 Layers and the Timeline

11 Bitmap and Vector Artwork

12 Using Artwork Created Elsewhere

13 Working with Vector Art

14 Using Text

15 Breaking Up a Project

CHAPTER 8

Laying Out Your Project

IN THIS CHAPTER

Creating a Template   63

Rulers   65

Using Guides   66

Using Guide Layers   66

Using and Editing the Grid   67

Summary   68

Sample Questions   68

Part of getting organized is developing a page or interface layout that you plan to use for much of your application. This is more than creating site maps; you need to sketch out what your interface is going to look like from point to point. Often called storyboarding, it's useful to not only have it drawn out somewhere on paper, but also in Flash, in special layers.

This chapter reviews the ideas behind laying things out in Flash and creating templates that you and everyone else in your team can use to maintain consistency throughout your application.

Creating a Template

In Chapter 4, "The Structure of Flash MX 2004," we glanced quickly at the templates that come with Flash, and quickly discussed making your own. In this chapter we're going to pay a little more attention to it.

When talking about creating a template, we're talking about saving a Flash editable file (with the .FLA extension) on our hard drive and in a special directory. When we build new documents from that file, we're essentially doing a glorified copy and paste; the original document is untouched, but the document we build from it will inherit all the master document's assets. In Flash, unlike in Dreamweaver, all parts of the document built from the template are editable.

The purpose of creating a template is so that you can build multiple documents that have the same appearance and in some cases, the same assets.

To create a template, you must first make a new document or open an existing FLA file. Then, select File > Save as Template.

TIP

Templates are not globally available. They're saved in a special place in your user directory, depending on your assets. On Mac,OS X, it's yourUserName/Library/Application Support/Macromedia/FlashMX2004/en/Configuration/Templates. In Windows 2000 and XP, it's on your C Drive, under Documents and Settings\Your User Name\Local Settings\Application Data\Macromedia\Flash MX 2004\en\Configuration\Templates.

When the Save as Template dialog box appears, you have several options to choose from:

- **Name.** Give your template an intuitive name.

- **Category.** You can save your template in any one of the pre-existing categories in Flash. You can also create your own category by simply typing something into the category box. Once you've made it, it will show in your Start screen, and will also be available from that point forward.

- **Description.** Type in a description of what your template does, is for, and why it's there. The more sensible information you have, the better off you'll be.

- **Preview.** If you have any assets in the template you're building, the preview window will show you what the template looks like.

To create a file based on your template, select File > New to open the New Document dialog box. Click the Templates tab, and then choose your template from whatever category you saved it from.

TIP

Flash does not have an Edit Template feature. To edit your template, you must open the FLA file from the template folder in your user directory. See the above tips to find it.

Once you've saved your file as a template, you can start building the layout you're going to use when you build documents from it. That means using rulers, the grid, and guide layers.

Rulers

Rulers in Flash help you to position graphics based on standard units of measurement. Which unit of measurement you use depends on what you're doing and what you prefer. So before you even start to work with rulers, you need to set your unit of measurement.

Ruler units are set in your Document Properties dialog box. To open the Document Properties dialog box, select Modify > Document, or click the Stage, then click the Size button on your Property Inspector.

➡ See Chapter 4, "The Structure of Flash MX 2004," for more information on document settings.

> **TIP**
> You can also right- or Control-click on the Stage, and choose Document Properties from the Context menu.

In the Document Settings dialog box, click the Ruler Units pull-down menu, then select the unit of measurement you prefer to use.

> **NOTE**
> The default is pixels.

To turn rulers on, select View > Rulers. The rulers will appear to the top and to the left of your document window, and the units of measurement showing will be based on the units you selected in your document settings. As you zoom in or out, your rulers will adjust to match your document.

> **TIP**
> To assist you in drawing, rulers will show tick marks that move with your cursor when a drawing tool is selected. Watch the tick marks as you're drawing to create more precise lines and shapes.

Rulers must be open in order to use guides. Guides work with rulers to aid in the positioning of graphics. However, once you have guides out on the Stage, you can hide the rulers, and the guides will remain visible.

Using Guides

Guides are vertical and horizontal lines dragged out of rulers, and they have three general purposes: to assist in the placement of objects, block off content areas, and assist in the drawing of graphics.

To create a guide, first make sure your rulers are turned on. Then, with your cursor over either a horizontal or vertical ruler, click and drag a guide out.

> **TIP**
>
> Guides, by default, are bright green, and do not publish with the final file. To change the guide color, select View > Guides > Edit Guides, and choose a new color from the color chip in the Edit Guides dialog box.

To position a guide, drag it to the desired location. To lock it in place so that it isn't accidentally repositioned, select View > Guides > Lock Guides. Deselect the option to unlock the guides.

By default, your cursor and all objects will snap to your guides. This helps position and draw, but you may not necessarily want the help. To shut snapping off, select View > Snapping and deselect the Snap to Guides option.

> **TIP**
>
> You can also select View > Guides > Edit Guides, and deselect the Snap to Guides option from the dialog box. What's more, you can edit the snap distance by choosing Normal, Must Be Close, or Can Be Distant from the Snap Accuracy pull-down menu.

To remove a guide, drag it back into the ruler. To shut off all guides at once, select View > Guides and deselect the Show Guides option.

Using Guide Layers

Guide layers are special layers that do not publish. They're used to draw mock-ups of the interface, or to trace graphics with the Pen tool in a different layer.

To create a guide layer, first insert a normal layer, then, double-click the layer's type icon to pull up the Layer Properties dialog box. Select the Guide option and press OK. The layer type icon will change to a T-square, indicating the layer is a guide layer.

> **NOTE**
>
> Guide layers are not the same as motion guide layers.

➔ For more information on motion guide layers, see Chapter 21, "Motion Tweening," and Chapter 10, "Layers and the Timeline."

Use guide layers to draw a page layout with the layout tools. You can use the rectangle tool to draw different colored content blocks that will indicate which areas will hold what kind of content.

> **TIP**
>
> Guide layers can really hold any kind of visual content. You can import a storyboard from a program like Fireworks or Freehand into your guide layer rather than draw a bunch of graphics, if you prefer.

While you're drawing content blocks in your guide layer, it's useful to have your grid visible so that you can refine your layout even further.

Using and Editing the Grid

The grid is another layout tool that helps you position visual assets. When you're designing a page layout in something like a template, it's even more useful, since it gives you a sort of visual road map to follow. The grid helps you decide what will go where, and how much space it will take up on the Stage.

To turn the grid on, select View > Grid > Show Grid. The grid will appear as a series of faint lines, like graphing paper. By default, the line colors are pale gray.

> **TIP**
>
> The grid area and spacing of the grid squares is based on your units of measurement.

To change the grid settings, select View > Grid > Edit Grid. In the Edit Grid dialog box, you can change the grid line color, shut the grid off, toggle snapping on or off, change the width and height of grid squares, and set snap accuracy.

> **TIP**
>
> Grid snapping can also be turned on or off by selecting View > Snapping and either selecting or deselecting the Snap to Grid Option.

> **TIP**
>
> If you're happy with your grid settings, you can click the Save as Default button in the Edit Grid dialog box.

Summary

To assist in the drawing of graphics and building page layout, Flash comes with several useful tools: rulers, guides, guide layers and the grid. None of these items are published with the final SWF.

Rulers help us position graphics based on a unit of measurement, which is set in the document properties. The ruler displays tick marks as you are drawing strokes and fills.

Guides are dragged out of the ruler, and are also used to position graphics on the Stage. Objects can be snapped to guides.

Guide layers are special layers that do not publish with the final SWF. They're used to create content blocks for layout, or to trace graphics in a different layer.

The grid is a useful planning and layout tool that superimposes a series of lines over the Stage. In appearance, it is much like graphing paper. Like guides, objects and graphics can snap to grid lines.

Page layouts and mock-ups can be saved in templates. Building from a template helps to ensure a consistent interface layout.

Sample Questions

1. How can using a grid to plan a page layout be helpful?

   A. It helps you determine ahead of time what will go where, and how much space it will occupy.

   B. Objects don't snap to the grid, so it's easier to align them.

   C. The grid is visible in the final SWF.

   D. Using the grid forces you to make the most use of your Stage space.

2. What are the three snap accuracy options for guides and the grid?

   A. Normal

   B. Don't Snap

   C. Must Be Close

   D. Can Be Distant

3. Why are guide layers useful (choose 2)?

   A. They keep the final SWF file size low.

   B. They don't publish.

   C. Content blocks can be drawn in them.

   D. They're invisible.

4. How can you create your own template category?

   A. Click the New Category button in the Save as Template dialog box.

   B. Enter a new name in the Category field in the Save as Template dialog box.

   C. You can't create your own categories.

   D. Select Modify > Templates > Template categories, and insert a new category.

CHAPTER **9**

Organizational Tools and Where to Find Them

IN THIS CHAPTER

The Library   71

Shared Libraries and Symbols   72

The Layer Pane in Brief   74

The Timeline in Brief   75

The Movie Explorer   76

The Info Panel   76

Summary   77

Sample Questions   77

This chapter covers the tools that you use to organize your Flash MX 2004 or Flash MX Professional 2004 document into logical content groups, as well as the tools that you use to manage your assets. We'll look briefly at the Layer panel and the Timeline, both of which will be discussed in depth in Chapter 10, and we'll pay special attention to the Library, the Movie Explorer, and the Info panel. Other panels will be treated in subsequent chapters.

The Library

The Library is your chief organizational tool for all the assets you import, create, or otherwise add to your Flash application. To launch the Library panel, select Window > Library, or use the keyboard shortcut Control-L (Command-L on the Mac). The Library panel is separated into a preview pane and a listing of your assets.

Stored in the Library are bitmapped images, symbols, sound files, digital video, and font symbols for sharing. The Library also stores components.

At the lower left corner of the library window are buttons that allow you to create a new symbol from scratch, add a library folder for organizing assets inside the library, view the properties of assets, and delete assets from the library.

To add an asset to the library, you can import it directly by selecting File > Import > Import to Library, or by dragging a graphic drawn in Flash into the Library panel.

> **TIP**
>
> When you drag a visual asset into the Library, it will be converted to a symbol, and the Convert to Symbol dialog box will appear. Select Movie Clip, Graphic, or Button as the behavior, and click the OK button. Anytime you create a symbol, Flash automatically stores it in the library.

If you want to make a new symbol using the Library panel, click the New Symbol button on the lower left corner of the panel, or choose New Symbol from the Library options menu. Either will bring the New Symbol dialog box up; choose the symbol behavior you want, and click the OK button. The symbol will be created, and you will be placed in symbol editing mode.

To organize assets, create a folder by clicking the New Folder button at the lower left of the panel, or selecting New Folder from the Library options menu. After you create the folder, name it, and drag items into it. Double-clicking on the folder will cause it to expand and collapse.

> **TIP**
>
> When organizing your library, you can automatically delete any items that are not actually being used by choosing Select Unused Library Items from the Library options menu, then deleting whatever is highlighted. Unused assets are not actually published with the SWF, so this isn't critical, but it can make managing things a little easier.

Shared Libraries and Symbols

In addition to storing assets, items in a document's library can be shared, either while authoring, or when the file runs. These are referred to as author time and runtime sharing, respectively. This way, you can centralize certain assets, such as business logos, and update numerous files without having to republish numerous SWFs.

If you are going to use shared symbols, it's a best practice to keep them all in one location, meaning a file dedicated to nothing but shared symbols. Symbols that are designated for runtime sharing will have to be published in an SWF that must be located on the web server, and symbols designated for author time sharing must be in an FLA file somewhere on your network.

To make a symbol runtime shared, select the symbol in your Library panel, and either right- or Control-click it, or select it and click the Library options menu. From either Context menu, choose Properties or Linkage. If you choose Properties, click the Advanced button to make sure the Linkage settings show.

In the Linkage Settings of the Properties dialog box, check the box that says Export for Runtime Sharing. Next, in the Identifier text box, give the symbol a name to be used for sharing; be sure to name it intuitively. Finally, in the URL field, specify the URL that the symbol will be located at on the server. For instance, if the symbol were going to reside in the root level of your web server, and the published SWF name was Shared, you'd type `Shared.swf`.

> **TIP**
>
> A shared symbol can be used in many SWFs; as all the SWFs that use the symbol are really just pointing to the shared library on the server. When you update the symbol in `Shared.fla`, for example, the symbol will update in any file that uses it.

> **NOTE**
>
> The FLA file containing the shared symbols must be published in order for SWFs using shared symbols to retrieve them.

To import a shared symbol for use in a different SWF, you can select File > Import > Open External Library, then open the FLA file that contains the shared symbols. Drag the symbols from the External Library into your document. It will automatically be set for runtime sharing.

> **NOTE**
>
> This way, you have a visual representation of the shared symbol on the Stage, although it won't update in the FLA when it changes in the shared Library. Updates to shared symbols will only be visible at run.

> **TIP**
>
> You can also create a symbol from scratch for import. When you are in the New Symbol dialog box, click the Advanced button, and in the Linkage Properties section, deselect Import for Runtime Sharing. You'll have to specify the shared symbol's identifier, set in the shared library, and the URL. When you use this method, you won't see a visual representation of the symbol on the Stage, but the symbol will show when you run it.

Author time sharing is just a little different. With author time sharing, you can specify a symbol in any FLA located on your network or hard drive as your source symbol when you create a symbol from scratch. In addition, you can replace a symbol with a source symbol from another FLA. The goal of author time sharing is to have an asset in the development environment shared. That asset may change from time to time, and the FLA that uses it will update when it's published.

> **NOTE**
>
> This is not the same as runtime sharing. In runtime sharing, changes to a symbol have to be published in a shared SWF, which is centrally located on the server. These are for deployment symbols. In author time, the file that USES the shared symbol must be published or manually updated for changes to register.

To use an author time shared symbol, in the Insert Symbol, Convert to Symbol, or Symbol Properties dialog box, click the Advanced button. At the bottom of the dialog box, in the Source section, click the Browse button to point to the FLA that contains the symbol you want to use as your source and click OK. From the Select Source Symbol dialog box, choose the symbol you want to use, and click OK. That imports the symbol into your document library.

To use the symbol, drag it and drop it on the Stage, just like any other symbol.

> **TIP**
>
> To ensure that author time shared symbols update to reflect the latest version of the symbol, check the Always Update Before Publishing box in the Symbol Properties dialog box.

To update the symbol, right-click it in the document library and choose Update from the dialog box, or select the symbol in the library, and choose Update from the Library options menu.

Other library options, such as selecting unused items in the library, can be retrieved from the Panel Options drop-down menu.

The Layer Pane in Brief

The Layer pane allows you to organize your assets after they're actually on the Stage. We'll look at layers in more detail in the next chapter. In this section, we're just going to focus on the pane itself.

The Layer pane is in the upper left corner of your document window, and is part of the Timeline. Each layer added to the Layer pane has its own Timeline.

To add layers from the Layer pane, click the New Layer button on the lower left corner. Next to that button is the Add Motion Guide button, and the New Layer Folder button. At the far bottom right of the pane is the Delete Layer button.

At the top right of the Layer pane are the Show/Hide All Layers, Lock/Unlock All Layers, and the Show All Layers as Outlines buttons.

Each layer in the Layer pane has an icon to show what kind of layer it is. In addition, each layer has a name and three dots that allow you to show or hide, lock or unlock, and show the layer as outlines respectively.

→ For more on types of layers, see Chapter 10, "Layers and the Timeline."

> **NOTE**
> Because the Layer pane is attached to the timeline, the Layer pane will also be collapsed or closed when the timeline is collapsed or closed.

The Timeline in Brief

The Timeline is an organizational tool that allows you to organize content at key points, to change the appearance of your interface over time, or to create animations. The Timeline is composed of layers, used to organize visual assets, keyframes, which specify content at critical points, and frames, which hold as placeholders for graphics.

To show different content along the Timeline, a red playhead moves from one point to the next, either in sequence with the frames, or by following ActionScript instructions that tells it where to go and when.

When you create a new Flash Document, by default the Timeline shows at the top of the document itself. When you create an application with screens, the Timeline either doesn't show or is collapsed. However, each screen has its own Timeline and layer structure.

> **TIP**
> Flash will remember where you placed the Timeline last, should you undock it and move it about. The next time you open Flash or make a new document, the Timeline will show it its last position.

If the Timeline is not visible, you can display it by selecting Window > Timeline.

The Movie Explorer

The Movie Explorer allows you to view the assets used in your document and their location. To launch the Movie Explorer, select Window > Other Panels > Movie Explorer.

The Movie Explorer has a functional aspect to it too. Double-clicking on text assets in the Movie Explorer allows you to change the text. Double-clicking on a symbol will launch you into symbol editing mode. Finally, simply selecting an item in the Movie Explorer selects the item on the Stage, provided the layer it's in isn't locked.

The Movie Explorer also allows you to search for things like blocks of text in your document, or lines of ActionScript. Enter a line of text or a snippet of code in the search block, and the Movie Explorer will automatically start searching.

➡ For more information on the Movie Explorer panel, see Chapter 6, "Panels."

The Info Panel

The Info panel is an organizational tool in that it gives you information about an asset if it is selected. The Info panel also allows you to change the width, height, and position of the assets, along with its registration point.

> **NOTE**
>
> The Info panel is really geared for working with symbol instances. However, it will work with any visual asset, symbols and editable graphics alike.

To change the position of an asset using the Info panel, select it, then launch Info panel by choosing Window > Design Panels > Info. The Info panel will show the asset's currently location in the x and y boxes. Enter new values for the x and y position by clicking into the box and typing the new value, hitting enter to lock the value in and reposition the asset.

When the object moves, it moves with respect to its registration point, which by default is the upper left corner of the asset. To switch it to the center of the asset, click the small white square in the Symbol Position squares.

To change width and height, enter new values into the width and height boxes.

When the Info panel is open and the Selection tool is chosen, the panel shows the current x and y coordinates of the Selection tool (registering to the tip of the arrow).

The Info panel also gives the RBG color percents of any asset that the Selection tool is over, much in the same way that the Eyedropper tool displays hexadecimal color numbers.

Summary

Flash MX 2004 comes with a number of tools that allow you to organize your project and its assets. The Library panel stores your audio and visual assets for use. The Layer panel allows you to organize your assets for production, and the Timeline allows you to change the appearance of your project over time.

The Movie Explorer is a tool that allows you to locate assets within your project that are being used on the Stage. In addition, Movie Explorer allows you to select items for editing and change text directly. The Info panel shows color information and x- and y-positions, and allows you to change width, height, and position of selected assets.

Sample Questions

1. Which of the following panels would you use to change the position of a visual asset?

    A. The Movie Explorer

    B. The Info panel

    C. The Transform panel

    D. The Property inspector

2. How do you make a symbol available for runtime sharing?

    A. Choose the symbol in the Library, and select Shared from the Library's options menu.

    B. Open an external library by selecting File > Import > Open External Library, then drag the symbol you want from that library into your document.

    C. In the advanced settings of the Symbol Properties dialog box, choose Export for Runtime Sharing, give it an identifier, and specify the URL that the shared library will be stored in.

    D. None of the above.

3. How do you insert a new layer from the Timeline (choose 2)?

    A. Click the New Layer button.

    B. Right- or Control-click on a layer, and choose Insert Layer from the Context menu.

    C. Click the Show/Hide Layers button.

    D. Alt- or Option-drag a layer that already exists.

4. Which Library option allows you to remove items from your document library that are not being used in your application?

    A. Compact Library

    B. Select Unused Items

    C. Select Unused Symbols

    D. Delete Unused Items

CHAPTER **10**

Layers and the Timeline

IN THIS CHAPTER

Adding and Removing Layers   79

Organizing Layers   81

Layer Types   81

The Timeline   83

The Playhead   83

Frames and Keyframes   83

Nested Timelines   84

Summary   85

Sample Questions   85

Layers are used to organize the visual content of your project (the stuff that the end user is going to see). They are transparent, and stack on top of each other, each layer containing graphics or other visual objects that will not interfere with the assets on other layers. Of course, graphics stored on layers higher in the stacking order will obscure graphics in lower stacking orders where they overlap (which can be used creatively to create perspective effects or the illusion of depth). In addition, layers are used to store ActionScripts and sounds.

Chapter 9, "Organizational Tools and Where to Find Them," looked at the Layer pane in general, indicating its use as an organizational tool. This chapter pays closer attention to it.

Adding and Removing Layers

To insert a layer, you can do one of three things: select Insert > Timeline > Layer, select the Insert Layer button in the lower left corner of the Layer pane, or Control-click on a layer name, and choose Insert Layer from the Context menu. When you add a new layer, it will appear above whatever layer is currently selected. To delete a layer, select the layer, and click the Delete Layer button in the lower right corner of the Layer pane, drag the layer into the trash can icon on the Layer pane or right- or Control-click on the layer name, and select Delete Layer from the Context menu.

To view a layer's properties, double-click on the Layer Type button next to the name, right or control click on the layer and choose Properties from the Context menu, or select Modify > Timeline > Layer Properties. In the Layer Properties dialog box, you can change the name of the layer, and select whether it is shown or locked. In addition, you can change the layer type, the outline color of objects on the layer when Show Outlines is selected, and whether the objects on the layer will be shown as outlines. You can also adjust the layer height.

TIP

You can also rename a layer by double-clicking the current layer name, then changing it when the input box appears.

To hide a layer, click the Hide Layer button immediately to the right of the layer; right-click or Control-click the layer, select Properties from the Context menu, and uncheck the Show Layer box; or select Modify > Timeline > Layer Properties, and uncheck the Show Layer box. The Show/Hide Layer button will be replaced by a big red X to indicate that it's hidden. To hide every layer but the one you're actively editing, right-click on the layer and select Hide Others from the Context menu.

TIP

To hide all of your layers at once, click the Eye icon at the top of the layer pane. All the layers will have a red X in their Show/Hide Layers column. To make them all visible again, click the Eye icon a second time.

To lock a layer, click the Lock Layer button on the layer; right- or Control-click the layer and select Properties, then check the Lock button; select Modify > Timeline > Layer Properties, and check the Lock button. To lock all the layers but the layer you're actively editing, right- or Control-click the layer and choose Lock Others from the Context menu.

TIP

To lock and unlock all of your layers at once, click the Padlock icon at the top of the Layers pane.

To view only the outlines of the graphics in a layer, click the View as Outlines button on the layer; right- or Control-click the layer and select Properties, then click the View Layer as Outlines option at the bottom of the dialog box; or choose Modify > Timeline > Layer Properties, and select the View Layer as Outlines button at the bottom of the Layer Properties dialog box.

TIP

In the Layer Properties dialog box, you can also change the outline color. Flash determines the colors by default.

TIP

To toggle all layers as outlines, click the View as Outlines icon at the top of the Layer pane (it's the rectangle).

Organizing Layers

Frequently, when you are working with many layers, it's helpful to organize them into logical groups (animations, text blocks, and so on). This is where the layer folder comes in.

Layer folders give us a way to organize our layers as well as the real estate in our Layer pane. A layer folder is added by clicking the Layer Folder button in the lower left corner of the Layer pane, or by selecting Insert > Timeline > Layer Folder. Layers are added to layer folders by dragging them in. Layer folders can be expanded or collapsed to show or hide their contents. Like individual layers, they can be hidden, locked, or shown as outlines; however, when one of these settings is applied to a layer folder, it affects all of the layers within the folder by default.

> **TIP**
> Within a layer folder, layers can be locked, hidden, or shown as outlines individually, whether or not these settings have been placed on the layer folder itself.

Layers and Layer folders are positioned by dragging them up or down the stacking order to their new locations. The topmost layer occupies the top of the stacking order, and graphics in that layer will obscure other graphics where the layers overlap. You can think of it as the layer that's closest to the user's eyes. See Table 10.1 for a list of layer types.

Layer Types

Table 10.1 lists the layer types.

Table 10.1 Layer Types

LAYER TYPE	PURPOSE
Normal	Organizes visual content and assets
Guide	Not published. Used to assist in layout in layers above the guide layer
Guided	Indicates whether the layer is associated with a motion guide
Mask	Indicates the visible portion of layers attached to the mask layer
Masked	Attaches a layer to a mask layer
Folder	Technically is not a layer, but rather a folder to which you can drag layers to organize them

Mask layers allow you to draw a graphic in the layer, and use that graphic to determine the visible area of the layer below, similar to placing a matte over an image.

> **TIP**
>
> Because the actual effect of masking is a layer property, you can use animations to create transition effects. For instance, if you want an image to be gradually revealed, in the layer above the image, you create an animation that gradually covers the image up. Remember that the graphics in the mask layer become windows to the content of the layer underneath, so when you change the layer from Normal to Mask, you'll have the effect of a gradual reveal.

To make a layer a mask, either double-click on the layer's icon and select Mask from the Layer Properties dialog box, or you can right- or Control-click on the layer name, and select Mask from the context menu. To add layers to the mask, drag them below the masked layer. If they do not automatically register to the mask, double-click on the layer's icon, and select Masked from the Layer Properties dialog box.

Motion guide layers have to do with motion tween animations. To insert a motion guide, either click the Motion Guide button in the lower left corner of the Layer pane, or select Insert > Timeline > Motion Guide.

➡ See Chapter 21, "Motion Tweening," for more on this kind of animation.

> **TIP**
>
> If you drag a layer beneath a motion guide, all objects in the layer will automatically snap to the guide if a motion tween has already been set up in the layer.

In the motion guide layer, a path is drawn with one of the line drawing tools. The object in the layer below the motion guide can be snapped to that path at the beginning and the end of the animation by the designer, and the path determines how the object animates. Like guide layers, motion guide layers are not published.

> **NOTE**
>
> The path must be a stroke.

➡ You can read more about motion guides in Chapter 21, "Motion Tweening."

Guide layers are another layer type, and they're generally used as assists in laying out content. Guide layers do not publish with the SWF.

To make a layer a guide layer, insert a new layer first. Then, double-click on the layer's icon, right- or Control-click on the layer and select Properties, or select Modify > Timeline > Properties to pull up the Layer Properties dialog box. In the Type category, choose Guide.

The Timeline

The Timeline shows at the top of any basic Flash MX 2004 or Flash MX Professional 2004 document.

> **TIP**
>
> You can move the Timeline, but Flash will remember where it was last placed, and the next time you open Flash and make a new document, the Timeline will be placed in its last known position.

When working with screens, the Timeline, by default, does not show. To display the Timeline, select Window > Timeline.

Primarily used for animations, the Timeline allows you to organize the appearance of your content over time, or to organize content at key points.

The Timeline is composed of different layers, frames, and keyframes. Keyframes and frames allow you to extend visual content out over time. You use keyframes to make changes and frames as place holders.

➜ For more information about keyframes and frames, check out Chapter 20, "Animation Basics."

The Playhead

The playhead controls playback on the timeline. When the timeline has more than one frame, the playhead moves down the timeline at a speed based on the frame rate (how many frames are flipped through per second), displaying the contents of each frame as it moves and thus creating the appearance of animation. You can also use ActionScript to control the position of the playhead.

➜ See Chapter 17, "Button Symbols," and Chapter 18, "The Movie Clip Symbol," for more details.

Frames and Keyframes

To insert a keyframe in a layer in the timeline, select Insert > Timeline > Keyframe. Use keyframes to designate how you want your content to appear at different points, such as the beginning and the end of an animation. When you insert a keyframe, any graphics in the keyframe before it will by default be copied into the new keyframe.

You can also insert blank keyframes, which are simply keyframes that do not copy graphics from the previous keyframe. In fact, any keyframe that doesn't have content is a blank keyframe. To insert a blank keyframe, select Insert > Timeline > Blank Keyframe, or right- or Control-click on the frame position you want to insert the blank keyframe in and choose Insert Blank Keyframe from the context menu.

> **NOTE**
> Keyframes (and blank keyframes) are the only frame types you can edit.

To convert a keyframe to a normal frame, select the keyframe in the timeline, and then select Modify > Timeline > Clear Keyframe.

> **TIP**
> Alternatively, you can right- or Control-click on the keyframe, and choose Clear Keyframe from the Context menu.

To insert a frame in a layer in the timeline, select Insert > Timeline > Frame, or right- or Control-click on the frame position you want to insert the frame in, and choose Insert Frame from the Context menu. Frames are used simply to display content, and not to display critical appearance at any point. An edit to a frame affects all the frames before and after it between keyframes.

> **NOTE**
> To remove frames or keyframes, select the frame or keyframe in the timeline, right- or Control-click, and select Remove Frames from the context menu, or select Edit > Timeline > Remove Frames.

Selecting a keyframe and pressing the Delete key on your keyboard deletes only the content of the keyframe. When you select the keyframe on the timeline, you also select all its content. When you select a frame and press the Delete key, you delete the contents of the keyframe to the left of the frame, and all frame contents in the next keyframe (on the right).

Nested Timelines

In Flash, the Movie Clip, Graphic, and Button symbols each have a timeline. Because they have their own timelines, you can add and organize content in those symbols much the same way you add and organize content in the main document window.

When you have a movie clip instance on the Stage, or a button or graphic symbol, you have essentially nested a different timeline in the main document's timeline. Nested Timelines allow you to make more complex animations as well as more complex interactive elements.

➜ We'll talk more about nested timelines in Chapters 16, "Graphic and Font Symbols," Chapter 17, "Button Symbols," and Chapter 18, "The Movie Clip Symbol."

Summary

Flash MX 2004 makes use of layers and timelines to organize visual content. The Layer pane and the timeline are integrated.

Layers in Flash can be added, removed, and organized to control the stacking order of assets. In addition, layers have special properties to mask content. Guide layers are used largely for positioning or tracing, and motion guide layers allow you to control the path of a motion-tweened object. Layer folders give you a way to maximize your layer pane space by dragging layers into them and then collapsing the folder.

The timeline is made of keyframes, frames, and layers. The playhead specifies the assets on the timeline that are visible at any given point in time, and can be controlled with ActionScript. You can use symbols to nest timelines.

Sample Questions

1. What two methods can you use to delete a layer?

   A. Drag the layer over the trash can icon in the Layer pane.

   B. Choose Edit > Timeline > Delete Layer.

   C. Right- or Control-click the layer and choose Delete Layer from the Context menu.

   D. Select the layer and press Delete on the keyboard.

2. If you are going to display a stationary graphic for 2 seconds, and your frame rate is 12 frames per second, which of the following should be inserted at frame position 24 if no changes to the graphic occur over that 2 seconds?

   A. A keyframe

   B. A frame

   C. A blank keyframe

   D. A scene

3. Guide layers (choose 2):

   A. Are used with motion tweens

   B. Are used to assist in the placement of graphics

   C. Do not publish

   D. Add file size to the final SWF

4. What do you use if you want graphics in a layer not to be visible after a certain point in time?

   A. Blank keyframe

   B. Keyframe

   C. Frame

   D. None of the above

CHAPTER 11

Bitmap and Vector Artwork

IN THIS CHAPTER

Bitmap Art   87

Vector Artwork   88

Using Trace Bitmap   89

Roundtrip Editing   90

Swapping Bitmaps   90

Runtime JPGs   91

Summary   93

Sample Questions   93

Visual assets make up the usable part of your interface. While you can draw most of what you want in Flash, often you'll import assets from other sources. When we talk about visual assets (as opposed to sounds, XML, and other things loaded into memory), we're generally talking about importing bitmapped artwork and vector artwork.

This chapter reviews the differences between those two types of art, and then focuses on some bitmap features that are particularly useful to a designer in need.

Bitmap Art

Bitmap artwork is anything saved in a pixel-type format. In bitmap artwork, color information is saved in pixels that combine to make a single image. The pixels are affixed to a grid, which itself remains constant. When you scale up the image, it scales up the grid, whose proportions are maintained. Because of this, you lose image quality when you scale bitmap images up (unless they've been saved at high resolutions).

Common bitmap formats on the web include:

- GIF. Graphic Interchange Format. Supports 256 Colors. Compression type is lossless.

- JPG and JPEG. Developed by the Joint Photographic Experts Group, the JPG format supports millions of colors. Compressing to JPG formats reduces quality, which is known as lossy compression.

- PNG. Portable Network Graphic; supports more colors than the GIF (which it is meant to replace), but is a lossless compression type, unlike JPGs.

> **NOTE**
>
> PNG formats aren't always compressed. Fireworks uses PNG as its native source format (the PNG is also intended to replace the TIF and TIFF formats).

Most of the time, bitmap formats are scanned or digital photographs, or artwork with complex tonality or color gradients created in a drawing tool like Macromedia Fireworks. Because of the complexity of color, bitmap images tend to be large, unless compressed into one of the formats listed above.

Very nearly every widely used bitmap format can be imported easily in Flash, although Fireworks PNG's have some special import considerations.

➜ See Chapter 12, "Using Artwork Created Elsewhere," for more detail.

Vector Artwork

What makes vector artwork different from bitmap artwork is how it's defined. Vector artwork is described by math, unlike the fixed grid system bitmap artwork has to adhere to. When you draw a vector circle, you're actually creating an equation. When you increase the scale of the graphic, you're really just modifying the equation.

Programs like Macromedia FreeHand and Adobe Illustrator are used to create vector art (and Macromedia Fireworks can do it, too). Some common vector file type extensions are:

- **FH10/FH11.** Macromedia FreeHand 10 and 11
- **AI.** Adobe Illustrator
- **EPS.** Adobe Illustrator/Macromedia FreeHand

Vector artwork is not viewable over the web without a plugin, as browsers don't support those kinds of file extensions. In order for vector artwork to be seen in a browser, a plug-in is required. Enter Macromedia Flash and the Flash Player.

> **NOTE**
>
> Vector artwork produced in other programs can be imported in Flash.

> **TIP**
>
> To edit vector artwork, use Flash's tools.

➜ For more on editing artwork with Flash tools, see Chapter 5, "Flash MX 2004 Tools."

Using Trace Bitmap

Occasionally, it's useful to convert bitmap artwork into vector artwork. This is usually done on simple bitmap files that don't contain a lot of colors, tones, or gradients, and is almost always done to save file size or to produce interesting visual effects. Generally speaking, vector artwork has a smaller file size burden, though that's not always true. The more vector objects you have to create a single cohesive image, the bigger your file size is going to be. When we convert bitmap artwork into vector artwork, similar colors are grouped together as a single color and a single vector object.

To convert a bitmap object on the Stage to vector art, select the image with the pointer tool, then select Modify > Bitmap > Trace Bitmap. The Trace Bitmap dialog box will appear. The dialog box options and what they do are summarized in the Table 11.1.

Table 11.1 Trace Bitmap Options

OPTION	PURPOSE
Color Threshold	Determines how many colors should be treated as the same color. Color selection occurs when two pixels are compared. If the difference in color is less than the color threshold setting, then the two colors are considered to be the same color. The value range is between 0 and 500.
Minimum Area	Sets the number of surrounding pixels to consider when determining a color. The value range is between 1 and 1000.
Curve Fit	Specifies how smoothly lines are drawn.
Corner Threshold	Determines whether or not sharp corners are maintained or smoothed out.

> **TIP**
>
> The fewer corners you have, the smaller the file size. Also, higher values for color threshold and minimum area will result in a smaller file size in the end, although the image will not be much like the original.

> **TIP**
>
> To produce an image nearly identical to the original image, color threshold and minimum are should be set to 1. However, you'll have a much bigger SWF when you publish.

Roundtrip Editing

In Flash, you can edit bitmap images in Fireworks directly from your Flash interface, and when done, Flash will update your graphic with the changes you made in Fireworks. This is an excellent feature for quick on-the-go edits, and a time saver, because you don't have to re-import anything.

To edit a bitmap from Flash using Macromedia Fireworks, select the image in the Library, and in the Library's options menu, choose Edit with Fireworks.

TIP

If you don't see Edit with Fireworks, choose Edit With, then select Fireworks as the editor. Once you've done it, Edit With Fireworks will appear in your library, and Fireworks will be selected as your default image editor.

NOTE

You can edit bitmaps with other programs choosing Edit With, but the roundtrip editing feature will obviously not work with something Adobe Image Ready.

Additionally, you can select a bitmap on the Stage, and click the Edit button on the Property inspector. Both will open Fireworks in a special editing mode. Make whatever changes or edits you want to make, and then click the Update button. Fireworks will minimize, and Flash will automatically update the image in the Library or on the Stage.

Swapping Bitmaps

Sometimes, you'll have on the Stage one bitmap image that you want to replace with another. You can quickly make the change using the swap bitmap feature, which allows you to exchange the item on your Stage with another from the Library.

To swap one bitmap with another, select the image on the Stage. On the Property Inspector, click the Swap button. The Swap Bitmap dialog box will appear, with a listing of all the bitmap images currently stored in your document library. Select the image you want to switch with, and click OK. The images are swapped.

TIP

You can also choose the bitmap on the Stage, and select Modify > Bitmap > Swap Bitmap.

Runtime JPGs

Flash is able to load JPG images dynamically, when the SWF runs. There are a number of advantages to using this feature, such as a reduction in the initial SWF download time, and easy updating of images. If you have images that change on a regular basis, you can simply replace them on the server (making sure they have the same names, of course, as the old files), and the SWF is automatically updated. No need to edit the FLA file.

The actions that load JPGs dynamically are `loadMovie` to load JPGs into an SWF in the Flash Player—or a movie clip instance within the SWF—while the SWF is still playing, and `loadMovieNum` to load JPGs into a level in the Flash Player.

> **TIP**
>
> You cannot load progressive scan JPGs into the Flash Player. Flash currently only supports standard JPG images.

> **TIP**
>
> The `loadMovieNum` action isn't really very useful to load JPG files dynamically, as the image will always load in the upper left corner of the Flash Player. That's great if that's where you want your images to appear, but not so useful if you want to be a wee bit more discriminating.

To load a JPG into a movie clip instance by attaching a script to a timeline, select the keyframe you want the action to trigger in, then type the following in your Actions pane in the Actions window:

```
targetMovieClip.loadMovie("myJPG.jpg");
```

Alternatively:

```
this.loadMovie("myJPG.jpg", targetMovieClip);
```

➜ For more on buttons, movie clips, and ActionScript, see Chapter 17, "Button Symbols," Chapter 18, "The Movie Clip Symbol," and Chapter 27, "The Actions Panel."

If you want the image to load on a button click, but are controlling the button from a script attached to a frame:

```
myButtonInstance.onRelease=function()
{
    targetMovieClip.loadMovie("myJPG.jpg");
}
```

If the script is attached to the button:

```
On(release)
{
    targetMovieClip.loadMovie("myJPG.jpg");
}
```

> **TIP**
>
> You can also use `_root.loadMovie("myJPG.jpg",targetMovieClip);`

> **NOTE**
>
> You can add the same action using the Behaviors Panel. To do so, select either a keyframe or button, click the Add Behavior button in the Behaviors Panel, and choose Load Graphic from the Movie Clip category.

Alternatively, you can use the `MovieClipLoader` class to load a JPG image into a movie clip. When you use the `MovieClipLoader` class, you have to create an instance of the class, and then use the `loadClip()` method of that instance to load either JPGs or SWFs into movie clips. The general syntax for the method is as follows:

```
movieClipLoaderClassInstance.loadClip(url, target);
```

> **TIP**
>
> The "target" parameter can either be a movie clip instance name, or a number indicating a level in the Flash Player. The URL can be absolute, or relative to the SWF.

The `MovieClipLoader` class is fairly complicated, and using it properly requires a more detailed understanding of ActionScript than we really need here. However, the general usage is as follows:

First, make an instance of the class, and data type it:

```
var myMovieClipLoader:MovieClipLoader=new MovieClipLoader();
```

Second, use the new instance to load an image into a target movie clip:

```
myMovieClipLoader.loadClip("myImage.jpg", targetMovieClip);
```

The advantage of using the `MovieclipLoader` class to load JPGs and SWFs is that you can track download progress with it, giving you a more flexible way of making preloaders.

➡ For more on how to use the `MovieClipLoader` class, see your Flash documentation.

Summary

Flash MX 2004 can use vector artwork and bitmap artwork. Bitmap formats contain color information in pixels affixed to a grid, and are not very scaleable. Vector artwork is defined by mathematic equations and is extremely scaleable.

Vector artwork in Flash can be easily manipulated with Flash drawing tools. To edit bitmaps, they have to be broken apart, or edited in an external program like Macromedia Fireworks. Flash is integrated with Fireworks and has a roundtrip editing feature.

Bitmap art can be converted to vector art using Trace Bitmap. Bitmap files on the Stage can be replaced by any other bitmap in the Library using Swap Bitmap. Finally, JPG images can be loaded from the server using the `loadMovie();` action, which loads the images into target movie clips, or the `loadMovieNum();` action, which loads them into a level on the Flash Player. You can write the action yourself, or use the Load Graphic behavior from the Movieclip category of the Behaviors panel. You can also load JPG images dynamically using the `loadClip()` method of the `MovieClipLoader` class, which allows you to track the progress of the download as it's occurring.

Sample Questions

1. When converting bitmap artwork into vector artwork with Trace Bitmap, what can you do to keep your file size as small as possible?

    A. Enter small values in the Color Threshold box.

    B. Enter small values in the Minimum Area box.

    C. Choose Few Corners from the Corner Threshold drop-down.

    D. Choose Tight from the Curve Fit drop-down.

2. What advantage does using the `loadMovie();` action have over the `loadMovieNum();` action to load JPG images when the SWF runs (choose 2)?

    A. There is no advantage.

    B. JPGs load quicker into target movie clips.

    C. You can position target movie clips anywhere you want on the Stage, having more control over where your images go.

    D. JPGs only load in the upper left corner of the Flash Player using `loadMovieNum();`

3. What is one advantage of using vector artwork over bitmap artwork in Flash?

   A. Vector artwork always has smaller file size.

   B. Vector artwork scales better.

   C. Vector artwork has more color choice options.

   D. None of the above.

4. What does the "target" parameter in the `MovieClipLoader.loadClip()` method signify (choose 2)?

   A. The position the loaded JPG or SWF should occupy on the Stage.

   B. A Movie Clip instance name for the JPG or SWF to load into.

   C. The name of the JPG image or SWF on the server.

   D. The name of a JPG image or SWF in the document library.

CHAPTER 12

Using Artwork Created Elsewhere

IN THIS CHAPTER

What Can Be Imported?   95

Import Options   96

Importing and Editing Bitmap
    Artwork   97

Importing and Editing Vector
    Artwork   98

Importing Fireworks PNGs   98

Importing PDF and EPS Files   99

Summary   99

Sample Questions   99

Macromedia Flash may have its own drawing tools, but you're by no means restricted to using them alone. In addition to producing your own visual assets in Flash, you can import artwork created in other graphic design or layout programs.

In Chapter 11, we reviewed the difference between vector and bitmap artwork, as well as the Trace Bitmap feature and retrieving JPG images when an SWF runs. In this chapter, we review importing and editing both bitmap and vector artwork.

What Can Be Imported?

Flash MX 2004 and Flash MX Professional 2004 can import very nearly any bitmap image format, vector formats, sounds, and digital video formats. Bitmap artwork and sound files import without any special considerations; vector and video files have other options to consider when you import them. This chapter covers how to import vector and bitmap artwork, as well as the factors to consider as you import the artwork. Table 12.1 provides a list of the types of files you can import.

Table 12.1 Graphic File Formats Supported by Flash MX 2004

FILE FORMAT	FILE EXTENSION
Adobe Illustrator	.ai, .eps, .pdf
Adobe Photoshop*	.psd
Macromedia FreeHand	.fh7 through .fh11
Macromedia Fireworks	.png
AutoCAD	.dxf
Enhanced Windows Metafile	.emf (Windows Only)
Future Splash Player	.spl
Compressed Formats	.gif, .jpg, .jpeg
Portable Network Graphics	.png
Flash Player	.swf (Version 6 and 7 only)
Windows Metafile	.wmf
Windows Bitmap	.bmp
MacPaint*	.pntg
QuickTime Image*	.qtif
Silicon Graphics Image*	.sgi
PICT, TGA, and TIFF*	.pct, .pic, .tag, .tif

> **NOTE**
> Files marked with an asterisk require QuickTime version 4 or later to be installed for the format to be supported.

Import Options

Flash offers several different ways to import artwork:

- File > Import > Import to Stage, which imports graphics directly to the Stage.

- File > Import > Import to Library, which imports graphics directly to the document library.

- File > Import > Open External Library, which allows you to open the library of a different document, and then drag and drop assets either directly to your document's Stage or library.

Importing and Editing Bitmap Artwork

After you have bitmap artwork in Flash, you can make use of it by dragging the artwork out of the library, and dropping it on the Stage where you want it, or you can import it directly to the Stage. You can also change an image's properties in the library.

There are three ways to alter an image's properties in the library: Select it and right- or Control-click and choose Properties from the Context menu, click the Properties button at the bottom of the panel, or select Properties from the library's options menu. In the image properties, you can change the image compression to either Photo (JPG) or Lossless (PNG/GIF).

> **TIP**
>
> If your image has complex colors and tones, choose Photo. If it has simple shapes and colors, choose Lossless.

If you have imported a JPG, you can choose to use the imported images settings by checking the Use Imported JPG Data check box. You can deselect the check box and enter a new quality setting in the Quality box.

If you select the Allow Smoothing check box, the Bitmap will be anti-aliased around the edges.

After you have a bitmap image on the Stage, you can change its width, height, or x- and y-position with the Property inspector. Likewise you can click the Swap button, which will allow you to swap the instance of the image on your Stage with a different image stored in the library. The Edit button on the Property inspector will launch Fireworks MX 2004 (if you have it) in a special editing mode that will allow you to modify the image while at the same time update it in Flash.

To scale, rotate, or skew bitmap art, you can use the Free Transform tool. To edit the image in Flash, select Modify > Break Apart to convert the image to a shape, and then use the Magic Wand, Lasso, or Polygon Lasso tools to select portions of the image to edit. When an image is broken apart, Flash treats it as though it were vector art, allowing you to fill in selections with color, erase portions of the image, or otherwise delete portions. A broken apart image on the Stage cannot be returned to its original state without selecting Edit > Undo.

Importing and Editing Vector Artwork

Vector artwork is artwork defined by mathematical equations, rather than color data affixed to a grid (like bitmap artwork). Flash, of course, has its own vector drawing tools, but in many cases, you may want to import vector artwork drawn in another program.

When you import files drawn in Adobe Illustrator that have the .ai extension, you will see a dialog box that asks you whether you want to preserve the file's original layer structure, flatten the layer, or distribute the layers to keyframes (effectively creating a frame-by-frame animation). You can also choose to include invisible layers. Many of the graphics in the file will be converted to graphic symbols.

When importing FreeHand files, Flash displays a different dialog box. Because FreeHand allows you to build pages, you'll be prompted to import your pages as scenes or keyframes so that you can build different content appearances at critical points. You can also preserve your FreeHand layers, import them as keyframes, or flatten them. You can import individual pages, a range of pages, or all pages, and finally, you can include invisible layers, background layers, and choose to maintain text blocks.

After vector artwork has been imported, you can edit it the same as any Flash vector art.

Importing Fireworks PNGs

Fireworks source files can contain both bitmap and vector artwork. Flash displays a different dialog box when importing Fireworks files than it displays for either Illustrator or FreeHand files.

To preserve the layer structure of a Fireworks file, import the file into a movie clip. Conversely, you can flatten the layers into a single layer in the current timeline (or scene).

You can rasterize objects in your Fireworks file (turning them into bitmaps), or you can keep them as editable objects. Likewise, you can rasterize text blocks or leave them editable.

Finally, you can import the entire Fireworks file as a single flattened bitmap. When you import a file in this fashion, Flash converts the file to a PNG image format—specifically, PNG32 (32 bits per pixel).

Importing PDF and EPS Files

When you import a PDF file, Flash looks at the underlying structure of it. You can import your pages as either scenes or keyframes, retain your layers, flatten them, or import them as keyframes, import all your pages or a range of pages, and finally, include invisible layers, maintain your text blocks, or rasterize everything.

If you decide to rasterize your PDF, you can specify the resolution at which Flash rasterizes it, either selecting from the pull-down menu, or specifying your own target resolution.

When you import EPS files, Flash confront you with the same dialog box and options.

Summary

Flash MX 2004 allows you to import from a number of bitmap and vector file formats, allowing you to use artwork created in different software products. You have three import options: Import to Stage, Import to Library, and Open External Library.

When you have imported bitmap artwork, you can edit its scale, rotation, position, and skew; you can also break it apart or convert it to vector art for further editing.

Vector artwork is defined by mathematical formulas and has different import considerations than bitmap artwork. When importing vector artwork, you can maintain layer structures and text blocks, or flatten the file into a single layer.

Sample Questions

1. When would you change an imported image's property to Lossless in the Image Properties dialog box?

   A. When the imported image has complex colors.

   B. When the imported image has many tones.

   C. When the imported image is a Fireworks PNG.

   D. When the imported image has simple shapes and colors.

2. Which of the following file types allows you to import multiple pages?

   A. Adobe Illustrator (.ai)

   B. FreeHand (.fh11)

   C. Fireworks (.png)

   D. Enhanced Windows Metafile (.emf)

3. To switch an image on the Stage with an image in the Library (choose 2):

   A. Click the Swap button on the Property Inspector.

   B. Select Modify > Bitmap > Swap Bitmap.

   C. Select Insert > Bitmap > Swap Bitmap.

   D. Choose Edit > Bitmap > Swap Bitmap.

4. The option that allows you to import assets from another FLA is:

   A. Import > Import to Stage

   B. Import > Import Library

   C. Import > Open External Library

   D. Import > Import Assets

CHAPTER 13

Working with Vector Art

IN THIS CHAPTER

Drawing in Flash   101

Manipulating Your Graphics   102

Using the Color Mixer   104

Using the Fill Transform Tool   105

Making Your Own Color Swatches   106

Summary   107

Sample Questions   108

In Chapter 12, we spent a lot of time reviewing the sorts of things you can do with bitmap art, and didn't really spend much time with vector art. Since Flash is a vector tool, it comes with an array of built in options that allow you to get pretty creative.

In this chapter, we're going to review vector tools and options. The drawing tools themselves are covered in detail in Chapter 5, "Flash MX 2004 Tools," so that information will not be repeated here.

Drawing in Flash

When we use the drawing tools in Flash, we're making vector objects. We can draw strokes, which are lines (or paths), and fill, which is area of color.

To draw an object, select the appropriate drawing tool and drag on the Stage. When you're drawing with the oval, rectangle, or polystar tool, Flash will draw both stroke and fill, unless you specifically shut one or the other off.

➜ For more on how to use the Oval, Rectangle, and Polystar tools, see Chapter 5, "Flash MX 2004 Tools."

> **TIP**
> Use layers to arrange your content spatially.

➜ See Chapter 10, "Layers and the Timeline," for more information about layers.

Stroke and fill are treated as two separate objects in Flash. Single-clicking a stroke will select either the entire stroke or just one line segment, depending on how the graphic is constructed and how many corners the line may have. Double-clicking on a stroke that has multiple corners will select the entire stroke. Single-clicking on fill will select just the area of fill, whereas double-clicking on the fill will select the entire graphic.

> **TIP**
>
> If you don't want to draw a stroke or a fill, with the oval, rectangle, or polystar tool selected, click the appropriate color chip in the Color section of the main toolbar, and select the white box with the red line through it. One of those tools has to be selected though.

Drawing with one of the drawing tools creates an editable object. An editable object can be changed with any of the drawing or transform tools, and when you click on it, a "hash" pattern appears to indicated it has been selected. When you have two editable objects on the same layer, and they overlap each other, the editable object in the higher stacking order will punch out (think cookie cutter) the editable object underneath of it. This allows a designer to create more interesting shapes.

> **TIP**
>
> Stacking order in a layer is determined by the order in which you draw the objects. The last drawn object always occupies a higher stacking order.

To prevent items from punching out, you can group editable objects after they're drawn. To group an object or a bunch of objects, select them, then select Modify > Group, or use the keyboard shortcut Control-G (Command-G on the Mac).

> **TIP**
>
> Editable objects that occupy separate layers do not punch out.

Manipulating Your Graphics

One you have drawn a graphic on the Stage, you can change its general appearance with a number of tools that come with Flash, including the Selection tool. There are two ways of changing the shapes of graphics to produce more visually compelling artwork: using the transform tools and options, or using the "natural drawing tools."

The natural drawing tools work with the Selection tool, and can alter the general appearance of any editable graphic.

When the Selection tool is hovering over the Stage, the cursor appears to be an arrow with a box in the lower right corner of it, indicating that selections can be made. As you approach an editable graphic that is not selected, the box will change to either a curvy line, or a right angle.

When the box has changed to a curvy line, you can bend a shape in or out (concave or convex) to produce curves. Press and hold down on the mouse key and drag to create the effect.

When the box changes to a right angle, you can change the position of corners or extend the length of lines. Press and hold down on the mouse key and drag to reposition a corner or drag an endpoint to a new position to lengthen a line.

> **TIP**
> This method only works if the graphic is not selected.

> **TIP**
> You can also drag corners in, or shorten a line, with the natural drawing tools.

Another way to alter the shapes of graphics to create new shapes is to use the Subselection tool. Any time you draw a graphic with the drawing tools, Flash automatically inserts anchor points, which can either be corner points for sharp angles, or curve points for curved lines. The Subselection tool allows you to manipulate anchor points and tangent handles to change the overall shape and appearance of graphics.

To use the Subselection tool, choose it from the tool panel, then click on any editable graphic on the Stage. When you choose an editable graphic with the Subselection tool, the anchor points will show for that graphic. If you click on an anchor point, its tangent handles will show.

To adjust the curvature of a line, drag and rotate tangent handles. To move an anchor point to a new position, drag it with the Subselection tool. You can also select the point with the Subselection tool and "nudge" it with the arrow keys.

> **TIP**
> Nudging refers to moving an item a few pixels in any direction with the arrow keys.

The Free Transform tool is also used to change the appearance and shape of graphics. The tool allows you to change scale, rotation, and skew of any object, as well as to distort editable objects.

To use the Free Transform tool, choose it from the tool panel and click on the graphic you want to transform. From the Free Transform tool options, choose Skew and Rotate, Scale, Distort, or Envelop to perform the appropriate task. For a full listing of the Free Transform tool's capabilities, see Chapter 5, where it is covered in detail.

In addition to using the Free Transform tool to change things like scale and rotation, you can use the Transform panel. To retrieve the panel, select Window > Design Panels > Transform. When a graphic is selected, you can enter values in to change width and height, rotation, and the skew of the graphic.

> **TIP**
>
> To constrain your proportions, click the Constrain button in the Transform panel, or click the padlock icon next to the Width and Height settings on the Property Inspector.

> **TIP**
>
> Transform settings can also be found in the Modify > Transform fly-over menu.

Using the Color Mixer

Part of making your own artwork means assigning color to your objects, whether it is stroke or fill. While we can assign colors via the Property Inspector, and the Color section on the main toolbar, those options are rather limited in scope. The Color Mixer, however, gives us plenty of options where color is concerned.

To use the Color Mixer, select Window > Design Panels > Color Mixer. The panel has two modes: HSB and RGB. To toggle between these two color modes, click the Color Mixer options menu, and select either HSB or RGB. The percentages for either will be listed in a column on the right of the panel, with Alpha being the last option.

The Color Mixer has Stroke and Fill settings. To select stroke color, click the color chip for the Stroke option and choose a color from the color palette that appears.

> **TIP**
>
> The default color palette is Web 216. To create a custom color palette, see the section below.

You can also simply highlight the stroke option, and choose a color from the color picker, enter in RGB or HSB values, or enter a hexidecimal number in the hexadecimal color box in the lower left corner of the color mixer. Changing the alpha will make the stroke color partially or entirely transparent, depending on what value is entered.

Fill color is set the same way, but with fill, you have several options: None, Solid, Linear, Radial, and Bitmap.

None and Solid more or less speak for themselves. Linear and Radial, however, don't, and they refer to two different gradient types. A linear gradient is a color progression from left to right, top to bottom, or corner to corner from one color to the next in line. A radial gradient progresses from a center point out. Choosing either of these options and clicking on a graphic with the Paint Bucket tool will apply a gradient to an editable object.

When you choose a gradient type, a gradient editor will appear in the color mixer, with several color chips along a bar of color that have arrows above them indicating their position. To change the color of a chip, click it and either select the new color from the color palette or alter the RGB mix, or enter a hexadecimal number. To add a color chip, click anywhere just beneath the color bar. Dragging a color chip away removes it from the gradient. Color chips can be moved about to change the range over which the color progression occurs between it and another chip.Bitmap fills can be applied to solid objects as well. When you select Bitmap from the fill option in the color mixer, you're presented with all of the bitmaps in your document library. Choosing one of the bitmaps will select it for fill. When you apply a bitmap fill to a graphic, by default, the bitmap will tile to fill the object.

How the bitmap appears inside of the object can be determined by the Fill Transform tool.

TIP

The Fill Transform tool can also be used to change the appearance of a gradient in a graphic.

Using the Fill Transform Tool

The Fill Transform tool allows you to change the angle, position, rotation, and scale of gradient and bitmapped fills. To use the tool, select it and then click an area of gradient or bitmapped fill. Control handles will appear indicate the center point of the fill and additional control handles will allow you to change the rotation and scale of the gradient.

TIP

When you mouse over a control handle, your cursor will change to reflect what that control handle does.

For gradients, you can change the center point, scale the gradient, and rotate it. The square control handle changes the scale when you drag it, and the center circle changes the center point of the gradient. When you're working with a circular gradient, you can also change the gradient's radius by dragging the middle control handle.

Bitmap fills are a little different. The Fill Transform tool will allow you to change the scale, rotation, and skew of the bitmaps filling the object.

When you select an object with a bitmap fill using the Fill Transform tool, the tiled bitmap that you clicked on will appear with three square control handles in its lower left corner, three circular control handles in its upper right corner, and a center point. Dragging the center point changes the position of the tile. Dragging the square control handle changes the scale of the tile; the corner square will maintain the proportions, while the two side squares change width and height. The corner circle control handle changes the rotation of the tiled fill, and the side circles skew and slant.

> **TIP**
>
> When a fill is locked, which is an option of the Paint Bucket tool, you will not be able to transform the fill.

Making Your Own Color Swatches

Very often, when you're working on a project, it is useful to have your own color swatches, if not your own color palette entirely. The Color Swatches panel gives you a way to construct your own palette, save it, and share it with other members of your team, who can then load it easily.

Open the Color Swatches panel by selecting Window > Design Panels > Color Swatches. By default, the Web 216 color palette is loaded; it can be cleared by selecting the Color Swatches option menu, then choosing Clear Colors.

> **TIP**
>
> This will clear every color but black and white.

> **NOTE**
>
> You can retrieve the Web 216 panel at any time by choose Web 216 from the Options menu. The Web 216 palette is important because it contains the 216 colors that work consistently between Mac, PC, and a variety of monitors with their varying color support.

To create your own swatch, choose the Fill option in the Color Mixer, or choose the Fill option from the Color section of the main tool bar. You can also select the Fill option from the Property Inspector. With the eyedropper, hover over an area of color on the Stage, and then click to select the color.

> **TIP**
>
> It's often useful to select colors from a bitmap image. You can also enter hexadecimal numbers in any of the fill options to create a color selection.

To add the swatch, place your cursor over the grey area in the Color Swatches panel, and click. Repeat this to add more colors.

To delete a swatch, select it in the Color Swatches panel, then select Delete Swatch from the Options menu.

To save your color swatches, select Save Colors from the Options menu. Flash saves color palettes with a CLR extension, which is a Flash color set.

> **TIP**
>
> You can make your color palette the default by choosing Save as Default from the Options menu.

To load a CLR, select Add Colors from the Options menu. This will not replace any colors currently in the Color Swatches panel, but will load your swatches at the end of whatever palette is currently loaded.

Summary

Flash MX 2004 is a vector tool that allows you to create and modify your own vector artwork. Vector artwork can be drawn and manipulated with a variety of tools.

Flash's natural drawing tools allow you to create new shapes by bending graphics with the selection tool, as well as modifying their corners and line lengths. The Color Mixer applies color settings for strokes, and color and fill settings for filled in objects. The fill settings are None, Solid, Linear and Radial gradients, and Bitmap fills. The gradient and bitmap fills of objects can be further altered with the Fill Transform tool.

The Color Swatches panel is used to create your own color swatches, or manage the color swatches that come with Flash. Custom color swatches that you build can be saved with a CLR extension, and saved as the default colors for your application.

Sample Questions

1. In what panel can you create your own custom color palette?

   A. In the Color Swatches panel

   B. In the Color Picker

   C. In the Color Mixer panel

   D. In the Fill Transform options

2. What tool allows you to move tangent handles to modify an existing shape?

   A. The Subselection tool

   B. The Pen tool

   C. The Stroke tool

   D. The Selection tool

3. How can you change the scale of a graphic (choose 2)?

   A. Modify > Scale

   B. With the Transform panel

   C. With the Free Transform tool

   D. Modify > Shape > Transform

4. What tool most efficiently draws three-sided shapes?

   A. The Rectangle tool

   B. The Polystar tool

   C. The Line tool

   D. The Pen tool

CHAPTER **14**

Using Text

IN THIS CHAPTER

The Different Types of Text   109

Adding Static Text   109

Breaking Text Apart   111

Using Input Text   112

Using Dynamic Text   114

Text Components   116

Font Issues   118

Summary   119

Sample Questions   120

The Different Types of Text

Flash uses three types of text in any application: Static, Input, and Dynamic text. Static text is hard-typed into the application, and never changes. Input text allows you to create fields that your end users can type information into. Dynamic text allows you to do things like display information retrieved from external sources in your application or otherwise change text through ActionScript.

Each type of text has different options to set on the Property Inspector, and these options can affect file size and quality.

Adding Static Text

To add static text to your application, select the Text tool from the Tool Bar. When the Text tool is selected, the Property Inspector will change to reflect the settings available for text.

First, in the upper left corner of the Property Inspector, make sure your text type is set to Static Text in the pull-down menu. Choose a font size, text color, style (bold or italic), text orientation (horizontal, vertical left to right, or vertical right to left), and text alignment (center, left, right, or block justify). Click on the Stage with the Text tool, and begin to type. Hitting Enter while typing in the text block will move you down to the next line.

TIP

When choosing color, the color of the text should have plenty of contrast with the background.

If you click and drag with the text tool, you can create a text area of a fixed size. Text will wrap in the text area when it exceeds the size you set. When you need to resize a text area, double-click on the text block with your text tool, then click and drag the control handle that appears in the upper right corner to resize.

> **TIP**
> The control handle appears as a small circle to indicate text boxes that aren't fixed width. If the text box is a fixed width, it will appear as a square. For dynamic and input text, it always appears as a square in the lower right corner of the text box.

> **TIP**
> If you try to change the size of a text area with the width and height options on the Property Inspector, it will distort the text.

To change leading or kerning, click and drag the slider in the leading/kerning box, or simply enter a value. Kerning is automatically turned on for most fonts. If you want manual control over kerning, deselect the Auto Kern check box.

> **NOTE**
> Leading is the space between lines in a paragraph. Kearning is the space between letters in a word.

> **TIP**
> Keep your fonts sizes big enough to be legible. Text sizes under 10 or 12 points can be difficult for end users to read.

To superscript or subscript text, select the text, then choose superscript or subscript in the pull-down menu on the Property Inspector. To change indenting, line spacing, and margins in a text area, click the Format button and enter the appropriate settings.

When you add static text to your application, two things happen. First, the font outline is ultimately added to the SWF that's produced. Second, the text displayed in your application is anti-aliased, which is fine for bigger font sizes, but not such a good idea for small text. You can toggle between aliased and anti-aliased text by clicking the Alias Text button on the Property Inspector. Aliased text is not smoothed, making smaller font sizes easier to read. Using this option does not prevent the font outline from being included in the SWF however.

To prevent a font outline from being embedded in the SWF, check the Use Device Fonts option on the Property Inspector. When this option is selected, text is automatically not anti-aliased, and the final SWF will look on the end user's computer for the font outline when the SWF runs. Because the font outline is not included, a smaller SWF is produced. The downside, however, is that the browser's default font will be used if the user doesn't have the font outline loaded on their computer.

Finally, you can make text hyperlinks in the Link section of the Property Inspector. However, unlike HTML, when you make text blocks hyperlink, they are not automatically changed in appearance. You must change the physical appearance of the text yourself in order to indicate to the user that the text is clickable.

Breaking Text Apart

Often on Flash web sites, you see text animate in and out, where individual letters pop into place to form whole words. Because you can only have one item at a time in a layer containing motion animation, each letter has to be on its own layer in order for these kinds of animations to work.

➡ See Chapter 21, "Motion Tweening," for more information on motion animation.

Rather than type a whole bunch of text blocks a single letter at a time, and then try to line them up, you can quickly break a line of text or a single word into individual letters. Select Modify > Break Apart once. Each letter that results is fully editable text.

To get each letter on its own layer, select Modify > Timeline > Distribute to layers.

If you want to convert text to paths, select Modify > Break Apart once, then Modify > Break Apart a second time. Once text has been converted to a path, it will behave as any editable vector object in Flash, and can be edited or otherwise altered with the tools.

TIP

Undoing will bring the text back. You can either select Edit > Undo, use Control- or Command-Z, or use the History Panel to undo.

Using Input Text

Input text allows a user to type into a text area. In general, input text fields are used to collect information from a user, and submit the information to dynamic text fields in your Flash application or to some technology that will do something useful with it. They have the same purpose, therefore, as input text fields in HTML.

To add input text to an application, select the text tool, and choose the Input Text option in the Property Inspector. On the Stage, click and drag to define an input text area. The basic formatting options of input text are the same as static text, with a few exceptions.

First, input text cannot be manually kerned. Likewise, input text can neither be superscripted nor subscripted. The hyperlink option is not available for input text as well.

As far as what you can do, input text can be set to be single line fields, multiline fields, multiline fields that don't wrap, and password fields.

NOTE

Password fields have nothing to do with encryption, and do not make the data typed into it secure. The field simply replaces any characters typed into the field with asterisks so that someone can spy over a user's shoulder.

Input text can be HTML tagged by selecting the Render as HTML Text button. If the input text field contains HTML version 1 tags, with no hard carriage returns, the text will render based on those tags.

Next to the Render as HTML Text button is the Show Border Around Text button. This will add a border and a background for the text field.

Font styles chosen for an input text field rely on the device fonts installed on an end user's machine by default. If you want to embed the font outline, you have to click the Character's button on the Property Inspector, and choose which portions of a font outline should be embedded. Use this option if you want a user to type in a font that may not be commonly installed on most computers. Embedding a character outline increases file size; in addition, text is anti-aliased as it's typed with this option turned on.

> **TIP**
>
> If you don't want the text to be anti-aliased, click the Alias Text button on the Property Inspector after embedding the outline. When the user types in text, the text will not be smoothed.

To assign a character limitation to the text field, enter a value in the Maximum Characters field.

> **TIP**
>
> Blank spaces in the text field count as characters, so be sure to keep that in mind when setting the limit.

Input text fields can be manipulated with ActionScript as well. As of Flash Player 6, input and dynamic text fields were brought into the fold of Object Oriented Programming; when you draw either with the text tool, you're making an instance of the TextField class. Because the text fields are objects, they can accept instance names, which are assigned in the Instance Name field in the Property Inspector. This allows you to manipulate the text field programmatically.

→ We'll cover this more in Chapter 27, "The Actions Panel," and Chapter 28, "The Basics of Action Script."

In addition to the Instance Name field, there is a Var field in the Property Inspector when you're working with Input Text. The Var field is used when authoring for Flash Player 5 or below, and is used to retrieve the text a person types into the text field for further processing. You should not use the Var field when you are also using the the methods and properties of the TextField class to control an input text field. In Flash MX and MX 2004, it is considered a bad practice.

Using Dynamic Text

Dynamic text in Flash is used to display information retrieved from some other source. Those sources can be ActionScript variables, hard-coded information (assigning a value to the field's text property), input text boxes, or external data sources such as XML, recordsets, Web Services, or name/variable pairs in text files.

To add a dynamic text field, select the Text tool, and in the Property Inspector, choose Dynamic Text from the text type pull-down menu. On the Stage, press and drag to create a text field.

> **TIP**
>
> The settings for a dynamic text field look an awful lot like the settings for input text fields. They can accept instance names, can be single line, multiline, or multiline with no word wrap. But unlike input text fields, they cannot be password fields and they can be hyperlinked (like static text).

Dynamic text fields, like input fields, do not automatically embed font outlines. To embed the font outline for a dynamic text field, choose the Character tab on the Property Inspector, and specify which portions of the font outline you want to embed. When a font outline is embedded, it behaves as static text, in that the font is anti-aliased by default.

The other options on the Property Inspector are:

- **Selectable.** When this button is toggled on, the text in the text field can be copied and pasted by the end user.

- **Render Text as HTML.** Displays HTML tagged text in the dynamic text field with the HTML formatting.

- **Show Border Around Text.** Creates a black border and white background by default for the text box.

Getting text into a dynamic text field requires a little bit of ActionScript. Dynamic text fields, in Flash Player 6 and above, can be named and directly manipulated through their text property. To add text to a dynamic text field with ActionScript, use the following syntax:

```
InstanceNameOfField.text="value"; for plain text, and:
InstanceNameOffield.htmlText="<b>value</b>" for HTML formatted text.
```

Where `InstanceNameOfField` is the name you add in the Property Inspector, `text` is the actual property of the field, and `value` is the text you want to display in the text field.

> **TIP**
>
> Like input text, dynamic text fields also have a Var field on the Property Inspector, which is used to assign text programmatically to a text field when publishing for Flash Player version 5.0 or below. When authoring for Flash Player 6.0 and above, the best practice is to use the .text and .htmlText properties.

Dynamic text fields can also retrieve their values for display from external text files by loading the information in those text files into a special object called the LoadVars object, built from the LoadVars class in Flash. This has to be done programmatically.

> **NOTE**
>
> The information in the text files has to be in `name-value` pairings. If you have more than one variable, you have to encase each pairing in "&" characters. For example: `&myCookie=Chocolate Chip&&myCookie2=Peanut Butter&` and so on.

First, select the keyframe that you want the ActionScript detailed below to trigger in. Then, launch your Actions window, and type the following in the Actions pane:

```
var myLoadVars:LoadVars=new LoadVars();
myLoadVars.load("myTextfile.txt");
```

The first line creates an instance of the LoadVars class (aka: a LoadVars object), gives it an instance name, and tells the Flash Player what kind of object it is. The second line loads the text file and all of its name-value pairings. Each variable becomes a property of the object, and each variable value becomes the new property value.

Next, you have to say what will happen with that information once it's fully loaded into memory. Use the following general syntax:

```
myLoadVars.onLoad=function()
{
    myDynamicTextfield.text=myLoadVars.variable1;
    myDynamicTextfield.text=myLoadVars.variable2;
}
```

The onLoad event is triggered when the data fully loads into memory and is stored in the LoadVars object. From there, you refer to the name-value pairings that were in the text file as though they were properties of the LoadVars object.

Read more about manipulating objects, including text field objects, in the chapters on ActionScript.

Text Components

Besides using text fields, Flash designers can use the text components that come with Flash. There are three text components: TextArea, TextInput, and Label. Each of these components can accept an instance name, so that they can be controlled using ActionScript. They also have properties that can be set using the Property Inspector, as well as ActionScript.

> **NOTE**
>
> Because controlling components using ActionScript is discussed in Chapter 19, "Components," it is not detailed here.

TextArea

The TextArea component is used to display multiline blocks of text, or to accept multiple lines of text when you are accepting user input, as in form fields that accept user comments. As a best practice, you wouldn't use the TextArea component for single lines of text. The TextInput component is considered better for that kind of task.

> **TIP**
>
> The TextArea component also has a built-in scroll bar that appears when the lines of text exceed the visible area of the component.

The TextArea component has the following properties that can be changed with the Property Inspector:

- **Editable.** The default is true. When set to true, a user can type into the TextArea.

- **HTML.** The default is false. When set to true, this property will render HTML tagged text with HTML formatting.

- **Text.** The text that the end user sees in the application.

- **WordWrap.** The default is true. This property indicates whether or not text can wrap in the TextArea's visible space.

To use the TextArea component, drag an instance of it from the Components panel to your Stage. If you have already used a TextArea in your document, you can drag it from your document library instead.

TIP

The TextArea component can be controlled using ActionScript. It's appearance can be modified with styles.

➜ See Chapter 19, "Components," for more information on using ActionScript with components.

TextInput

The TextInput component is used to display single lines of text, or to accept single lines for text from a user. It doesn't support carriage returns, so if you need multiple lines of text or user input, use the TextArea component.

The TextInput component has the following properties that can be modified using the Property Inspector:

- **Editable.** The default is true. This permits a user to type information into the component. When set to false, the component is used for displaying text.

- **Password.** The default is false. If this property is set to true, anything a user types into the field will be hidden, and an asterisk will replace each character typed.

- **Text.** The text the user sees.

TIP

The password property does not encrypt data. For instance, if you are building a form and you send the contents of the field to something using the GET method, the value of the field will show in the URL string.

To use an instance of the component, drag it from the Components panel and onto the Stage. If you have already used an instance of the TextInput component in your document, you can drag it out of your document library instead.

Label

The Label component is used any time you need to label another component in something like a form. Of course, you can use static or dynamic text to do the same thing, but there's an advantage to using the label component. If you're using styles to control the appearance of your components and the fonts that they use, they can easily be applied to the Label component to keep appearance consistent.

➜ For more information on applying styles to components, see Chapter 19, "Components."

The following properties can be set on the Property Inspector for any given instance of the Label Component:

- **AutoSize.** The default is none. When set to left, the right and bottom sizes of the component will resize to fit longer text. When set to center the bottom of the label resizes. When set to right the left and bottom sides of the label resize.

- **HTML.** The default is false. This property will render HTML tag text within the Label. However, if this option is set to true, you cannot use styles to format the component.

- **Text.** The text that the user sees. The default is Label.

To use an instance of the Label component, drag it out of the Components panel and onto your Stage. From there, you can adjust the properties in the Properties Inspector.

TIP

If you have already used the Label component in your document, you can drag it out of the library.

Font Issues

When you're working with Flash, there are a number of things you have to keep in mind. Some of them are specific to Flash, some are general multimedia design problems.

Let's summarize them here:

- Use sans-serif fonts whenever possible. Serif fonts are hard to read, because they look blurry at smaller sizes.

- Use device fonts for static text, if possible. Using device fonts keeps your file size smaller. Don't forget _sans, _serif, and _typewriter give you a way of using a system's default font in the appropriate category.

- Avoid using fancy or special fonts that might prevent you from using device fonts.

- Do not anti-alias small font sizes, as it makes text blurry and difficult to read. You can toggle aliasing on and off on the Property Inspector, even if you're going to use embedded fonts for static text.

Scaling also presents a problem for Flash designers. As a user resizes a browser, your Flash application may scale to accommodate the new browser size. If it scales too small, your text may not be legible. If it scales up, you may lose quality. You have two types of scaling choices in Flash, which can be set in the HTML tab of the Publish Settings dialog box, and which in turn will help you to keep your text legible.

In the Dimensions pull-down menu of the HTML tab, you can select pixels or percent.

If you choose percent, you're using a relative window scaling, because as a user resizes a browser window, your Flash document will resize to fit the percentage of the browser you said it should occupy.

If you choose Pixels, you're setting an absolute size, so this is an absolute scaling method. When a user resizes the browser, your Flash application will remain the set amount of pixels, whatever you chose it to be.

> **TIP**
> You can turn off scaling in the HTML tab by choosing No Scale from the Scale pull-down menu.

Summary

Flash MX 2004 has three types of text commonly used: static, dynamic, and input text. Static text is written directly in the application, and is used to display information that won't change. Dynamic text allows the application to retrieve information from an external source and display it, allowing for changes to be made outside the application without creating a need to republish the SWF. Input text allows the application to collect information from a user.

Each type of text field has different settings that can be altered in the Property Inspector, which affect the display of the text, whether or not the font is embedded in the final SWF, and whether or not the font is anti-aliased. Some of these settings also affect file size.

Things like scaling and anti-aliasing can make text difficult to read. Small font sizes should not be anti-aliased. Scaling can be made relative or absolute in the HTML tab of the Publish Settings dialog box. Relative scaling means your Flash application will resize when the browser resizes and absolute scaling means the dimensions of the Flash application will not alter as the browser resizes.

Text components duplicate much of the functionality of input and dynamic text fields, and can be added to your document by dragging and dropping them on the Stage.

Sample Questions

1. Which of the following is a disadvantage of using device fonts for static text?

   A. File size is kept at a minimum.

   B. Device fonts anti-alias.

   C. Special fonts can't be used because the end user may not have them.

   D. Device fonts are embedded in the SWF when the Flash file publishes.

2. Which of the following objects is used to load name-value pairings from a text file on the server for use in dynamic text fields?

   A. Movie Clip object

   B. LoadVars object

   C. XML Object

   D. None of the above

3. Which option prevents static text from being copied and pasted from your Flash application?

   A. Modify > Text > Not Selectable

   B. Text > Font > Not Selectable

   C. The Selectable button on the Property Inspector.

   D. Static text is always selectable.

4. What properties of input and dynamic text fields should you use to assign text for display using ActionScript (choose 2)?

   A. txt

   B. text

   C. var

   D. htmlText

CHAPTER **15**

Breaking Up a Project

IN THIS CHAPTER

Breaking a Project into
  Multiple SWFs   121

Loading an SWF into a Movie Clip   122

Loading an SWF into Levels   125

Preloaders   126

Runtime Sharing   127

Summary   128

Sample Questions   129

There are a number of ways to organize your application in its final form. In the old days, people used to develop all of their content in Scenes, load the entire SWF into the end user's browser all at once, then jump the playhead from point to point via animation and ActionScript. As Flash becoma more complex, a best practice emerged, and that was to break your project up into smaller, content related SWFs that don't load into the interface until they're needed.

This chapter reviews that best practice and the ActionScript you need to make things work.

Breaking a Project into Multiple SWFs

There are many different ways of building an application in Flash, but not all of them are necessarily the most efficient. In Flash, it's considered a best practice to take a single application and break it up into several modules, each of which will be its own independent SWF. Each module is separated by unique content, and may be further broken down. The idea is to have as many different SWFs as web pages, and then to integrate them in a single end user environment.

I like to use this as an example:

Say you're building a Web-based application for a pet company. You have dog owners, cat owners, and other small-pet owners coming to the site to look up information on feeding, or to buy products related to their pets. That's a lot of information. If you build all the dog information and all of the cat information, and all of the small pet information (ferrets, etc.) into a single SWF, your end user is going to be waiting for a LONG time for that SWF to load into the browser before they can actually use it. It makes more sense, then, to separate the project into a series of smaller SWFs that relate to each other by content. The main dog section would be its own SWF, then the dog food section, the dog toy section, feeding information, health tips, and so on, would each have their own SWFs. They don't load until a user clicks on a button that calls them.

The advantages to this approach include:

- Smaller initial download time for your interface.

- Only the relevant content displays when the user wants it.

- The ability to work in a team environment, where multiple people can work on the same project (just different aspects of it).

When you build everything into a single SWF, only one person at a time can work on the project. Breaking it up spreads the workload.

There are two ways to load multiple SWFs into a single interface. One is to load the external SWF into a Movie Clip somewhere in the application; the second is to load the external SWF into a level in the Flash Player.

> **TIP**
>
> It's generally better to load into a target movie clip, as you have greater control over things like position and appearance. The movie clip inherits the SWFs timeline, but the SWF inherits everything else, like scale, rotation, and alpha.

Loading an SWF into a Movie Clip

The first way to load an SWF external to your main application is by loading it into a Movie Clip in a timeline. The Timeline can be the main—or root—timeline, or it can be the timeline of another Movie Clip, depending in what it is you want to do. We'll discuss Movie Clip timelines in Chapter 18, "The Movie Clip Symbol."

To load an SWF into a Movie Clip, you must have the Movie Clip on the Stage. You can create the Movie Clip visually, or using ActionScript, with the `createEmptyMovieClip` action.

> **TIP**
>
> The Movie Clip should be empty; if you have any content in the Movie Clip, it will be replaced by the SWF that loads into it.

To create a Movie Clip with ActionScript, use the following syntax:

```
this.createEmptyMovieClip("newInstanceName",depth);
```

Depth, in the above example, is the stacking order of the new Movie Clip in relation to the other elements on the Stage, and this is the main timeline.

To create a Movie Clip visually, select Insert > New Symbol, choose Movie Clip as the Behavior type, and click Ok. That will place you into Symbol Editing mode. To keep the Movie Clip empty, return to Scene 1 without adding content, then drag and drop the empty Movie Clip into a layer on the Stage.

> **TIP**
>
> Remember, you're loading external content into this Movie Clip. Paying attention to the layer is important, so critical data is not obscured.

Movie Clips created visually must have an instance name. An instance name identifies the Movie Clip for use in ActionScript, and is different than the Library name (which is really only an internal name so that a user can organize assets). To assign an instance name to the Movie Clip, select it on the Stage, then add the name in the Instance Name field of the Property Inspector. Instance names must begin with a letter, can contain any combination of letters and numbers, but can't have special characters or spaces.

Once the Movie Clip has been named, you can select either a frame or a button to add the behavior that will load the SWF into the interface. One way to do that is with the Behaviors Panel. The Behaviors Panel is detailed in Chapter 26, "The Behaviors Panel." For now, we'll just review the specific behavior that executes the action.

Open the panel by selecting Window > Development Panels > Behaviors. In the panel, click the Add Behavior, and from the categories, select Movie Clip. The behavior to use is Load External Movie Clip.

In the dialog box that appears, type the URL of the SWF that you're going to load into the interface. This can be an absolute reference (http://www.domain.com/whatever.SWF), or it can be relative (folder/whatever.SWF or simply whatever.SWF if both movies are in the same directory).

> **TIP**
>
> The only restriction here is that the SWF loading into the interface must be in the same domain that the interface is in, by default. We call that the Sand Box rule. If you need to load SWFs, you need to create a Cross Domain Policy. For more information, check out Macromedia's website.

If you added the behavior to a frame, then you won't be able to change the triggering event. In that case, the SWF will load when the playhead enters the frame that has the behavior. If you added the behavior to a button, then you can change the event to any of the mouse events in the Events pull down menu in the Behaviors panel. The default is onRelease, which is when someone clicks and then let's go of the mouse button.

Once the SWF loads into the Movie Clip, the Movie Clip will inherit the SWFs timeline. That is to say, they become one and the same. What's more, unless you've set the Movie Clip's width and height using ActionScript, and after the behavior that loads the external SWF, the Movie Clip will resize to fit the content loaded into it. Anything in the Movie Clip already will be replaced.

TIP

Using this method, it doesn't matter what the Stage size of the external SWF is. Once it's in the Movie Clip, you can change things like size, position, scale, opacity, and anything else that can be done with a Movie Clip.

NOTE

Keep in mind that wherever the Movie Clip is in the layer structure is where your SWF will show. Make sure your container Movie Clip is in the right layer for the right purpose

You can also load an SWF into a target Movie Clip using the MovieClipLoader class. To use the class you must first make an instance of it using ActionScript:

```
var instanceName:MovieClipLoader=new MovieClipLoader();
```

The general syntax to load an SWF using the MovieClipLoader instance you create is:

```
movieClipLoaderInstanceName.loadClip(url, target);
```

An example of how that might look in an actual application follows:

```
var myLoader:MovieClipLoader=new MovieClipLoader();
myLoader.loadClip("content.swf",myMovieClip);
```

TIP

The MovieClipLoader class is fairly complex and can be used to do things like check the download progress of an SWF or JPEG image as it's loading. For more information on the proper use of the MovieClipLoader class, check out the ActionScript Dictionary from the Help menu, and move the MovieClipLoader class entry.

Loading an SWF into Levels

The Flash Player is broken up into levels, each of which can contain and play an SWF. This gives you another way to organize your application into content modules. When an instance of the Flash Player is created inside of an HTML page, you can stack movies up on top of each other from zero to 16,382. The first SWF to load into the Flash Player (the first one called by the EMBED tag, that is) occupies level zero, and sets the size of the Flash Player, and the background color as well. What that ultimately means is if you play movies one on top of the other in an HTML page in levels, any movie loaded above level zero will inherit the Flash Player size and the background color determined by whatever's in level zero.

Levels always remind me of the Mylar sheets you see in encyclopedias for human anatomy. Each sheet contains something different (skin, muscle, bones, and so forth), and when you remove one sheet you see the different content. However, in order for things to look right, each sheet has to be the same size, and positioned the same way. Also, their upper left corners have to match, as well as the size of the sheet.

Likewise, when you're loading movies into levels, each SWF that you create should have the same Stage size to get things lined up properly. When the SWF loads into a level, it will automatically match its upper left corner with the movie in level 0. In fact, it doesn't really have a choice.

To load an SWF into a level, you need to use a little ActionScript. The behaviors don't work so well with this option. First, select the item that you want to use to trigger the ActionScript. If it's a button, you can do it one of two ways, either giving the button an instance name, and then controlling it from a frame, or by adding the script directly to the button. Both methods are listed below, and the scripts must be typed into the Script Pane of the Actions Panel.

First, from a frame:

```
MyButtonInstanceName.onRelease=function()
{
    loadMovieNum("SWFname.SWF",level number);
}
```

Next, on the button itself:

```
on(release)
{
loadMovieNum("SWFname.SWF",level number);
}
```

If you want the script to execute when the playhead rolls over a frame, then add the script directly to a keyframe, selecting it and typing in the Script Pane of the Actions Window:

```
loadMovieNum("SWFname.SWF",level number);
```

This will load the movie into a level in the Flash Player.

> **NOTE**
>
> Remember, levels are not the same thing as layers. Layers are part of an actual Flash document. Levels are part of the Flash Player.

> **NOTE**
>
> Only one thing can be on a level at a time. If you load an SWF into the same level as something else, what was already there will be replaced with the new content.

Preloaders

When you're delivering Flash content over the web, preloaders are a must. A pre-loader mitigates extended download times by providing the end user with information about the progress of the download, or by otherwise letting them know that something is in fact happening. When you've broken a project up into multiple SWFs, and are loading them into target Movie Clips or levels in the Flash Player, preloaders are a must for every SWF loading in.

There are multiple ways to create preloaders. Many people create an animation in a Movie Clip, and place an instance of the Movie Clip in the first frame of the movie. The remaining content for the movie begins on the second frame. You use an ActionScript to make the Movie Clip instance play until the SWF is fully loaded. When the SWF is fully loaded, the Movie Clip stops playing and the movie progresses. Other methods for making preloaders include using scenes, or building a preloader in a completely different SWF.

The following block of ActionScript demonstrates a very simple preloader using a Movie Clip in the first frame of a movie:

```
stop();
var preLoadMC:MovieClip;
preLoadMC.onEnterFrame = function() {
    if (_root.getBytesLoaded()<_root.getBytesTotal()) {
        this.preText.text =
Math.round((_root.getBytesLoaded()/_root.getBytesTotal())*100)+"%";
    } else if (_root.getBytesLoaded() == _root.getBytesTotal()) {
        _root.play();
        delete this.onEnterFrame;
    }
};
```

The first action stops the movie from playing until the SWF fully loads into the Flash Player. The Movie Clip monitoring progress has the instance name preLoadMC, and inside of the Movie Clip is a dynamic text field with the instance name preText. The onEnterFrame event of the MovieClip class is used to drive the preloader, since it executes based on the frame rate. In the case of this script, the frame rate was 12 frames per second, so the event executed every 12th of a second. So every 12th of a second, preLoadMC checks to see whether the amount of bytes loaded into the Flash Player is the same as the total amount of bytes for the SWF. If not, then it divides the two, rounds the number, and multiples the number by 100 to get the percent of the SWF that's loaded. The product is displayed in the preText text field. Otherwise, when the two numbers become the same, the movie plays and the enterFrame event is deleted to save CPU.

> **TIP**
>
> When breaking your project into multiple SWFs, and using a preloader strategy like the one above, you should place the preloader in every SWF that will be loaded in the interface. Of course, this isn't the only method, and there are other ways of authoring preloaders so that you can have one that can be reused for each SWF loading into the interface.

Another way of creating preloaders is to use the MovieClipLoader class. This is a more complicated way of doing things, and requires a keener understanding of ActionScript. When you use an instance of the MovieClipLoader class, you can load JPEG images or SWFs into Movie Clip instances, and check the progress of the load.

> **TIP**
>
> Using the MovieClipLoader class allows you to create a preloader as a separate SWF, then load the content into the preloader itself! While the content is loading, the preloader will work its magic.

➜ For more information on how to use the MovieClipLoader class to preload SWFs and JPEG images, check out the ActionScript dictionary under the MovieClipLoader class entry.

Runtime Sharing

Runtime sharing is another technique that you can use to make sure your file sizes are as small as possible. We talked about runtime sharing in Chapter 9, "Organizational Tools and Where to Find Them." We'll review it here.

First, the idea is to share assets such as symbols or bitmaps from one SWF and use them in multiple SWFs. In this fashion, the shared assets are not actually brought into an SWF until the file runs. The general steps are summarized here:

1. Select the asset that you want to share from the document library.

2. Right- or control-click it, and choose Linkage from the context menu.

3. In the Linkage Properties dialog box, check Export for Runtime Sharing, and give the asset a Linkage Identifier.

4. Save and publish the document with the shared asset.

5. To use the shared asset in a different file, choose File > Import > Open External Library.

6. Open the FLA file that contains the shared asset.

7. Drag the shared asset from the external library into your document library or onto the Stage.

8. Save and publish the file that uses the shared asset

TIP

Remember, the SWF with the shared symbol must be published with the SWF that uses it.

Summary

Flash applications can, and should be, separated into multiple SWFs, with each SWF containing related content. Each SWF can then be called into the interface when an end user wants it, or when we specifically need it to load.

External SWFs can be loaded into Movie Clips or into levels of the Flash Player. To load an SWF into a Movie Clip, first, give the Movie Clip an instance name, and then, use the Load External Movie Clip behavior from the Behaviors panel. To load an SWF into a level, add the `loadMovieNum()` method to a frame or to a button using the Actions Panel. External SWFs and JPEGS can also be loaded with the MovieClipLoader class.

Preloaders should be used to indicate to your end user that a file is loading into the interface. Preloaders can be made a variety of ways, including using Movie Clips, Scenes, or completely different SWFs. The MovieClipLoader class can be used to create preloaders that monitor the download progress of an SWF or JPEG image loading into a Movie Clip instance.

Runtime sharing can be used to optimize applications by sharing assets across SWFs. Shared assets must be exported for runtime sharing, and must have a linkage identifier.

Sample Questions

1. What is the default restriction to loading external SWFs from the server into either Movie Clips or levels?

   A. All calls to the SWF must be absolute, using
   `http://www.yourDomain.com/my.swf.`

   B. All SWFs must be the same size as the first SWF loaded into the Flash Player.

   C. All SWFs must be loaded from the same domain that calls them.

   D. There are no restrictions.

2. What is an advantage to loading external SWFs into target Movie Clips or levels?

   A. You don't have to make preloaders for your SWFs.

   B. You don't have to worry about file size using this method.

   C. You can't use Scenes when you're loading external SWFs.

   D. The end user can load only the content relevant to him or her in, keeping your initial download time low.

3. Which of the following actions loads SWFs into target movie clips?

   A. `loadMovie();`

   B. `loadMovieNum();`

   C. `createEmptyMovieClip();`

   D. `load External Movie Clip`

4. What is a Movie Clip's depth?

   A. The layer that the Movie Clip is in.

   B. The level that the Movie Clip is in.

   C. The Movie Clip's stacking order with respect to the other visual assets.

   D. The size of the Movie Clip after an external SWF is loaded into it.

PART 3

Symbols in Depth

16 Graphic and Font Symbols

17 Button Symbols

18 The Movie Clip Symbol

19 Components

CHAPTER 16

Graphic and Font Symbols

IN THIS CHAPTER

Graphic Symbols Explained   133

Creating a Graphic Symbol   134

Using a Graphic Symbol   135

Editing a Graphic Symbol   136

Graphic Symbol Capabilities and
 Limitations   137

The Font Symbol   138

Summary   139

Sample Questions   139

In Macromedia Flash we make animations and design interfaces, and that means we have to reuse visual assets for any number of reasons. It can be as simple as using a corporate logo in several different areas, or as complex as animating the corporate logo across the screen. To keep our file sizes as small as possible, we put these visual assets in symbols, which can be used as often as we need to without adding significant file size. The Graphic symbol is ideal for reusing static visual assets.

What's more, in some cases, we may need to share special fonts that not everyone may have on their computers. Enter the Font Symbol, often neglected, but always ready to lend a hand.

In this chapter, we review the Graphic symbol, and some of the instance effects we can use with them when animating. We'll also review the Font Symbol, from creation to sharing.

Graphic Symbols Explained

Simply put, Graphic Symbols, and in fact all symbols in Flash, are reusable assets. Anything visual can be a graphic symbol, whether it's a bitmap image, a vector drawing, a block of text, or individual letters. All we have to do is take one of those visual assets and put it inside the graphic symbol, or create a graphic symbol from scratch and import or draw our assets into it. From there, we can use the symbol and its assets as many times as we need to without having a significant impact on file size. That's pretty important when you consider that many tasks in Flash require multiple instances of assets; motion animation, for instance, requires that you take one visual asset and slightly adjust its position in multiple frames over time.

TIP

When you create a graphic symbol, you are essentially wrapping an asset in a container, and storing it in the library. When you use the symbol on your stage, you're creating an instance of that symbol; a pointer to the symbol definition in the library, the same way image tags in HTML don't actually copy and paste an image in the HTML document, but point to its location on the server for retrieval.

Creating a Graphic Symbol

There are two ways to create a graphic symbol. First, you can take an asset that's already on the stage and convert it to a graphic symbol. Second, you can create it from scratch and add content to it.

To convert an asset to a graphic symbol, select the asset on the stage, then select Modify > Convert to Symbol, or drag and drop it into your document library. Additionally, you can right- or Control-click the asset, and select Convert to Symbol from the Context menu. The keyboard shortcut to convert an asset to a symbol is F8.

NOTE

You can convert more than one asset at a time to a symbol. Merely select all the assets to be included in the symbol, then convert. The assets don't have to be on the same layer, either; they'll be collapsed into a single symbol that will occupy the topmost layer that the assets were in.

When the Convert to Symbol dialog appears, you select the Graphic option from the Behavior section; in the name section, give the symbol a name to be used in the library. In addition, you can change the symbol's registration point by clicking on one of the little white squares in that section. Click OK to create the graphic symbol.

TIP

The library name is an internal organizational name, and isn't used by Flash or ActionScript. It's for human types only.

Once you've converted an asset to a graphic symbol, an instance of that symbol will automatically be placed on the stage, and the symbol definition in the library.

To make a new symbol from scratch, choose Insert > New Symbol, or click the New Symbol button on the lower left corner of the document Library Panel, or choose New Symbol from the Library Options pull-down menu. This will place you in symbol editing mode, where you can now import and organize assets.

> **TIP**
>
> When you're in symbol editing mode, you'll see a crosshair on the Stage. That's the symbol's registration point.

Using a Graphic Symbol

When you want to make use of a graphic symbol in your Flash document, drag it out of the library window and drop it on the stage in the layer and the keyframe you want it to be in. This creates an instance of the symbol.

Symbol instances essentially point to the symbol properties in the library, and draw a copy on the stage without duplicating the whole asset. This is what keeps our file size low. But just because it's a reference to a master asset doesn't mean that it can't be changed. In fact, symbol instances have their own special properties we can modify with the Property Inspector (in the case of graphic symbols).

To modify a symbol instance's properties, select it on the Stage. See Table 16.1 for the Graphic symbol instance properties.

Table 16.1 Graphic Symbol Instance Properties

PROPERTY	PURPOSE
Behavior	Tells you what kind of symbol it is, and allows you to change the behavior without affecting the symbol's definition in the library. The options are Graphic, Button, and Movie Clip.
W	Used to change the width of the symbol asset.
H	Used to change the height of the symbol asset.
X	Used to specify the X coordinate where the symbol should be located.
Y	Used to specify the Y coordinate where the symbol should be located.
Swap	Allows you to switch out one symbol instance for a different instance of a different symbol in the library.
Loop	If the symbol instance contains animation, loop will play the animation continuously for as many frames as the symbol instance occupies.
Play Once	If the symbol contains animation, the animation will play one time, regardless of how many frames the symbol instance occupies.
Single Frame	If the symbol contains animation, this setting allows you to specify a frame to show, skipping the animation entirely.
Color	Allows you to change brightness, tint, alpha (opacity), or, under the advanced option, a combination of RBB and Alpha.

In addition to the settings you change in the Property Inspector, you can change scale and rotation of a graphic symbol using the Free Transform tool, Transform panel, or by choosing an option from Modify > Transform.

To disassociate a symbol from its definition in the library, select the symbol and choose Modify > Break Apart. This will break the symbol back down into its constituent assets, but will not retain the symbol's layer structure. Everything will be placed in the layer that the broken apart symbol was already in.

Editing a Graphic Symbol

Graphic Symbols, like all symbols in Flash, have their own timelines that are tied to the main document timeline, their own layer panels, and their own set of X and Y coordinates.Inthe graphic symbol's timeline, you can add layers, import graphics, draw your own graphics, and add text assets if you want. You can even add animations, but it isn't recommended, since the graphic symbol is dependent on and uses the main document's timeline, as well in the next section.

After you have added assets to a new graphic symbol, or converted an asset to a graphic symbol, you can edit the contents of the symbol by double-clicking the symbol icon in the library, or by double-clicking the symbol on the Stage. Both of these methods will take you into symbol editing mode, with one very big difference; double-clicking a graphic symbol on the Stage opens the symbol definition in what's called Edit in Place Mode. Any change you make here (in normal symbol editing mode) makes a change to the master properties of the symbol. Ultimately, that means all instances of the symbol being used on the Stage will also be affected. Their individual instance properties, however, will be maintained.

When you enter symbol editing mode using either of the methods listed above, you will see a crosshair in the center of the symbol. The crosshair you see in symbol editing mode represents the symbol's absolute center, and as a result, the symbol's registration point.

For that registration point, 0, 0 is the center of the crosshair. Positive X values extend to the right, positive Y values down. Negative X extends right, negative Y, up. When you convert an asset to a symbol, and specify its registration point as the upper left corner, it matches the upper left corner of the asset to the center of the crosshair in its lower right quadrant.

> **NOTE**
> You can also enter symbol editing mode by right or control-clicking on the symbol on the Stage, and selecting either Edit, Edit in Place, or Edit in New Window. Edit and Edit in Place bring you to one of the above symbol editing modes. Edit in New Window opens symbol editing mode in an entirely different window, which can be rather useful at times.

In addition to editing a graphic symbol's assets in symbol editing mode, you can change the behavior of the master symbol itself. To do this, select the symbol in the library window, and either right- or Control-click the symbol, and choose Properties, or select Properties from the library's Options pull-down. This allows you to change the symbol from one type (graphic) to another (movie clip or button).

> **NOTE**
> When you change a symbol's properties in the library, it doesn't automatically update the symbol instance on the stage. If you change a graphic symbol to another symbol type in the library, you must select the symbol instances on the Stage, and also change their behaviors in the Property Inspector to match the new master symbol.

Graphic Symbol Capabilities and Limitations

To do motion animations in Flash, an asset first has to be a symbol. So if you want to animate an asset, you can immediately convert it to a graphic symbol, and then animate the whole symbol.

As mentioned before, graphic symbols have their own timelines, and as a result, can contain anything that a normal Flash document can contain. That means that you can create nested animations (animations inside symbols, added to the Stage).

Graphic symbols, like other assets, can be used with runtime sharing as a way to optimize your SWFs, both for file size and ease of updating.

➡ For more on using assets for runtime sharing, see Chapter 9, "Organizational Tools and Where to Find Them," and Chapter 15, "Breaking Up a Project."

While it has its own timeline, the graphic symbol is dependent on the main timeline. In essence, graphic symbols use the main timeline as their own. Therefore, there has to be at least as many frames on the main timeline as there is inside the graphic symbol in order for an animation inside a graphic symbol to display start to finish. And that's just from where the instance starts in the main timeline in the document. Therefore, graphic symbols are not the ideal vehicle for nested animations.

By and large, graphic symbols are used to contain static graphics that we then animate on the main timeline, or animate in the timelines of movie clip symbols. We also use them simply to display non-moving graphics throughout an application.

The Font Symbol

The Font Symbol is a fourth, and often forgotten, symbol type in Flash. It's primarily used to share fonts with between Flash documents with runtime sharing, or to export fonts to Flash documents.

> **TIP**
>
> Using a font symbol with runtime sharing allows you to use the same font across multiple Flash documents without adding the font outline to every single one of the SWF's, keeping file sizes at a minimum. Remember, Static Text automatically embeds the font outline in the SWF when the file publishes, adding file size.

To create a font symbol, from the Library panel's Options menu, select New Font. The Font Symbol Properties dialog box appears. In the Name field, enter a name for the font. This can be anything you want. In the Font menu, choose the font that you want to use for your font symbol. If you want to apply a style to the font, check the Bold or Italics check boxes, and specify a size (optional). Click OK to create the font symbol.

To use a font symbol for runtime sharing, select the font symbol in the document library, right- or Control-click it, and choose Linkage from the Context menu. In the Linkage Properties dialog box, do the following:

1. Check the Export for Runtime Sharing Checkbox

2. Assign the symbol a Linkage Identifier

3. Click OK

4. Save, publish, and close the file containing the symbol to share.

To use the shared symbol in another document:

1. Select File > Import > Open External Library

2. Select the FLA file that contains the shared symbol that you want to use

3. Drag the symbol from the external library to your document library

4. Create a Static, Input, or Dynamic text field on the Stage

5. In the Property Inspector, choose your font symbol from the Font menu.

> **TIP**
>
> Your font will appear in the menu in alphabetical order, with an asterisk next to the name. The asterisk indicates that the font is a font symbol from the library.

> **TIP**
>
> To import the font without runtime sharing, don't give the font symbol a linkage identifier, and follow the steps above to import. If you've already dragged in the symbol as a shared symbol, simply open the Linkage Properties dialog box, and deselect the Import for Runtime Sharing checkbox.

Summary

Graphic symbols are used to create reusable assets. Reusable assets do not significantly increase file size. Because graphic symbols have their own timeline, and therefore layer structure, you can build complex graphics inside the symbol. You can also create animations inside the symbol; however, because the graphic symbol's timeline is dependent upon the main timeline, this isn't always a recommended practice.

Graphic symbols can be edited in place (on the Stage), in symbol editing mode, or in symbol editing mode in a completely different window. Changes to a graphic symbol's master properties affect all symbol instances on the Stage.

Individual graphic symbol instances can have their own property set, including scale, brightness, tint, opacity, and position, without affecting the master properties of the symbol.

Graphic symbols are mostly used for static graphics.

Font symbols are another symbol type in Flash. These symbols are most often used for using fonts with runtime sharing, or to share fonts across Flash documents.

Sample Questions

1. What graphic symbol property allows you to create animated fade-in, fade-out effects?

   A. Opacity

   B. Alpha

   C. Tint

   D. Brightness

2. How do you make a font symbol available for runtime sharing?

    A. Check the Export for Runtime sharing box in the Linkage Properties dialog box.

    B. Select the font symbol in the library and choose Export for Runtime Sharing in the document library's Options menu.

    C. Right- or Control-click on the symbol in the document library, select Properties, and check the Export for Runtime Sharing checkbox.

    D. Select File > Import > Open External Library, and drag the font symbol into your document library. Flash will automatically set the font symbol to be runtime shared.

3. When you are in symbol editing mode, what two things does the crosshair on the Stage represent (choose 2)?

    A. The symbol's absolute center.

    B. The x and y location of the symbol on the Stage.

    C. The symbol's registration point.

    D. Where the snap ring will appear when you drag the object on the Stage.

4. How do you convert an editable visual asset to a graphic symbol (choose 2)?

    A. Select Modify > Timeline > Convert to Symbol.

    B. Select Modify > Convert to Symbol.

    C. Drag the asset into the Library.

    D. Drag the asset onto the Property Inspector.

CHAPTER 17

Button Symbols

IN THIS CHAPTER

Button Symbols Explained   141

Creating Buttons   142

Creating More Complex Buttons   144

ActionScript and Buttons   145

Button Best Practices   149

Summary   149

Sample Questions   150

Buttons are one of the more important symbol types in Flash, if for no other reason than they allow a user to build in interactivity. Without them, we wouldn't have much of an application. In this chapter, we'll go over how to make buttons, and what to do with them after they are created. We'll also review how to make your buttons more compelling.

Button Symbols Explained

Button symbols allow users to interact with your Flash application. They consist of a hit state, which serves as a hot spot, and three optional aesthetic states which can be used to provide a visual feedback mechanism to a user, indicating that the button can be clicked. Those states are Up, Over, and Down, which we'll discuss in the section on making buttons.

In Flash, buttons are objects, and that means that they be controlled by ActionScript. This can be accomplished either through the Behaviors panel or the Actions panel, and both practices will be addressed in the "ActionScript and Buttons" section later in this chapter.

Finally, because buttons are symbols, they're reusable, which means you can create one or two types of buttons and use them multiple times throughout your application without adding any significant file size. Each instance of a button is unique.

Creating Buttons

There are multiple ways to create buttons in Flash. You can take an asset that's already on the Stage, and convert it to a button symbol by selecting Modify > Convert to Symbol. You can drag the asset into the Library panel, which will convert it to symbol by default. You can also use the keyboard shortcut F8, or right- or Control-click on the asset on the Stage and choose Convert to Symbol from the Context menu. Any one of those methods will bring up the Convert to Symbol dialog. Choose Button in the Behavior section, give the button a name, and click OK when done. That creates the symbol in the library.

> **NOTE**
> If you don't add any other graphics in the button timeline, the Hit state becomes defined by whatever graphic is in the Up state.

The other way to create a button from scratch is to select Insert > New Symbol, click the New Symbol button on the Library panel, or choose New Symbol from the Library's Options menu. This will bring up the New Symbol dialog, which looks identical to the Convert to Symbol dialog. The only difference is that when you hit the Ok button this time, you will automatically be placed in Symbol Editing Mode.

In Symbol Editing Mode, you'll be placed in the Button's timeline. Buttons only have four frames to work with. Those are:

- **Up.** The button appearance when the application first loads.

- **Over.** The button appearance when the mouse rolls over it.

- **Down.** The button appearance when the user clicks on it.

- **Hit.** A graphic that creates a hotspot, determining the active area of the button.

The Up, Over, and Down states aren't really needed, but the Hit state IS the button. Without it, your button won't work. Any graphics in the Hit frame are completely invisible, which is what makes the Hit state a hotspot, so to speak. If you convert an asset to a button but don't add anything else, then whatever is in the Up frame will be used to determine the active area of the button.

To build the other graphic states of the button, first select the frame in which you plan to place a graphic, then insert a keyframe by selecting Insert > Timeline > Keyframe, or right- or Control-click, depending on your platform, on the empty frame position and choose Insert Keyframe from the Context menu. Then import a graphic, draw a graphic, or drag and drop an asset from the Library. Assets in the different frames will only be visible when their respective events are executing. In the case of the Up frame, that's the SWF simply being fully loaded into the interface, before the end user interacts with the button. For the other frames, either place the mouse over the button (which makes the Over frame visible), or click on the button (which makes the Down frame visible). When you place a graphic in the Hit frame, you'll want to be sure that it's big enough to cover your visual assets. You can turn on Onion Skinning to check.

> **TIP**
>
> You don't really want to have just text in the Hit frame. The graphic portion of text is the physical letter. If you're mousing over the edge of an "O" for example, the button is clickable. But when you're in the center of the "O," you're just out of luck. The button won't work.

To use an instance of the button symbol, drag it out of the library, and place it on the Stage. To make the button do something (like go to a web page), see the section on "ActionScript and Buttons" later in this chapter.

> **NOTE**
>
> If you don't place a graphic in the Up frame, but do in the Over and Down frames, then the button is sort of invisible, as the graphics in the other frames will become visible when you mouse over the hot area. If you only place a graphic in the Hit frame, then the button is totally invisible. In the editing environment, you'll see a translucent blue version of the button to indicate that it's there in both cases, so that you know where it is.

In the Control pull-down menu, there is an Enable Simple Buttons option, which makes the button behave as if it were in the deployment environment (with two exceptions). That means that when you mouse over it, you'll see your Over state, and when you click it, you'll see your Down state. However, if the button has no graphic in the Up state, but does have graphics in the Over and Down states, you won't see it until you mouse over it. Likewise, if the button only has a Hit state, you won't see anything at all. Deselecting Enable Simple Buttons will bring back the translucent blue rectangles.

> **NOTE**
>
> You cannot move buttons while Enable Simple Buttons is toggled on. However, you can draw a selection box around it with the Selection tool, then move it with your arrow keys. If you hold down the shift key while you use your arrow keys, the button will move 10 pixels at a time.

Creating More Complex Buttons

Buttons can be as complex and rich as any graphic in Flash. For starters, button timelines can support multiple layers, the same as any timeline. You can use layering to make a more interesting and visually compelling button. To insert a layer in a button from its timeline, click the Add Layer icon in the Layer panel, or choose Insert > Timeline > Layer. Then add your graphics to keyframes in the appropriate state.

Sounds can also be added to buttons; these are most often used for "click" sounds. As a best practice, sounds should occupy their own layers in a button. To add the sound, add a keyframe to the appropriate state (most often Over or Down), and drag a sound out of the library and anywhere on the Stage with the keyframe highlighted. You won't see a visual representation of the sound on the Stage, but you should see a little oscillation pattern in the keyframe.

> **TIP**
>
> If you add the sound to the Up frame, in the Sync menu on the Property Inspector, you can set the sound to Stop. In the Over frame, you can set the sound to Start. That way, the sound will always stop when the user rolls off the button. For more on sound and sound settings, see Chapter 24, "Sound."

Buttons, having only four frames, can't directly support any kind of animation (meaning you can't actually build an animation in the button itself). But because buttons are symbols, you can nest other symbols in them, so long as they aren't button symbols.

To make an animated button, you first need to build an animation in a Movie Clip symbol (discussed in Chapter 12, "Using Artwork Created Elsewhere"). Then, in the button timeline, insert a keyframe in the state that you want the animated symbol to appear in. Drag the Movie Clip symbol out of the library and onto the Stage in the keyframe. In most cases that's the Over frame. This means you'll want a static version of the first graphics to appear in the button's Over frame. That way, you have a seamless transition from button-sitting-around to button-animating.

You'll want to bear in mind, of course, that as you're making your button more complex, that you're also adding to its file size. You'll want to use short sounds when at all possible, and try to restrict the amount of color gradients you're using. What's more, if you're using Movie Clips to animate a button state, be aware that Movie Clips must fully download in order to actually animate (but then again, so do buttons). The more complex the animation inside the movie clip, the more file size you'll wind up with. I know; there's always a catch, isn't there?

ActionScript and Buttons

To make the most of a button, you need ActionScript. You can add ActionScript directly to a button instance, or you can control a button instance from ActionScript added to a frame. What's more, you can add ActionScript using either the Actions panel, or the Behaviors panel. We cover ActionScript in more detail in a later chapter, so the thing to focus on here is not ActionScript, but rather how to add it to a button.

The Behaviors Panel

The Behaviors panel was introduced in Flash MX 2004, and it closely mirrors the Behaviors panel in other Macromedia Products. The idea behind it is that you add a behavior from the panel to an object or frame, fill out a few parameters in a dialog box, and then go on with your life. It's a great tool, although a little limited in scope, which is quite all right since it wasn't supposed to be TATE (The Answer To Everything). The Behaviors panel is broken down in Chapter 26, "The Behaviors Panel," so we won't address all its features here. We will, however, tell you what to do with it.

To open the Behaviors panel, select Window > Development Panels > Behaviors.

The first step in adding a behavior is to select a button instance on the Stage. Behaviors can be directly applied to buttons. To add the behavior, choose the Add Behavior button in the Behaviors panel, and it will pull up a menu of categories. Each category will have one or more behavior in it. Choose the behavior you want from the category you need, and it will open a dialog (in most cases) that will prompt you to fill out some additional information to complete the behavior.

The most common behaviors you add to buttons are: Go To Web Page From the Web Category, and Go To and Play At Frame or Label, Go To and Stop at Frame or Label, and Load External Movie Clip, Movie Clip Category. To add the Go To Web Page behavior, you choose the Web category and the Go To Web Page behavior, the resulting dialog that appears requests the URL you want the button to navigate to, and the Target (how it should open in the browser). Click OK, and the behavior is added to the button.

When you have the behavior added, you'll want to make sure that the trigger user event is correctly set. By default, it's onRelease, which is when a user clicks and lets go of the mouse button. To change it to something else, like a rollover event, click the pull-down menu in the Event section of the Behaviors panel. The different events are listed in Table 17.1.

Table 17.1   Mouse Events for Buttons

EVENT	WHEN IT'S TRIGGERED
Release	Called when a user clicks and lets go of the mouse over top of the button's hit area.
Release Outside	Called when the user has pressed on a button, but releases the mouse off the button's hit area.
Key Press	Called when the user strikes a key on the keyboard.
Key Down	Called when the user is holding down a key on the keyboard.
Roll Over	Called when the user rolls into the hit area of the button.
Roll Out	Called when the user rolls off of a button's hit area
Drag Over	Called when a user has pressed and is holding down the mouse, and then drags into a button's hit area.
Drag Out	Called when the user has pressed and is still holding down on the mouse key, but drags off of a button's hit area.
Press	Called when a user presses and holds down on the mouse and on the button.

Which mouse event you use depends on what you're hoping to accomplish.

> **NOTE**
>
> Using the Behaviors panel, you can't nest mouse events on the button. Sometimes you need more than one (`release`, and `releaseOutside`) in order to cover all your bases; you'll have to get into the ActionScript window and add the additional event yourself to make it happen.

To edit the behavior, double-click on the action in the panel. To remove a behavior altogether, select it in the panel, and click the Minus icon.

Now, if you want to see what's *actually* happened when you add a behavior, with your button still selected, open the Actions window. You'll see that the Behaviors panel has written ActionScript on to the button with the details you provided. If you're ActionScript savvy, you can add to it from there. But don't delete anything from the script itself. You'll see two comments that begin and end the behavior; for example, the Go to Web Page behavior placed directly on a button looks like this:

```
on(release)
{
    //Goto Webpage Behavior
getURL("http://www.macromedia.com/","_self");
    //End Behavior
}
```

The comments, indicated by the two forward slashes, are what tells Flash that this script is a behavior added from the behaviors panel. If you delete the comments, the behavior vanishes from the behaviors panel. You can add script before or after the comments safely, as well as add other mouse events inbetween the parentheses without breaking anything.

To test the behavior, either choose File > Preview in Browser, or choose Control > Test movie, and see how well things work out.

You can also control a button from a frame in the timeline, which is really the preferred way of doing things. Placing a behavior directly on a button attaches the ActionScript directly to that object, which is a little like making a chore chart for kids or roommates and pasting their chores directly to their shirts. Sure, they know what they have to do, but there's no central resource to find what the chores are and who's doing what. Not a best practice at all. When you control a button from the timeline, you assign a button an instance name, and then tell it what to do from that central location. So your chore chart is in one place, and the chore responsibilities are indicated by name. You can find them much easier that way, and modify them more easily too. Of course, the people doing the chores may not be so happy about that.

ActionScript

The other way to add interactivity to buttons is to write your own ActionScript, which should be your goal in any event. Behaviors are nice, but limited. ActionScript is only limited by technology and imagination. We have two ways of writing scripts that affect our button: Writing the script directly on the button, or writing the script on the frame and specifying which button it's referring to. Relax, it's easy.

Let's look at the big picture first.

When you are writing a script for a button, you have to specify an event that will trigger an action. The action that the event triggers is called the event handler. We have a syntax to follow that's slightly different depending on whether the event handler is written on the button or on a frame.

First, on the button:

Select the button instance on the Stage, and then launch the Actions panel. The Actions panel will show you all of the categories of ActionScript that currently exist, and in those categories are a host of functions, events, properties, and so on. The script pane is the big white document-looking section of the panel where you will write all of your code.

Write your triggering event:

```
on(whateverTheEventIs)
```

Next, you want to open a curly brace. Actually, it's useful if you open one, hit enter a few times, then add a close curly brace to build the shell of your event handler. That way, you don't have to forget about adding the close curly brace when you're all finished. The curly braces hold the instructions that Flash has to execute when the event occurs.

Inside the curly braces, write whatever is going to happen when the event triggers. That can be just about anything, from getting a URL, to making the playhead stop moving, or to loading an SWF into your application from off the hard drive:

```
{
    Do Stuff();
};
```

Here's a snippet of actual code to give you a better idea of what's going on:

```
on(release)
{
    _root.loadMovie("dogNutrition.swf", container_mc);
}
```

The above example loads a SWF from the server (or hard drive), and into a Movie Clip on the Stage.

Now, all that is adding code right on the button, which I've mentioned is not a best practice, for several reasons. First, it makes it hard to find and update the code when you need to do that. Second, you can't really use find-and-replace to make broad changes to your ActionScript. Third, it makes it a pain to call functions or variables that may be floating around somewhere else. So let's look at what's considered the best practice; naming the button then controlling it from a script on a frame.

To do this, first you have to select the button on the Stage, and in the Property Inspector, assign it an instance name. The instance name is critical; because this is how you differentiate one button instance from the next. Imagine, for instance, that you're at a birthday party for your niece. Twenty kids are running about the living room doing what kids do, which is making a lot of noise and mess. Exhausted, frazzled, you call out a command: "Hey kid! Go to the refrigerator and get me a soda!" Which of the 20 hyperactive children is going to go and get you a soda? Several of them? All of them? None of them? Your results would be unexpected.

It would make more sense to be specific, right? You would say, "Hey, Cheyenne, go to the refrigerator and get me a soda!" to make sure that only one kid gets your refreshing beverage. What you've done is call an instance of the Kid object, and activated its getSoda(); method. Pseudocoded, it would look like this:

```
Cheynne.onUncleRequest=function()
    {
        getSoda("fridge","Coke","UncleJim");
    }
```

So let's apply that to our buttons, shall we? When we're scripting a button from a frame in the timeline, we have to specify the button instance name and triggering event. Our event handler will be defined in what's generally termed an anonymous function, which really just means that the event handler is only for this single button instance. We'll talk more about that syntax in the ActionScript unit. And all of this has to be in a keyframe in the timeline where it can access the button.

```
ButtonInstance.onSomeEvent=function()
{
    doStuff();
}
```

An actual usage might be:

```
NYTimesNav.onRelease=function()
{
    getURL("http://www.nytimes.com/");
}
```

And that's how it's done.

Button Best Practices

When working with buttons, we need to keep a number of things in mind to be sure that we're keeping file size down, and making buttons that are actually useful. The list below details some button best practices:

- Make reusable buttons, avoiding using text inside the button itself
- Avoid making overly complex buttons
- Assign buttons instance names and control them from a frame script
- If you must use sound, use short, non-intrusive sounds
- Limit the use of animated movie clips in your buttons to short animations

Summary

Buttons are symbol types in Flash that are both reusable and able to be controlled with ActionScript. We use buttons to add interactivity to a Flash application.

Buttons have four frames that can contain graphics. Those are the Up, Over, Down, and Hit frames. The Hit frame itself is invisible; the graphics in the hit frame determine the interactive area of the button. You can make your buttons more compelling by adding graphics, as well as animated movie clips and short sounds.

To make buttons interact with other aspects of your published Flash file, you must add ActionScript from either the behaviors panel, or by writing your own. You can add ActionScript either directly to the button, or to a frame, controlling the button by name. It is a best practice to control the button from a frame.

Sample Questions

1. In order for a button to respond to ActionScript written in a frame, what must the button have?

   A. An Over frame

   B. An instance name

   C. A Hit frame

   D. A behavior added from the Behaviors panel

2. When you add your own ActionScript to a button, the instructions must be within:

   A. An event handler

   B. Parentheses

   C. The Hit frame

   D. None of the above

3. To make a reusable invisible button that works like a hotspot, what should be the only button frame that contains a graphic?

   A. Up

   B. Over

   C. Down

   D. Hit

4. What behavior in the Behaviors panel redirects a user to a Web page?

   A. Load Page

   B. Load External Movie Clip

   C. Go to Web Page

   D. None of the above

CHAPTER **18**

The Movie Clip Symbol

IN THIS CHAPTER

Movie Clips Symbols Explained   151

Creating a Movie Clip   151

Movie Clip Timelines   153

Movie Clip Properties   155

Movie Clip Methods   156

Movie Clip Events   157

ActionScript and the Movie Clip   158

Summary   161

Sample Questions   161

Movie Clips Symbols Explained

In Macromedia Flash, the Movie Clip symbol is the true workhorse of any application that you're going to build. In fact, the symbol is the foundation for your application; your Stage is actually a Movie Clip whose properties and capabilities have been hidden. Movie Clips are ActionScript objects, and can be controlled, made, and removed by ActionScript, in addition to being created visually. Movie clips can hold anything that your main timeline can hold, and can contain ActionScript, or have ActionScript written directly on them.

We use Movie Clips to create nested animations, to respond to user-driven events, to hold assets so that we can reuse them without adding file size, and to add interactivity to our Flash Applications. They're without a doubt the most versatile object in Flash (well, besides the generic Object object).

Creating a Movie Clip

There are two ways to make a movie clip in Flash; visually, or programmatically, using ActionScript. Let's start with the visual part.

To create a Movie Clip visually from scratch, select Insert > New Symbol, click the New Symbol icon in the Library panel, or choose New Symbol from the Library Options menu. When the New Symbol dialog appears, give the symbol a library name, choose the Movie Clip behavior, and finally, click OK. This is, of course, in simple mode. Advanced mode we'll talk about later.

> **NOTE**
>
> The name of the symbol in the library is not the same as its instance name on the Stage. The library name is for people, used for organization, and has no meaning to ActionScript. The instance name, on the other hand, is used by ActionScript to control a movie clip's properties, methods, and so on.

Once you've clicked the OK button, you'll be placed in symbol editing mode. The crosshair you see on the screen represents the center of the symbol, and the registration point of the symbol once you've added graphics to it. Movie Clips have their own timelines and layer structures which operate independently of the main timeline, unlike graphic symbols.

> **NOTE**
>
> If you'll recall, graphic symbols are dependant on the main document timeline. See Chapter 16, "Graphic and Font Symbols," for more on graphic symbols.

> **TIP**
>
> Because movie clips don't have this restriction, they're ideal for nesting animations. More about that later in this chapter.

In symbol editing mode, place graphic assets, sound assets, and whatever else you want in the timeline just as you would do in the main document window. To use the symbol in your application, drag it out of the library and on to the Stage.

The other way to create a Movie Clip symbol visually is to select an asset on the Stage, and choose Modify > Convert to Symbol, or drag it into the library. Give the new symbol a name, select Movie Clip as the behavior, choose a registration point, and click OK. To edit the symbol, double-click it on the Stage to enter Edit in Place mode, or double-click the symbol's icon in the library to enter symbol editing mode. To return to the main document timeline, select Scene 1 on the info bar (or whatever it's named, if you've changed the name in the Scenes panel).

To make an empty movie clip that will later hold JPG images or external SWFs called into the interface from a button, choose Insert > New Symbol, make it a movie clip, then immediately return to the main document timeline without adding content. Of course, you'll have to drag and drop your empty symbol onto the Stage, but it won't be invisible. You'll see it out there as a dot when it's selected, or a crosshair when it's not.

To create a movie clip programmatically, you have to attach ActionScript to a frame or an object. It makes more sense to do it from a frame, so we'll specify the command with that in mind.

First, highlight the keyframe on the timeline where you want the movie clip to be created. Then launch your Actions panel. In the script pane, type:

```
this.createEmptyMovieClip("newInstanceName",depth);
```

this refers to the main timeline in the current example. In other circumstances, it would refer to the timeline that you are in. The method, createEmptyMovieClip(); is a method of the Movie Clip class, and takes two arguments, which is the instance name of the movie clip that you're creating, and the depth (stacking order) that it will occupy. Usually, positive depths are assigned, and you have from –16,384 to 1,048,575 to work with.

> **NOTE**
> When you publish your file to an SWF, layers are converted to depths, and items in the layers are assigned a depth as well, from the bottom up. Objects in the lowest layer occupy the lowest depth, and that starts at –16,384. Only one asset can occupy a depth at a time.

Now, of course, when you're creating a Movie Clip with ActionScript, you can't really get into its timeline and edit it visually. You have to load stuff into it using ActionScript as well, like JPG images and SWFs. There are times, however, when the movie clip will not have any content, but is being used as a sort of controller to do a number of things automatically.

We'll discuss how to load external images and SWFs later in this chapter.

Movie Clip Timelines

Movie Clip timelines, as I've mentioned, are completely independent from the main document timeline. What that means for us as designers of an application is that we can nest animations in the main timeline, such as animated pull-down menus, without affecting the other content on the Stage. It also gives us a way to add interactive elements, create more complex navigation, create sound toggles, and a whole host of other things.

Because the main Stage is also a movie clip, the movie clip timeline is identical to the main document timeline. The only real difference is the size of the Stage; inside a movie clip symbol, there is no work area. Apart from that, the layer panel is the same and the timeline is the same. You can add ActionScript to frames or buttons, and you can add other movie clips to layers and frames as well.

> **NOTE**
> You can't place an instance of a movie clip symbol inside itself. Not only is that a bad idea, but Flash won't let you do it.

Authoring content for a Movie Clip is a lot like making another Flash application all by itself, only one which will work with the larger application as a whole. I like to think of it as a television in a living room. The television has a whole lot of things happening inside of it while the folks in the living room interact with it independently to control what the television is showing or how loud it is.

Movie Clips can communicate with other timelines using ActionScript, with the goal of controlling those timelines, calling ActionScripts that may live in those other timelines, or responding to things that happen on other timelines. Those timelines can be the main document timeline, or other movie clip timelines. To communicate, those timelines have to be pointed to, or pathed, correctly.

When we are in a movie clip timeline that sits in the main document timeline, and we want to refer to the main document timeline with an ActionScript, we usually refer to _root. That always points to the main document timeline, no matter where you are in a series of nested movie clips. _parent always refers to whatever timeline the movie clip is resting in. So if you have a movie clip inside of a movie clip resting on the main timeline, you can use _parent to refer to one timeline out. This is useful when you're dynamically loading movie clips or SWFs into other movie clips.

If you want to point to other movie clips specifically, you have to know where they are in the grand scheme of things. If, for instance, from one movie clip timeline, you want to control a movie clip in the document's main timeline, you would use:

```
_root.movieClipToControl.whatever=value;
```

If you want to point to a movie clip inside of a movie clip on the main timeline:

```
_root.movieClip1.movieClipToControl.whatever=value;
```

If you want the Movie Clip to refer to the timeline it's in, whatever that may be, use:

```
_parent.someMethod();
```

> **NOTE**
> _parent always refers to the timeline that the Movie Clip is contained in.

If you want to control a Movie Clip that's inside the Movie Clip you're adding ActionScript to:

```
this.movieClipToControl.property="value";
```

> **TIP**
>
> The keyword `this` is a self-reference, saying "look inside this object" more or less. It can also mean other things, which we'll discuss when we get into ActionScript.

Occasionally, you'll want a movie clip's timeline to act like it's the main document timeline. Movie Clip timelines have a special property, `_lockroot`, that has a true or false value. When `_lockroot=true;` the movie clip's timeline will behave as though it's the main document timeline, which can be useful in data-driven applications.

Movie Clip Properties

Movie Clips, as ActionScript objects, have their own special properties. In addition, they have instance properties when they're visually created and on the main Stage. Of course, the instance properties and ActionScript properties are the same, but the difference is the amount of properties that you use. The properties say how a Movie Clip should appear and where it should be, generally.

Instance properties are set on the Property Inspector, and show when a Movie Clip symbol instance on the Stage is selected. The instance properties are:

- Behavior (Movie Clip, Graphic, or Button)
- x and y position
- Width and height
- Color (brightness, tint, alpha, and advanced)

These options change how an individual instance looks and where it's positioned. You can also change width, height, rotation, and skew with the Free Transform tool.

Of course, because Movie Clips are ActionScript objects, their properties can be controlled through ActionScript as well. Changing properties with ActionScript is obviously very different than changing properties with the Property Inspector. For starters, we have more options to choose from.

> **TIP**
>
> You can see all the properties of the Movie Clip in the Actions panel's Categories pane. Select Built In Classes > Movie > Movie Clip > Properties to see the full list.

To find out what a property does, you can look it up in the ActionScript dictionary by choosing Help > ActionScript Dictionary, then looking up the Movie Clip class and its properties. Or you can select the Property in the Actions panel's Categories pane, and right- or Control-click on it, choose View Help from the Context menu. If you aren't a right- or Control-click fan, you can highlight the property, and click the View Help button in the upper right corner of the Actions Window (it's the book with the little "?" on it), or choose View Help from the Options menu of the Actions window. Either way, it will bring you directly to the entry for that property in the ActionScript Dictionary. The entry will tell you the earliest version of the Flash player that the property can be used with, what the property does, and give you a sage example.

To change the properties of a movie clip using ActionScript, use this general syntax:

```
MovieClipInstance.name.property=new value
```

For example, if I wanted to change the opacity of a movie clip on the Stage when the application first loads up, on the first keyframe of my main timeline, I would add the following block of code:

```
MyMovieClip._alpha=65;
```

That makes the object 65 percent opaque. But then, you knew that already.

Properties don't have to be changed from frame scripts of course; they can also be changed when a user clicks a button, when data loads in, and so on. The following example shows a change in a Movie Clip's position when a user clicks a button:

```
MyButton.onRelease=function()
{
    myMovieClip._x=100;
    myMovieClip._y=100;
};
```

This simply highlights the fact that movie clips can be changed on the fly, based on user interaction.

Movie Clip Methods

Methods are the kinds of things an object can do. Movie clips, as ActionScript objects, can do all kinds of things, and there are quite a number of them.

> **TIP**
>
> To view a complete list of methods for the Movie Clip class, select Built In Classes > Movie > Movie Clip > Methods from the Actions panel's Categories pane.

Generally speaking, Movie Clip methods have to be called with ActionScript that you write, although some of the methods can be used through the Behaviors panel, eliminating the need for you to write your own code. We'll show you how to do that when we get to the section, "ActionScript and the Movie Clip."

Methods are functions attached to objects or classes of objects. Because of that, when we call a method, we call it similar to a function that has a name:

```
InstanceName.methodCall(arguments);
```

A real example follows:

```
MyClip.loadMovie("dogNutrition.swf");
```

The instance name of the movie clip is self-explanatory. The method is what the movie clip will do, and the arguments modify how the method executes. In the above example, the movie clip MyClip is loading an external SWF into its timeline.

Movie clip methods can be invoked on a keyframe in a timeline, or in the event handler of an object such as a button.

Movie Clip Events

Events are essentially things that objects listen for, then when they hear them, execute a block of code. Movie clips react to numerous events, including mouse events that happen "on" the object.

Events trigger event handlers, as we'll see in more detail in the Chapter 28, "The Basics of ActionScript." Here, we'll focus on movie clip events.

When you want to execute something based on an event, you can do it from a frame in the timeline, or directly on the movie clip object itself. When you are going to execute ActionScript directly on a movie clip object, there are special considerations. We'll talk about them here in this section.

First, to specify events when you are working from a frame in the timeline, use the following syntax:

```
MovieClipInstance.onWhateverEvent=function()
{
    doStuff();
}
```

For instance, if you want something to happen when a user clicks a movie clip that is acting as a button:

```
MyMovieClip.onRelease=function()
{
    getURL("http://www.motionovertime.com","_self");
}
```

> **TIP**
>
> Besides button type events, movie clips have their own special events, including the very important onEnterFrame event, which is often used with animation. These events can be looked up in the Actions panel's Categories pane by selecting Built In Classes > Movie > Movie Clip > Events. The onEnterFrame event is detailed in Chapter 23, "Animating with ActionScript."

ActionScript and the Movie Clip

In this section, we'll focus on how the movie clip works with ActionScript to get things done. First, we'll look at the ActionScript capabilities you can add to movie clips from the Behaviors panel. Then, we'll look at how things are accomplished when hand-coding.

From the Behaviors Panel

When you want to attach functionality to a movie clip that's out on the Stage, you can do so through the Behaviors panel. The Behaviors panel has a category for movie clips alone.

The Movie Clip category of the Behaviors panel contains actions used for:

- Controlling a movie clip's timeline
- Loading and unloading external SWFs
- Controlling a Movie Clip's depth
- Loading graphics
- Making Movie Clips draggable and droppable

To add a behavior to a movie clip, select the Movie Clip instance on the Stage. In the Behavior's panel, click the Add Behavior button, and add the behavior from the category you want. For instance, if you want to make a movie clip draggable, select the Start Dragging Movie Clip behavior.

The Start Dragging Movie Clip Dialog box will prompt you to select a movie clip to drag (usually the movie clip you've selected). Click OK to make the Movie Clip draggable.

If you're going to make it draggable, make sure you can drop it, too. With the Movie Clip still selected, choose the Stop Dragging Movie Clip behavior, which will call up an alert box that tells you that the behavior will stop the dragging of any movie clip.

> **NOTE**
>
> Behaviors can also be added to Movie Clip timelines

Like Buttons, when you add a behavior to a Movie Clip, it will populate with a default event to trigger the behavior. The events that trigger the behavior are the same as are available for buttons. Those events are summarized in table 18.1.

Table 18.1 Movie Clip Events in the Behaviors Panel

EVENT	WHEN IT'S TRIGGERED
Release	Called when a user clicks and lets go over top of the Movie Clip.
Release Outside	Called when the user has pressed Movie Clip, but lets go of the mouse off of Movie Clip's visual area.
Key Press	Called when the user strikes a key on the keyboard.
Key Down	Called when the user is holding down a key on the keyboard.
Roll Over	Called when the user rolls over the Movie Clip.
Roll Out	Called when the user rolls off of a Movie Clip.
Drag Over	Called when a user has pressed and is holding down the mouse, and then drags over top of a Movie Clip.
Drag Out	Called when the user has pressed and is still holding down on the mouse key, but drags off of a Movie Clip.
Press	Called when a user presses and holds down on the mouse and over top of a Movie Clip.

> **TIP**
>
> Movie clips have more events than buttons, but they can only be added by writing your own ActionScript. The Behaviors panel limits Movie Clip events to mouse types. For an exhaustive list of Movie Clip events, check the documentation.

Adding Actions from the Actions Panel

When you want to add ActionScript to a Movie Clip that is more sophisitcated than what the Behaviors panel currently supports, you have to use the Actions panel. We can add the ActionScript directly to the Movie Clip object, or to a frame in the timeline that refers to the Movie Clip by name.

To add ActionScript directly to a movie clip, select the movie clip instance on the Stage, then launch the Actions panel. You have to be careful here, because any time you add code to a movie clip, it has to be in the context of an event, meaning that something has to tell the object that it must execute the ActionScript it carries. Those events are generally referred to as Clip Events, and they can be as simple as a button type, like on(release), or as complicated as one of the Movie Clip events, such as on(enterFrame). No matter what, though, there has to be an event. The rest of the code is written between curly braces.

TIP

The enterFrame event executes based on the document frame rate. If the frame rate is 12 FPS, then the enterFrame event will execute every 12th of a second. It's CPU intensive, so once you're finished, it should be removed with delete this.enterFrame.

When you want to make a movie clip functional, but you don't want to place code directly on an object, do it from a frame. Simple property changes don't require any type of clip event, and in some cases, simple method calls don't either. It all depends on what you're doing. If the movie clip is to react to something, however, you must specify one of the events available to movie clips.

In any case, you first must give the movie clip that you're trying to control an instance name. Remember, the instance name differentiates it from every other movie clip on the Stage, even though they may be instances of the same symbol.

Second, select the keyframe that you want to add the ActionScript to, and in the Actions panel, write the script you want to use. The following example sets a movie clip alpha to 65% initially, and then changes it to 100% when someone rolls over the movie clip itself:

```
MyClip._alpha=65;
MyClip.onRollOver=function()
{
this._alpha=100;
}
```

Remember, which event you use will depend on what it is you're trying to accomplish.

If you place ActionScript directly on a Movie Clip instance, it must be done within an event handler. The following example makes a Movie Clip draggable:

```
on(press){
this.startDrag();
}
```

Summary

Movie clips are special objects in Flash that can be created visually or by using ActionScript. Movie clips have their own timelines, which operate independently of the main document timeline, making them ideal for adding interactive elements or nested animations.

As ActionScript objects, movie clips have properties, which determine their general appearance and location. They also have methods, which are what movie clips do, and events, which movie clips respond to. All of these things can be controlled using ActionScript, either by placing ActionScript directly on a movie clip, or by controlling it from a frame in a timeline.

To edit a visual movie clip, double-click on its icon in the library to enter symbol editing mode. Conversely, you can double-click on the Stage, which brings you to Edit in Place mode. To return to the main document timeline, select Scene 1 on the Info bar.

Sample Questions

1. Which Movie Clip behavior from the Behaviors Panel must be used to load an external SWF?

   A. `loadMovie()`

   B. Call External SWF

   C. Load External SWF

   D. Load External Movieclip

2. One Movie Clip is nested in another. The parent Movie Clip is named mcHolder, and the nested Movie Clip is named mcChanger. If you click the nested Movie Clip, you want the mcHolder Movie Clip to become slightly transparent. Which is the correct ActionScript to use in an `on(release)` event handler (choose 2)?

   A. `this.mcHolder._alpha=70;`

   B. `_parent._alpha=70;`

   C. `_root.mcHolder._alpha=70;`

   D. `mcHolder._alpha=70;`

3. Movie Clip timelines are:

   A. Dependent on the main document timeline.

   B. Independent of the main document timeline.

   C. Cannot have ActionScript in them.

   D. Cannot contain other Movie Clip symbol instances.

4. What does the enterFrame event do?

   A. Checks to see if conditions are true.

   B. Deletes objects from memory.

   C. Executes continually based on the frame rate.

   D. Changes the position of contents in a frame.

CHAPTER 19

Components

IN THIS CHAPTER

Component Types   163

Changing Component Parameters   165

Adding Data to Components   168

Changing Component Appearance   169

Handling Events on Components   170

Summary   171

Sample Questions   171

Flash MX introduced components to the Macromedia family. In Flash MX 2004, components have grown to a much more sophisticated level, speeding up development of interfaces.

In this chapter, we review what components are, how to add them to your Stage, and how to get some data into them. We also review the basics of what to do when a user interacts with one of them.

→ The media components will be reviewed in Chapter 24, "Sound," and Chapter 25, "Video."

Component Types

With Flash MX Professional 2004, you get three categories of components that you can use:

- **Data.** These components allow you to connect to and use external data sources.

- **Media.** These components are used with digital video in FLV format, and MP3 files, for streaming over the Web.

- **UI.** These are pre-built user interface elements.

With Flash MX 2004 standard, you get UI components only.

TIP

The FLV format is a proprietary format for video compression, and stands for Macromedia Flash Video. It is used for streaming video through the Flash player, and is available in most current digital video editors.

> **NOTE**
>
> The data components are non-visual; that is to say, there is no visual representation of the components in the published file. They contain all of the ActionScript needed to communicate with external data sources and bring the data into Flash.

These components give developers and designers a way to use common resources without reproducing functionality. Each component has parameters that can be modified, methods and properties like any Flash object, and events that they can respond to.

> **TIP**
>
> All components are ultimately built off of the Movie Clip class in Flash.

To use a component, open the Components panel by selecting Window > Development Panels > Components. Drag the component you want to use from the panel and onto your Stage in whatever layer and keyframe you want to place it in.

The component you added will show in the library, and can be reused from there. However, the assets that make up the visual part of the imported component is a special file called an SWC, which is a compiled, or published, file. What you see on the Stage is a live preview of the component as it would behave in the Flash Player, since the component has essentially already been published. You can shut that off and see an outline indicating the component's position on the Stage by selecting Control > Enable Live Preview. If Live Preview is unchecked, you will only see a black outline of the component position. If it's checked, you'll see more or less what the component will look like on the Stage.

> **TIP**
>
> The Kind column in the library will show as a compiled clip.

When you add an instance of a component to your document, you get the core functionality of all components. This will add somewhere between 25 and 30K to your file. Once you have it, though, adding additional components will not add significantly to your file size.

> **NOTE**
>
> Most of the visual components use assets in common. The only file size increase comes when a component has visual assets unique to it.

Changing Component Parameters

All components that come with Flash have parameters that can be changed either in the Property Inspector, or the Component Inspector. The Component Inspector is a special panel that not only sets parameters, but also creates data bindings from one component to another, and shows the structure, or schema, of components. To open the Component Inspector, select Window > Development Panels > Component Inspector.

Because every component has its own parameters, we'll look at some of the more widely used components as examples: the ComboBox, the Button, and the TextArea. Also, because the Parameters tab on the Property Inspector is the same as the Parameters tab in the Component Inspector, we will review the Component Inspector exclusively.

To set the parameters of a component, select it on the Stage and launch the Component Inspector. The Inspector has three tabs: Parameters, Bindings, and Schema. Choose the Parameters tab.

Parameters for the ComboBox component are:

- **Data.** Assigns data to the component. Data is used for processing either locally, or will be sent to a server.

- **Editable.** Has a true or false value. If set to true, a user can click on a selection in the ComboBox and type into the field that appears. If set false, the ComboBox displays information and does not allow a user to enter new data.

- **Labels.** Sets the text that a user sees. The labels should match the data.

- **rowCount.** Sets the amount of viewable rows in the ComboBox when a user expands it. When the amount of data exceeds the viewable rows, a scroll bar will appear to allow end users to view the rest of the information.

- **Enabled.** True or false value. When set to true, a user can click on it and otherwise interact. When set to false, the component is grayed out and not useable.

- **Visible.** True or false value. When set to true, it's visible on the Stage. When set to false, it's transparent.

- **minHeight.** Sets the minimum height for the component.

- **minWidth.** Sets the minium width for the component.

> **TIP**
>
> `minHeight` and `minWidth` are measured in pixels. `Data` and `labels` accept data as arrays.

> **TIP**
>
> The Property Inspector does not display `enabled` through `minWidth`.

Parameters for the Button component are:

- **Icon.** Allows you to display a movie clip in the library in the button. The movie clip in the library must have a linkage identifier.

- **Label.** Sets the visible text on the button that the end user will see. The default label is Button.

- **labelPlacement.** Center, right, or left justifies the button label in relation to the icon you're using, if you're using one. Also places the label at the top or bottom of the button.

- **Selected.** Works with the toggle parameter. If set to true, the button will appear in its down state, appearing to be depressed.

- **Toggle.** Accepts a true or false value. If set to true, the button works like an on/off switch. When selected, it will stay in its down state until clicked again.

- **Enabled.** True or false value. When set to true, a user can click on it and otherwise interact. When set to false, the component is grayed out and not useable.

- **Visible.** True or false value. When set to true, it's visible on the Stage. When set to false, it's transparent.

- **minHeight.** Sets the minimum height for the component.

- **minWidth.** Sets the minium width for the component.

> **TIP**
>
> The Button component will not resize if either the label or the icon is larger than the current button size. You must resize the button with the Free Transform tool or the Property Inspector.

> **TIP**
>
> The Property Inspector does not display from `toggle` through `minWidth`.

Parameters for the TextArea component are:

- **Editable.** True or false. If set to true, allows end users to type information into the TextArea component.

- **HTML.** True or false. If set to true, the component will render HTML tagged text. If set to false, it will show the text as it is.

- **Text.** Sets the text for display in the component. Whatever is typed here will be seen in the SWF.

- **wordWrap.** True or false. If set to true, allows text to wrap in the component. If set to false, text will not wrap.

- **maxChars.** Sets the maximum amount of characters that can be typed inside the component.

- **Restrict.** Determines the kind of characters that can be entered into the field. The default is Undefined, which means any kind of characters can be entered by a user.

- **Password.** When set to true, whatever an end user types in the field is replaced with the * character.

- **Enabled.** True or false. When set to true, a user can click on it and otherwise interact. When set to false, the component is grayed out and not useable.

- **Visible.** True or false. When set to true, it's visible on the Stage. When set to false, it's transparent.

- **minHeight.** Sets the minimum height for the component.

- **minWidth.** Sets the minium width for the component.

> **TIP**
>
> The Property Inspector does not display from `maxChars` through `minWidth`.

> **TIP**
>
> Password does not encrypt the actual password.
>
> Restrict can accept strings like "A-Z 0-9" which allows only capital letters, numbers, and spaces. For more information on Restrict, see Flash Help, under Using Components.

> **NOTE**
>
> While it may seem so from the above, not all components have `enabled`, `visible`, `minheight` and `minWidth` parameters in the Component inspector, though very nearly all of them have those control-lable ActionScript properties.

To change a parameter's value, click the input box next to its name, and enter the new value, either by typing the new value in, or selecting it from a pull-down menu, as in the case of the true/false values.

Adding Data to Components

There are two ways, more or less, to add data to user interface components, such as the ComboBox and the TextArea: using the Property or Component Inspector, or using ActionScript.

To add data to a ComboBox component using the Property Inspector or Component Inspector, select the component instance on the Stage. In either inspector, click on the Data parameter and then the Browse icon that appears in the box, or double-click the parameter. The Values dialog box will appear.

To add a data value in the Values dialog box, click the Add Value button (the plus icon), and replace the defaultValue text with meaningful data. To remove a value, highlight it and click the Remove Value button (the minus icon). Values can be reordered using the Up and Down arrow buttons in the dialog box.

Click OK to populate the ComboBox with the values you added.

> **TIP**
>
> Remember, the order in which your data appears in the dialog box should match the order in which the labels appear.

To add labels to your ComboBox, click the Label parameter, then the browse icon that appears in the box, or double-click in the Label Parameter. Either way, you will pull up the Values dialog box again. Add labels the same way you added data.

Any component that has data or label parameters works essentially the same way.

Besides adding data using the Property Inspector or Component Inspector, you can also use ActionScript, which is much more flexible. Most of the User Interface Components use the following methods (and one property) to add data:

- **dataProvider.** This component property uses an array to get its values for either label, data or both. An array is like a variable that can store more than one value. There are a couple of ways we can use this property. The following examples assume a frame script.

  ```
  myComboBox.dataProvider=["value 1","value 2","value 3"];
  ```

  or

  ```
  var myArray:Array=new Array("value 1","value 2","value 3");
  myComboBox.dataProvider=myArray;
  ```

  > **TIP**
  > Arrays can store objects as well as simple string values.

- **addItem().** The `addItem()` method will add labels and/or data to the very end of the component. For example, if a ComboBox already has items Orange, Banana, and Watermelon, and you wand to add Pear to the end of the list, write the method as follows:

  ```
  myComboBox.addItem("Pear");
  ```

- **addItemAt().** This method does the same thing as `addItem()`, but you get to say where in the list the item goes. The top of the list starts at 0 and numbers from there (0, 1,2, 3, 4, and so on). If you wanted to add something in the middle of the list, pushing everything else down, you would type:

  ```
  myComboBox.addItemAt(3,"new item");
  ```

Most of the UI components have at least `addItem()`, `addItemAt()`, and `dataProvider`. Some (like the CheckBox component) may be a little different, but they're all essentially cut from the same cloth. That's the idea, after all.

➡ For more information on ActionScript, see Chapter 27, "The Actions Panel," and Chapter 28, "The Basics of ActionScript."

Changing Component Appearance

Changing component appearance means using ActionScript. It's best to write the ActionScript that accomplishes this task in a frame, usually the first frame in a layer named Actions, so that the components are changed right away.

There are three different ways to change appearance: using styles, creating a theme, or creating new skins (those are the graphic assets).

Styles can be applied to single component instances, all the instances of one particular type of component, or all the components that appear in your document.

To apply a style to a component, you use the `setStyle()` method, which takes two parameters: the style that you want to set, and the value. For example, to change the font in a ComboBox from Arial to Impact, type the following:

```
myComboBox.setStyle("fontFamily","Impact");
```

To change all the ComboBoxes to have Impact, type:

```
_global.styles.ComboBox.setStyle("fontFamily","Impact");
```

To make *all* components use Impact:

```
_global.style.setStyle("fontFamily","Impact");
```

Handling Events on Components

In order for components to be of use in your application, they need to do something, and generally, that means that users have to interact with them. All of the UI components have some kind of event that they can respond to (even the TextArea component), and we can handle those events rather easily.

To handle events on components, first identify what event you want the component to respond to. In the case of a Button component, that may be a mouse click, or in the case of the ComboBox, that could be the selection of an item.

TIP

Events for components can be found in the Actions panel. Choose the Components category, the component whose event you're looking for, and the Events sub-category to get a listing. If you aren't sure what one of the events is or how to use it, right- or Control-click it and select View Help from the Context menu.

Once you've identified the event, write a handler for it using the following syntax:

```
componentInstance.eventHandler=function()
{
    instructions
}
```

The event part is what the component is going to respond to, and must be in lower case. The text Handler=function() is required, and the H must be capitalized.

The following is an example of an event handler for a Button component that loads a Web page when a user clicks the button:

```
myButton.clickHandler=function()
{
    getURL("http://www.macromedia.com");
}
```

Summary

Flash comes with a number of components that speed up development of applications. Data components communicate with external data sources. Media components are used to stream sound and video, User Interface components are things like menus and buttons.

All of the components have editable parameters that can be changed in the Property Inspector or the Component Inspector. Data and labels can be added in either inspector, or by using ActionScript.

User Interface components can react to user events in an event handler.

Sample Questions

1. On the Property Inspector, what property of the ComboBox component is used to populate it with information?

   A. Data

   B. dataArray

   C. dataProvider

   D. Text

2. Which of the following lines of ActionScript change the appearance of all components in a document?

   A. `_global.Components.setStyle();`

   B. `_global.styles.setStyles();`

   C. `_global.style.setStyles();`

   D. `_global.setStyles();`

3. The `addItem()` method of the ComboBox:

   A. Adds an item to the beginning of the ComboBox.

   B. Adds an item to the end of the ComboBox.

   C. Adds an item in the position you specify.

   D. Only adds labels to the ComboBox.

4. Which of the following is not a property of the Button component?

   A. Restrict

   B. Toggle

   C. Icon

   D. Label

PART 4

Animation

20 Animation Basics

21 Motion Tweening

22 Shape Tweening

23 Animating with ActionScript

CHAPTER 20

Animation Basics

IN THIS CHAPTER

The Three Animation Types   175

Necessary Items   176

Onion Skinning   178

Summary   179

Sample Questions   180

One of the things that makes Macromedia Flash such a cool tool is its animation capability. When combined with Flash's other abilities, animation helps you to build a more complex interface that behaves the same as desktop type applications. Of course, animation is also used to make cool effects that have nothing to do with interface designs, but just think about where you can take things in terms of application development.

In this chapter, we review the necessities of animation, as well as the different kinds of animation you can do.

The Three Animation Types

There are three ways of animating elements in your Flash application:

- Frame-by-frame positioning

- Motion tweening

- Shape tweening

All of these animations require frames and keyframes, but where and how you use them varies.

First, frame-by-frame animations require that you insert a keyframe in every frame you need to alter to produce the illusion of animation. This is a tedious process at best, and can result in larger file sizes if you aren't using symbols. There are some circumstances where you will need to use this type, but hopefully, not very often.

Motion animation in Flash means you take an object and change its position, scale, rotation, and/or opacity over time. You can create the effect of motion with a frame-by-frame animation, but it's in its own category because you can have Flash take care of that tedium for you.

Shape animation is a way to change the physical shape and appearance of an editable object over time. Shape animation, like motion animation, can be done manually, but Flash can do it for us as well. Shape animation requires making alterations to the physical appearance of an object, like changing a triangle into a star, and as a result usually creates larger file size and higher CPU processing burdens. As a best practice, use shape animation sparingly, and make these animations simple.

> **TIP**
> Shape tweening can't be done on layers that contain symbols or grouped objects.

Because motion and shape tweening have their own chapters, we'll go over them in Chapters 21 and 22 in detail. This chapter is more devoted to what we need to get started.

Necessary Items

To make an animation, you need keyframes, frames, visual assets, and organization. Keyframes, however, are most critical.

A keyframe indicates a position in time where something is going to change, whether it's the contents of the frame, a sound that's going to play, or an ActionScript that's going to execute. To insert a keyframe in a layer on the timeline, choose the frame position, then select Insert > Timeline > Keyframe, right- or Control-click on the frame position and choose Insert Keyframe from the Context menu. You can also use the keyboard shortcut F6.

There are two types of keyframes: blank keyframes, and normal keyframes. When you insert a keyframe, it will copy the graphic from the previous keyframe into the new one. If you insert a blank keyframe, no graphic is copied at all (hence, the word "blank"). To insert a blank keyframe, select Insert > Timeline > Blank Keyframe, right- or Control-click and choose Insert Blank Keyframe from the Context menu. You can also use the keyboard shortcut F7.

> **NOTE**
> Blank keyframes are often used to prevent assets from being visible after a certain point in time.

In a frame-by-frame animation, you insert a keyframe in every frame position from the beginning of the animation to the end of the animation. In motion or shape tweens, you insert the keyframe only at critical points, allowing Flash to do the rest. For instance, insert a keyframe at the start, midpoint, and end of the animation sequence, and Flash draws all the frames in between.

To delete a keyframe, select Edit > Timeline > Remove Frames. You can also right- or Control-click on the keyframe and choose Remove Frames from the Context menu.

> **NOTE**
> If you select a keyframe and hit Delete on your keyboard, it only deletes the contents of the frame. That has the effect of turning your keyframe into a blank keyframe, which can also be done by choosing Modify > Timeline > Convert to Blank Keyframe.

To convert a keyframe to a normal frame, select Modify > Timeline > Clear Keyframe. Additionally, you can right- or Control-click on the keyframe, and select Clear Keyframe from the Context menu. That turns the keyframe into a normal frame.

Frames hold content, and that's all they do. If we edit the content in a frame, it affects all the frames before it and after it until a keyframe is encountered. We use frames to display content over time if the content isn't animating, or holding content still until it's supposed to animate. To insert a frame, select Insert > Timeline > Frame, right- or Control-click on a frame position and choose Insert Frame from the Context menu. You can also use the keyboard shortcut F5.

To delete a frame, select it, and then select Edit > Timeline > Remove Frames. Or, right- or Control-click on the frame you want to delete, and choose Remove Frames from the Context menu.

> **TIP**
> As with keyframes, when you highlight a frame and hit Delete on your keyboard, it will remove the contents of the frame. Unlike keyframes, however, it will also remove the contents of every frame before it or after it until it encounters keyframes.

Frames and keyframes can be cut, copied, pasted, and reversed. To copy frames, select Edit > Timeline > Copy Frames (with the frames selected, of course). To paste frames, highlight the frame positions you want to past the frames in, and select Edit > Timeline > Paste Frames.

> **NOTE**
> You can also cut frames to the clip board by selecting Edit > Timeline > Cut Frames.

To reverse frames and keyframes, highlight the frames that will be reversed on the timeline, and select Modify > Timeline > Reverse Frames. If you reverse the frames of an animation, you change the order in which the animation plays.

> **TIP**
>
> To reverse frames and keyframes, select them in the timeline, right- or Control-click anywhere on the selection, and choose Reverse Frames from the Context menu.

When you have created an animation, and need to reposition the entire thing after it's been set, you can use the Edit Multiple Frames feature. First, unlock all the layers that contain the animations or graphics that you want to reposition. Second, click the Edit Multiple Frames button on the Timeline, which will pull up the onion skin markers. Drag the onion skin markers so that they span all the frames you're going to move, then select Edit > Select all. From there, drag the animation to its new position anywhere on the Stage.

How fast or slow an animation plays is determined in part by the frame rate. The frame rate indicates how quickly the playhead moves over frames and keyframes in the timeline. Of course, the other determining factor is how many frames an animation spans.

> **TIP**
>
> To quickly add frames to slow an animation down or otherwise extend the amount of time the animation plays, select as many frames as you want to add. From the Insert pull-down menu, select Timeline > Insert Frames. Flash will insert as many frames as you have selected.

The default frame rate in Flash is 12 frames per second. 10 frames per second is the slowest you can go and still appear as almost natural motion. The higher the frame rate is, the more smoothly an animation will occur. Bear in mind, however, that higher frame rates will consume more CPU time, and in some cases, can result in higher file size, especially if you're not using symbols in your animations.

Onion Skinning

Onion skinning allows you to see the contents of frames other than the one you're currently working on. You can see the contents of previous frames, or frames after your current selection, depending on how you set the onion skin markers.

Using this technique allows you to fine-tune animations, especially when you're using the frame-by-frame method. It also helps you when you have to worry about positioning elements over time.

The onion skin options are on the timeline, at the bottom of the Timeline panel. They start at the second button from the right. There are three buttons: Onion Skin, Onion Skin Outlines, and Modify Onion Markers. To turn on onion skinning, choose either the Onion Skin or the Onion Skin Outlines button.

When you turn on Onion Skinning, the Onion Skin Markers will appear on either side of the playhead. There's a left and right control handle that will allow you to click and drag the marker to expand how many frames show at any given time to either the left or the right of the playhead or both.

Whatever the span of frames is, the contents of those frames will show as shaded out, indicating the position of assets in those frames at that point in time. When Onion Skin Outlines is showing, you'll see the outlines of the graphics instead of a shaded-out version.

The Modify Onion Markers button contains settings for how many frames show by default (two or five), and an option for anchoring the onion skin markers in place, no matter where the playhead is positioned.

Summary

In Flash, there are three different types of animation that we use: frame-by-frame animations, motion animations, and shape animations. Inserting one keyframe after the other, and altering visual assets in each of those frames over time manually produce frame-by-frame animations. Motion animation involves changing the position of a visual asset over time, as well as scale and rotation. Motion animation can be accomplished manually or by using Flash's automated functionality. Shape animation involves changing the physical appearance or shape of a visual asset over time, and this animation type can also be animated. Manual animations create bigger file sizes.

Onion skinning is an animation tool that shows assets in frames other than the one you're actively editing. The two onion skin options are Onion Skin, which shows grayed-out versions of assets on other frames, or Onion Skin Outlines, which shows the outlines of assets in other frames. Modify Onion Markers allows you to change onion skin settings, or you can manually adjust onion skin settings by pressing and dragging onion skin markers over a span of frames.

All animations require frames and keyframes. Keyframes specify critical points in time where a change is going to occur. When you insert a keyframe, it copies the graphics from the previous keyframe on that layer into the new one. Blank keyframes do not copy graphics into the new keyframes. Keyframe and blank keyframe content can be edited. Frames are placeholders, and hold visual assets over time. Frame content cannot be edited without affecting the contents of all frames before and after it until the next or previous keyframe.

Sample Questions

1. Which of the following inserts a keyframe?

    A. Insert > Keyframe

    B. Insert > Timeline > Keyframe

    C. Modify > Timeline > Keyframe

    D. Edit > Timeline > Keyframe

2. What option in the timeline allows you to move entire animations to a different position on the Stage?

    A. Modify Onion Markers

    B. Center Frame

    C. Edit Multiple Frames

    D. Onion Skin

3. Which of the following is used to delete a keyframe?

    A. Modify > Timeline > Remove Frames

    B. Edit > Timeline > Remove Frames

    C. Select the keyframe and press the Delete key on your keyboard.

    D. Select the keyframe and drag it into the Trash can icon in the Layers panel.

4. What option allows you to reverse the sequence of frames and keyframes in the timeline?

    A. Modify > Timeline > Reverse Frames

    B. Edit > Timeline Reverse Frames

    C. Commands > Reverse Frames

    D. Insert > Timeline > Reverse Frames

CHAPTER 21

Motion Tweening

IN THIS CHAPTER

What Can Be Motion Tweened?   181

Setting Up   182

Turning On the Tween   183

Tween Settings   185

Motion Guides   185

Mask Effects   187

Summary   187

Sample Questions   188

Motion tweening is probably the more widely used type of animation in Flash. It's used for everything from animated menus to animated characters. In this chapter, we'll review motion tween steps and settings, and Motion Guides besides.

First though, we need to remember that whenever we talk about a "tween," we're talking about Flash doing most of the work for us. We specify what something should look like in the beginning of the animation, and what it should look like at the end, and Flash draws the in-between steps for us.

What Can Be Motion Tweened?

When we are building motion tweens, we must first convert our visual assets into symbols, as only symbols can be motion tweened. Button symbols, Movie Clip symbols, or Graphic symbols, it doesn't matter, whichever is handier for the type of animation you're building.

> **NOTE**
> If you try to motion tween an asset that is not a symbol, Flash will convert it to a graphic symbol automatically, in each keyframe that the symbol appears. These symbols will show in your library as Tween 1, Tween 2, and so forth.

The reason for restricting this type of animation to only symbols has to do with file size. If we could motion tween anything, and if you want to animate, say, a business logo from one corner to the next over a one second period of time, and your frame rate is 12 frames per second, that means that your logo has to appear in two keyframes and 10 frames. If your logo happened to be 100K, you'd wind up with a 1.2 megabyte file instantly. Because symbols are reusable, we don't have to worry about file size quite so much, as the symbol is stored in the library once, and every use of it on the stage is more or less a reference to that symbol in the library.

When we speak about motion tweening, we're talking about changing the position of a symbol over time. However, we can also use motion tweening to change scale and rotation over time. This allows a designer to create perspective effects.

Apart from position, scale, and rotation, instance properties can also be altered using motion tweening. That's alpha, brightness, and tint, as well as RGB and alpha mixes and percentages. To fade things in and out, use symbols and the alpha instance property.

> **NOTE**
>
> Using motion tweening to change instance properties over time is a CPU intensive thing, and should be used sparingly.

Finally, when you are motion tweening, the graphic that you are going to motion tween must occupy its own layer. What's more, there can't be anything else in the keyframes and frames that the asset occupies in that layer (although there can be plenty of graphics in the layers above it and below it). So that asset essentially has to be isolated on its own layer, the sole occupant of the frames and keyframes that it will animate over in that layer.

Setting Up

Before creating a motion animation, you need to know how long the animation is going to run, when you want it to start, and when you want it to end. Animations can occur at different times in an application, so you'll want to be careful about how you plan things out.

First, choose which layer your motion tween is going to happen in, or insert a new layer to start the animation there. You must also decide when, in time, the animation will occur, and insert a keyframe at that point on the timeline.

➡ For more about keyframes, see Chapter 20, "Animation Basics."

> **NOTE**
> When you create a layer in Flash, a keyframe is automatically inserted for you in frame 1.

Draw or add your visual asset to the keyframe, and be sure that it's a symbol before you go any further. If you've dragged and dropped a symbol out of the library, you're good to go. If you drew your visual asset with the Flash drawing tools, or imported a graphic from somewhere, you'll probably have to convert your asset to a symbol using Modify > Convert to Symbol or the keyboard shortcut F8. Once it's a symbol, it can be animated.

Make sure your asset is positioned where you want the animation to begin. Then, based on the frame rate and what it is you want to happen, insert a keyframe in the next position on the timeline where a change will be reflected. When you insert a keyframe, it automatically copies the symbol instance from the previous keyframe, so all you'll have to do at the new keyframe is make changes to the asset. Remember, the playhead plays from left to right, so the new keyframe there will represent a more current point in time than the previous.

So with at least two keyframes, you have a starting position and an ending position. From there, it's just a matter of making the animation happen.

> **TIP**
> Once you've created the motion tween, you can go back and add keyframes anywhere along the animation. This lets you make adjustments to how the animation executes.

Turning On the Tween

To tell Flash to animate between two keyframes, we have to turn on motion tweening specifically. There are a couple of ways to do that.

First, you can select the beginning keyframe on the timeline. With that keyframe selected, look at the Property Inspector; it will show Tween in the frame properties. The Tween pull-down menu has three options: None, Motion, and Shape. Choose Motion.

Second, you can right- or Control-click in between two keyframes and choose Create Motion Tween from the Context menu.

Finally, you click between the two keyframes in the timeline and select Insert > Timeline > Create Motion Tween.

Flash will build the motion tween, and the frames between your two keyframes will shade blue and show a solid arrow pointing right. This indicates a successful tween. If something was amiss, you'd see a dotted line in the blue fill.

TIP

In addition to the dotted line, the Property Inspector will display an Alert button to let you know something's wrong. Click it to get more information about what's not working.

To play the animation, hit Enter or Return on your keyboard. You can also drag the playhead over the timeline to see the animation execute.

NOTE

Dragging the playhead through the timeline is called "scrubbing."

TIP

You can see how the animation would look to your end user by selecting Control > Test Movie, or File > Publish Preview > Default (or Flash or HTML or whatever other format you're going to publish in).

To produce the effect of fading in, choose your symbol instance in the first keyframe of the animation. In the Property Inspector, choose Alpha from the Color pull-down menu, and set the alpha to 0. Make sure that the symbol instance in the keyframe where you want the symbol to become completely visible in the animation has its alpha set to 100%.

To produce the effect of fading out, choose your symbol instance in the last keyframe of the animation (or the keyframe in which it should be completely invisible) and set the alpha of the symbol instance to 0. Make sure that the instance in the first keyframe of the fading sequence is set to 100%.

Tween Settings

The Property Inspector with includes a number of settings that alter how the animation executes. Those settings are summarized in table 21.1.

Table 21.1 Motion Tween Settings

SETTING	PURPOSE
Ease	Alters the speed of the animation in the beginning or end. To begin the animation slowly and accelerate towards the end, choose a value between –100 and –1. To begin the animation quickly and slow down towards the end, choose a number between 1 and 100. The total time of the animation remains constant.
Rotate	Rotates a symbol during animation. Auto-rotates the symbol at least once in the direction requiring the least amount of motion. CW rotates clockwise, CCW rotates counter-clockwise.
Times	The amount of times an object should rotate.
Orient to Path	Used with motion guides. Causes the baseline of the symbol to align with the stroke drawn in the motion guide layer.
Sync	Used with graphic symbols that contain animation. Causes the graphic symbol's tweens to match the number of frames the graphic symbol animates over in the main timeline.
Snap	Used with motion guides. Snaps a symbol to a stroke in a motion guide by the symbol's registration point.
Scale	Scales symbols between two keyframes in a motion animation, if the instance in the second keyframe has a different scale than the one in the first.

> **TIP**
>
> Sync can also be set by selecting the first keyframe of the animation in the main document timeline and selecting Modify > Timeline > Synchronize Symbols.

Motion Guides

Motion guides alter how an animation executes without necessarily adding more keyframes. They have their own special layers, contain strokes to specify the path of the animation, and must be on top of a layer or layers that contain an animation.

To add a motion guide, set up a motion tween between two symbol instances in two or more keyframes. Select the layer with the animation, and click the Insert Motion Guide button on the Layers panel, or choose Insert > Timeline > Motion Tween.

> **NOTE**
>
> You can also right- or Control-click on the layer that has the animation and choose Insert Motion Guide from the Context menu.

Flash will create a Motion Guide layer immediately above the selected layer that spans at least the same amount of frames as the layer containing the animation. Using the Straight Line Tool, the Pen Tool, or the Pencil Tool, draw a stroke in the Motion Guide layer.

> **TIP**
>
> It's helpful to lock your animation layer first so that you don't accidentally draw the stroke in the animation layer. When you've finished drawing the stroke, lock your Motion Guide layer, and unlock the animation layer to complete the following steps.

Next, in your animation layer, grab your symbol by its center, and snap it to the path in the Motion Guide layer in each keyframe and position that the symbol occurs in.

> **TIP**
>
> It's easiest if you grab by the center, although you can certainly drag and snap by the symbol's registration point.

> **TIP**
>
> Make sure Snap to Objects is turned on. This way, you can see the snap ring and make sure the symbols are snapped to the path.

To remove a Motion Guide layer, you can highlight it and delete it in the Layers panel, or access the layer properties for the Motion Guide layer and set it to Normal, or finally, you can drag the Animation layer above the Motion Guide layer (or vice versa).

→ See Chapter 10, "Layers and the Timeline," for more information about deleting layers and changing layer properties.

Mask Effects

You can use motion tweening to create mask effects in Flash, which can serve as transition for static images or embedded video. In Chapter 10, "Layers and the Tmeline," we saw that masking was a property of a layer, which makes it ideal for making transition effects.

To make a proper mask effect, you'll need two layers. One layer will contain the animation, which will serve as the transition. The other will be the layer that the transition affects.

To transition in, build your animation so that it scales over or otherwise gradually covers up the contents of the layer beneath it. To transition out, build your animation so that the contents of the layer being masked are gradually exposed. One you have either animation set, right- or Control-click on the animation layer and choose Mask from the Context menu to produce the transition effect.

TIP

You can also select Modify > Timeline > Layer Properties, then choose Mask from the Layer Properties dialog box; the same dialog box can be retrieved by double-clicking on the layer's type icon.

Summary

Motion tweening is used to create the effect of motion, changes in scale or rotation, or changes in opacity or coloration over time. Motion tweening can only be enacted upon symbols.

To turn on motion tweening between two keyframes, select the first keyframe in the animation sequence and choose Motion from the Tween pull-down menu in the Property Inspector. You can also choose Insert > Timeline > Create Motion Tween, or right- or Control-click between two keyframes and choose Create Motion Tween from the Context menu.

Motion tweens can be altered using the easing and rotations options. Additionally, Motion Guide layers can be used to control the path of an animation.

Finally, motion tweens can be used to create mask effects, which produce transitions in and out for images or video.

Sample Questions

1. To fade a symbol in with a motion tween:

   A. Set its alpha in the color mixer to 0 in the first keyframe of the animation sequence.

   B. Set its alpha to 0 in the Property Inspector in the last keyframe of the animation.

   C. Set its alpha to 0 in the Property Inspector in the first keyframe of the animation.

   D. Set its alpha in the color mixer to 0 in the last keyframe of the animation sequence.

2. _____ can be motion tweened:

   A. Movie clips only

   B. Graphic symbols only

   C. Button symbols only

   D. Any symbols

3. Flash animates between symbol instances in what?

   A. Frames

   B. Keyframes

   C. Blank keyframes

   D. None of the above

4. Which of the following is not the correct way to add a Motion Guide layer?

   A. Edit > Timeline > Add Motion Guide

   B. Click the Add Motion Guide button on the Layers panel

   C. Select Insert > Timeline > Motion Guide

   D. Right- or Control-click on a layer with an animation and choose Add Motion Guide from the Context menu.

CHAPTER 22

Shape Tweening

IN THIS CHAPTER

What Can Be Shape Tweened?   189

Setting Up   190

Shape Tween Settings   191

Shape Hints   192

Summary   193

Sample Questions   193

In the last chapter, we reviewed motion tweening, which involved changing the position, scale, rotation, and opacity (as well as other instance properties) of an asset over time. Shape tweening differs in that we change the physical shape of an asset over time, so that its appearance completely alters.

In this chapter, we will review what you need to do to create a shape tween, as well as its unique settings.

What Can Be Shape Tweened?

The only kinds of assets that Flash can shape tween are editable objects. That means that they can't be symbols, text, or otherwise grouped. It includes any kind of vector artwork, and cannot be used with bitmaps. The idea is to change from one shape into another over time, although things like position and color can also be changed.

> **TIP**
> An asset is editable if it has a has a pattern indicating that it's been selected when you click on it. If you see a blue box, your asset isn't editable.

Artwork that you draw with any of the drawing tools is editable by default, unless it's been grouped or converted to a symbol. If you have an asset that you want to shape tween, you must first break it apart.

To break apart symbols and grouped objects, select the graphics with the selection tool, and select Modify > Break Apart. To break apart text so that it can be shape tweened, choose your text block, and choose Modify > Break Apart twice.

> **TIP**
>
> As a rule, you want to shape tween simple assets. Shape tweening can be processor intensive; the more complex the graphic, the more CPU will be consumed, and the more likely you'll get unpredictable results in between steps.

In addition to changing the shape of an asset, color and opacity can be changed over time using shape tweens. What's more, you can change position and scale (size) as well, creating effects similar to motion tweens.

→ For more detail on motion tweening, see Chapter 21, "Motion Tweening."

> **TIP**
>
> Shape tweens, because they don't use symbols, can result in larger file sizes. Use them sparingly.

Setting Up

Shape tweens, like motion tweens, are executed by Flash between keyframes, so you must have a beginning shape and an ending shape (and any shapes in between) in mind before you start.

In general, it's a good idea to change the shape of one thing at a time, but unlike motion tweening, you aren't restricted to that. If you want to change the shape of multiple items at a time, they must all be on the same layer.

> **TIP**
>
> While you can change multiple shapes at a time, it's still a best practice to put each tweening item on its own layer, unless you're using multiple objects to create a special effect, like a bunch of dots combined to create a word.

To set up the animation, draw or add an editable asset in the first keyframe where the animation sequence will begin. If the asset you have added is grouped or is a symbol, break it apart before you proceed. Next, insert a keyframe in the frame position where the animation sequence is going to end.

> **TIP**
>
> Since you're going to add or change the shape of the object, it's useful to insert a blank keyframe rather than a keyframe. Remember, blank keyframes do not copy graphics from the previous keyframe. See Chapter 20, "Animation Basics," for more information.

In the new keyframe, change the shape of the object, or replace it with an entirely new object. Onion skinning can be turned on to see what the previous frames look like, so that you can adjust the shape and position of your new asset accordingly. To turn on Onion Skinning, click the Onion Skin button on the Timeline panel.

When you have the object in the last keyframe of the sequence constructed, you're ready to turn on shape tweening. To turn the shape tween on, select the first keyframe of the animation sequence, and in the Property Inspector, select Shape from the Tween pull-down menu.

> **TIP**
>
> Shape tweening will not work if there are any grouped objects or symbols in the layer.

Shape Tween Settings

Shape tween settings on the Property Inspector modify how the tween executes. They're pretty straightforward:

- Easing. This option either speeds up the animation and slows down at the end when a positive number is selected, or slows down an animation and speeds it up toward the end when a negative number is selected. The animation still executes over its given amount of time.

- Blend. This option determines how smooth the animation appears when animating, and has two settings:

  - Distributive. Smoothes the in-between shapes as they animate.

  - Angular. Maintains straight lines and corners as the animation executes.

> **TIP**
>
> If tweening shapes don't have any sharp corners or straight lines, Flash will use the distributive mode.

Shape Hints

Shape tweens are very hard to get right. Shape hints give you a way to exercise some control over how a shape tween executes by adding control points at the beginning and end of the sequence. Control points at the end of the sequence become targets for the animating shapes; the starting shape hint should end up at its counterpart's final position, essentially.

When you add a shape hint, you must do so at the starting keyframe of the animation sequence, and the layer has to be editable. First, highlight the starting keyframe and select Modify > Shape > Add Shape Hint. This will place a shape hint on the Stage. Drag it to some position on your shape (generally along the edge of the graphic). This is the beginning shape hint, and it should be red, with a letter. The first shape hint will be lettered "a," of course.

> **TIP**
>
> When you place the hint into position, it will turn yellow in the starting keyframe.

Next, click on the last keyframe; Flash has already inserted the ending shape hint, represented by a green circle of the same letter. Drag it to the position on the graphic where it should appear.

> **TIP**
>
> As you add shape hints, position them in a way that makes sense. If your starting shape hint is in the shape's upper left corner, dragging the end shape hint to the shape's lower right corner in the next keyframe doesn't do a whole lot of good.

> **TIP**
>
> You can have up to 26 shape hints.

As you add more shape hints, arrange them in a counter-clockwise fashion. That seems to make things run a little bit more smoothly.

To make shape hints invisible in the editing environment, select View > Show Shape Hints to deselect. The shape hints will become hidden on the Stage. To turn them back on again, select View > Show Shape Hints a second time.

To delete a shape hint, drag it off the Stage. To get rid of all your shape hints, select Modify > Shape > Remove All Hints.

> **TIP**
>
> Macromedia recommends that you use intermediate shapes in multiple keyframes when you want to create complex shape tweens. Shape hints are great, but they'll only take you so far.

Summary

Shape tweening allows you to change one shape into another, while at the same time changing its position, scale, color and/or opacity. Like motion tweening, shape tweening is turned on in the Property Inspector, and has Easing settings, which control the rate at which the animation begins and ends while maintaining the overall time that animation executes. Blend modes determine how smoothly the animations in between steps are drawn when the shapes have sharp corners and straight lines.

Shape hints impose a limited amount of control over how the animation executes. When they are added to the first keyframe of the animation, Flash automatically adds them to the next (last) keyframe. Shape hints should be positioned counterclockwise, and start and end positions should make sense.

Sample Questions

1. Which of the following items can be shape tweened (choose 2)?

   A. An oval drawn with the oval tool

   B. A block of text

   C. Text that's been broken apart into editable objects

   D. Grouped vector art

2. The blend mode Angular is used for what kinds of shapes?

   A. Shapes that have sharp angles and straight lines.

   B. Shapes that don't have sharp angles and straight lines.

   C. Shapes that have color gradients.

   D. Shapes that don't have color gradients.

3. How do you add a shape hint to the first keyframe of a shape animation?

   A. Insert > Shape > Add Shape Hint

   B. Insert > Timeline > Add Shape Hint

   C. Modify > Timeline > Add Shape Hint

   D. Modify > Shape > Add Shape Hint

4. How do you make a block of text able to be shape tweened?

   A. Text is already able to be shape tweened

   B. Select Modify > Break Apart Once

   C. Select Modify > Break Apart Twice

   D. Select Modify > Ungroup

CHAPTER 23

Animating with ActionScript

IN THIS CHAPTER

What Can Be Animated with
ActionScript?   195

Using the onEnterFrame Event   196

Using the setInterval Event   198

Summary   199

Sample Questions   199

In Flash, the Movie Clip, Button, and Component symbols have instance names, and X and Y properties that can be changed programmatically. Anything whose position can be changed programmatically can be animated using ActionScript, thanks to the onEnterFrame event of the Movie Clip class, and setIinterval.

In this chapter, we review animation using ActionScript.

What Can Be Animated with ActionScript?

Any visual asset that can assume an instance name can be animated with ActionScript. This includes buttons, text fields, and components, as well as Movie Clips.

> **TIP**
> Only movie clips can respond to the onEnterFrame event.

Using ActionScript, you can change the position of a named object over time. You can also change scale, opacity, and rotation, or any other property that can be accessed via ActionScript. The primary thing to remember is visual change over time.

Because ActionScript is so flexible, it gives a way to create more interesting effects than you may be able to create using the timeline. In addition, because ActionScript events are processed in memory, largely speaking, animating with ActionScript eliminates the need for multiple keyframes in a timeline, which means that your final SWF file size will ultimately be lower.

> **TIP**
>
> Animating with ActionScript can create a processor burden. We'll see how to control that in this chapter.

Using the `onEnterFrame` Event

The `onEnterFrame` event is an event that Movie Clips respond to based on the frame rate of your document. The `onEnterFrame` event broadcasts continually to the movie clip instance that you specify an event handler for. If you tell a Movie Clip to respond to an `onEnterFrame` event, and your frame rate is 12 frames per second, the `onEnterFrame` event will broadcast approximately every twelfth of a second.

Because this event is continuously executing, it makes it ideal for animation. You can have a movie clip respond to the event by writing an event handler directly on the object, or in a keyframe on the timeline. The general syntax for both follows:

Keyframe:

```
movieClipInstance.onEnterFrame=function(){
    InstructionsToExecute();
}
```

Directly on movie clip:

```
onClipEvent(enterFrame){
    _parent.InstructionsToExecute();
}
```

> **TIP**
>
> When you are using ActionScript on a Movie Clip instance that needs to respond to an event, you must do it with an `onClipEvent` handler, and specify the event within open and close parentheses. The syntax `onClipEvent` is synonymous with the "on" handler for a button instance with a script directly attached to it.

When you want to create an animation, you'll change some property or properties over time. Sometimes, that requires that you set a condition with an "if" statement.

➜ For more conditional statements, see Chapter 28, "The Basics of ActionScript."

The following example is a frame script that animates a movie clip to the right until it reaches the position it should be in.

```
myMovieClip.onEnterFrame=function()
{
    if(this._x<300)
        {
            this._x+=10;
        }
    else
        {
delete this. onEnterFrame;
}
}
```

Movie clips can also animate other objects, acting as controllers in that regard. The following example creates a movie clip using ActionScript (See chapter 18, "The Movie Clip Symbol," for more information), makes it animate a text area component on the Stage, and deletes the onEnterFrame event since it is no longer needed.

```
this.createEmptyMovieClip("controllerMC",1);
controllerMC.onEnterFrame=function()
{
    if(taTextArea._x<300)
    {
        taTextArea._x+=10;
    }
    else
    {
    delete this.onEnterFrame;
    }
}
```

Using the `setInterval` Event

Like the `onEnterFrame` event, `setInterval` executes continuously over a period of time unless it's cleared. Unlike `onEnterFrame`, the period of time that it executes is not dependent on your main document frame rate. You get to decide how often it happens, in milliseconds.

> **TIP**
>
> Because the time interval is set by you, be aware that it is easy to make other items animating `onEnterFrame` out of synch with the animations you create using `setInterval`. Generally, it's best to use one or the other, but maybe not such a good idea to use all three in a single SWF.

The key thing to know about `setInterval` is that it is a function that calls another function, named or anonymous, that you write.

➡ For more on functions, see Chapter 28, "The Basics of Action Script."

Here are the two required parameters that `setInterval` accepts:

- `functionName`. A named or anonymous function that will be called when `setInterval` executes.

- Interval. The amount of time, in milliseconds, between each execution of `setInterval` (or how often the function specified in the `functionName` parameter will be called).

Here is an example of using `setInterval()` to move a TextArea component to the right every 10 milliseconds until it's reached its final location:

```
myInterval=setInterval(textAreaMove, 10);
function textAreaMove() {
    if (textAreaInstance._x<300) {
        textAreaInstance._x += 10;
    } else {
    clearInterval(myInterval);
    }
}
```

> **TIP**
>
> Like `onEnterFrame`, `setInterval` will eat up memory and CPU unless you specifically clear it. In the above example, the interval is named, and is cleared when `textAreaInstance`'s x position is no longer less than 300 pixels.

Some things to know about setInterval:

- When your interval is smaller than your frame rate, the screen will not refresh right away. Your SWF screen refreshes based on the frame rate. To force things to refresh, you have to use the updateAfterEvent() function, which allows you to specify when the screen should be refreshed.

- When your interval is greater than the frame rate, the interval will be called as close as possible to the time you set whenever the playhead enters a frame, so that way CPU and memory are not gobbled up.

Summary

Animation can be created using ActionScript, instead of using the timeline or motion or shape tweens. One advantage of using ActionScript for animation is that it can keep file size lower. You can animate position, rotation, opacity, and scale of any object that can accept an instance name.

To use ActionScript to animate, you can use an onEnterFrame event or setInterval. The onEnterFrame event is an event that Movie Clips can respond to, and executes continuously based on your document frame rate. When you use setInterval, you determine the amount of times between execution, and the function that gets called.

When using either method, it is important to delete the interval or onEnterFrame in order to save memory and CPU usage. Both will otherwise continue to execute, even if the movie is stopped.

Sample Questions

1. When using onEnterFrame with a script on a Movie Clip instance and not on a frame, which syntax do you use?

   A. on(enterFrame){instructions;}

   B. this.onEnterFrame(){instructions;}

   C. onClipEvent(enterFrame){instructions;}

   D. this.onClipEvent(enterFrame){instructions;}

2. What is a best practice when using `onEnterFrame` for animation?

   A. Only use it to animate movie clip instances.

   B. Delete the event when it's no longer needed.

   C. Use it with empty movie clips to control other objects.

   D. Use it to change the position of an asset only.

3. What are the two required parameters of `setInterval`?

   A. functionName and Interval

   B. Interval and triggering event

   C. functionName and triggering event

   D. functionName and target

4. Which is a best practice when using `setInterval`?

   A. Name the interval so it can be cleared later.

   B. Use only one interval per SWF.

   C. Never use an interval less than your frame rate.

   D. Never use an interval greater than your frame rate.

PART 5

Sound
and Video

24 Sound

25 Video

CHAPTER 24

Sound

IN THIS CHAPTER

Adding Sound to Your Application   203

Sound Settings   206

Sound Events   208

The Sound Object   208

Summary   210

Sample Questions   210

The inclusion of sound in web sites often adds value for the end user. While some sites use it for entertainment, or to create an atmosphere, other sites and applications use it to provide feedback to the user, indicating that they have done something, clicked on something, or otherwise interacted with the site.

In this unit, we review how to add sound, and what to do with it once you've done so.

Adding Sound to Your Application

There are several ways to add sounds to your application. You can import it directly and use it on the timeline, stream it from the server using the Sound class, or use Flash MX 2004 Media Components to stream MP3 files from the server.

> **TIP**
>
> When using the Sound class in Flash, you can only stream MP3 files. Any other type of file requires import.

To import a sound in Flash, select File > Import > Import to Library. In the Import dialog, find your sound file, and click the import button.

The sound formats supported by Flash MX 2004 include:

- AU
- WAV
- AIFF
- MP3

Once you have sound imported, you can make use of it in a couple of ways. First, you can add sound directly to the timeline, or you can use a sound behavior to attach a sound from the library and play it, eliminating the need to have it in the timeline.

To add a sound to the timeline, you should have a layer for it. As a best practice, sounds should generally have their own layers. Sounds, like everything else, must live in a keyframe, so insert a keyframe in the position you want the sound to start playing in. Then drag the sound out of the library and drop it on to the Stage.

By default, when the playhead strikes the keyframe that the sound first appears in, the sound will begin to play, and will continue to do so until it is complete, whether or not there are other sounds playing at the same time. When we look at the section on sound settings, we'll see how to have a little more control over things.

To remove a sound from the timeline, select the keyframe that the sound is in, and choose None from the Sound pull-down menu in the Property Inspector.

To use a sound behavior to make a sound play, select the sound in the library. Right- or Control-click the sound, and select the Linkage option from the Context menu, or select Linkage from the Library options menu. Give the sound a linkage identi-fier that's intuitive, and click OK.

Next, select either the keyframe you want the behavior to execute in, or an object (like a button) that you want to trigger the behavior. From the Behaviors panel, click the Add Behavior button (the plus icon), and from the Sound category, choose Load Sound from Library.

In the Load Sound from Library dialog box, type the linkage identifier that you set in the library, and an instance name for the sound that's being attached (so ActionScript can manipulate it). If you want the sound to play right away, make sure that the Play Sound Loaded check box is selected. Click OK to add the sound.

> **TIP**
>
> If you're adding the behavior to an object like a button, make sure that the Event is showing the event you want. The default is On Release, which means a user has clicked and released the button.

→ For more about the Behaviors panel, see Chapter 26, "The Behaviors Panel."

If you have Flash MX Professional 2004, you can use a Media component to stream an MP3 file from the server. The easiest one to use is the Media Playback component. Drag it and drop it on the Stage to make use of it, then launch the Component Inspector with either the Property Inspector, or by selecting Window > Development Panels > Component Inspector.

> **TIP**
>
> When you use the Media Playback component, the properties for it can only be set with the Component Inspector. For this reason the Property Inspector will display a Launch Component Inspector button in the parameters tab when an instance of the Media Playback component is selected on the Stage.

In the Component Inspector with the Media Playback Component selected, click the Parameters tab. Select the MP3 Radio Button, which will remove all of the video options. In the URL dialog box, type the URL where the MP3 file resides.

> **TIP**
>
> This doesn't have to be an absolute reference like `http://www.somePlace.com/tb3.mp3`. It can be relative to the SWF, such as `"sounds/tb3.mp3"`.

Select the Automatically Play option if you want the MP3 file to play when the component is fully loaded in the SWF. Control Placement specifies the position you want the playback controls to be located, and the control visibility determines whether the controls are always visible or if they appear when you mouse over the component.

> **TIP**
>
> You can use the Media Display component to stream MP3's as well, but without the playback controls. This is useful for things like instructional voice-overs.

Sound Settings

Adjusting sound settings can be done either with the Property Inspector, or using the Sound Properties dialog box, retrieved from the library. Of course, ActionScript can be used to change sound properties as well.

To change sound settings in the Library, select the sound file, then either right- or Control-click and choose Properties from the Context menu, or choose Properties from the Library options menu, or select the Information button at the bottom of the Library panel. This will bring up the Sound Properties dialog box.

The Sound Properties dialog box contains summary information about the sound, including how long it is and what format it is in. In this dialog box, you can also set your sound compression properties, the default of which is MP3 at16 kilobytes per second.

To change the default compression settings, click the Compression pull-down menu, and select a new compression. You can choose ADPCM, RAW, MP3, or Speech. You'll never guess what Speech compression is best used with.

> **TIP**
>
> Device sounds let you specify sounds for use with mobile devices. The sound formats that mobile devices use is not supported by Flash, so you use a temporary sound in its place. Click the Device Sounds folder icon and browse to the folder that contains the mobile device sounds you're using in development.

> **TIP**
>
> You can also adjust sound compression in the Publish settings. For more on that, see the chapters in Part 7," Optimization and Publishing."

You can also control sound settings such as volume and other effects in the Property Inspector, when the sound has been added to a keyframe in the timeline.

Select the keyframe in the timeline that contains the instance of your sound. The Property Inspector's sound section will highlight. If your sound is not already selected in the Sound pull-down menu, choose it. This selects the sound you want to make changes to using Flash.

Next, in the Effects menu, you can choose from a number of pre-built fade effects, which are:

- None
- Left Channel
- Right Channel
- Fade Left to Right
- Fade Right to Left
- Fade in
- Fade Out
- Custom

You can create your own fade effect using the Edit button, which also allows you to adjust the sound's volume over time when it is in the timeline. When you click the Edit button, it pulls up the Edit Envelop.

TIP
The Edit Envelop is also retrieved by selecting Custom from the Effects menu.

The Edit Envelop has two sound channels to work with. The top channel is the left channel, the bottom is the right, and between them is a bar that shows either frames or time, and is essentially a ruler indicating at what point in time a section of the sound occurs. In both channels there is an oscillation pattern with a line through it that indicates average volume, and white control handles over the top, which have the purpose of controlling sound volume at that point. Dragging the handles from the top towards the center decreases volume.

You can add control handles by clicking anywhere on the line that stores them, and remove them by dragging them away. When you have more than one control handle, you can produce fade in/fade out effects. Control handles placed from lower left to upper right fade a sound in. Control handles placed from upper left to lower right fade a sound out. When all of the control handles are at the bottom of either channel, the channel has no sound.

TIP
There can be a total of up to 8 handles in the Edit Envelop.

Click OK to get out of the Edit Envelop.

Sound Events

In the Property Inspector, there is a Synch pull-down menu, which contains options for the following:

- **Event.** Triggers when the playhead enters the keyframe the sound is in. It is meant to convey the idea "event in the animation," and is what you may choose when you place a sound in the down frame of a button timeline, for example. If the sound is already playing, a new instance of the sound will begin, and they will overlap.

- **Start.** Works the same as Event; however, if the sound is already playing, using the Start option will prevent a new instance of it from playing again.

- **Stop.** Turns off the sound specified in the Property Inspector.

- **Stream.** Used for Web content, Stream forces the timeline to keep up with the sound. In order for it to work, the sound layer must be extended to the appropriate amount of frames in the timeline that the sound plays over. The rest of the content for your piece must add up to that number of frames. To keep your animations and your sound synchronized, Flash kicks out random frames in the timeline (but not keyframes).

Also in the Property Inspector are loop options: Repeat, in which you enter a value to cause the sound to repeat a fixed number of times (the default is 1, so that the sound plays at least once), or Loop, which causes the sound to repeat for as long as the SWF is open.

The Sound Object

In Flash, Sound is a class of objects that can be used to control sounds in an application. To make use of it, you first must create an instance of the class:

```
var mySound=new Sound();
```

Next, you load a sound into it, either from the document library, using the attachSound method, or an MP3 from the hard drive using the loadSound method.

> **TIP**
> The sound object cannot control a sound playing in the timeline.

To load a sound using the attachSound() method and play it, use the following syntax on an object in an event handler, or in a frame script:

```
mySound.attachSound("libraryIdentifier");
mySound.start(0,0);
```

> **TIP**
>
> The first parameter is seconds offset and is a number that determines when the sound should start. The second parameter is loop, and is also numeric. It determines how many times the sound should repeat, and can go up to a value of 999.

To load an MP3 from the hard drive:

```
mySound.loadSound("myMP3.mp3",true);
```

> **TIP**
>
> The first parameter is the URL parameter, and must be within the same domain as SWF that calls it. The second is isStreaming, which can be either true or false. If isStreaming is set to true the MP3 file will play as it downloads. If set to false, the MP3 file must fully downloaded before it can play.

To stop a sound from playing, either in a frame script or an event handler, use:

```
mySound.stop();
```

To stop all sounds from playing, use:

```
mySound.stopAllSound();
```

> **TIP**
>
> The sound object also has a setVolume() method, which accepts a value from 0 to 100 to adjust the volume of a sound playing.

When a sound played through the Sound object stops playing it broadcasts an event, called the onSoundComplete event. Use this event to do things like synchronize sounds to sequential events, create jukebox-style playlists, or create slide shows that only move to the next slide after a voice-over has finished.

The following example creates a new Sound Object, loads a sound from the library, plays it, and sends a message to the Output window when the sound is done:

```
var mySound:Sound=new Sound();
mySound.attachSound("csSound");
mySound.start(0,0);
mySound.onSoundComplete=function()
{
    trace("Sound done");
}
```

Summary

Sound in Flash gives designers a good way to add value to a Web application. Sound files can be imported to the document and placed in the timeline, or they can be streamed off the server if they are in MP3 format.

The Behaviors panel contains a sound category, which in turn contains behaviors to do things like attach a sound from the Library and play it right away.

In Flash, Sound is also a class of objects that can be created and controlled with ActionScript. Objects created from the Sound class can load sounds from the Library, or can stream MP3 files from the server. The onSoundComplete method of the Sound class triggers when a specific sound has finished playing, and is very useful for things like slide shows or events that must trigger when a sound is complete.

Sample Questions

1. What synch setting must be selected in order for sound and animation to match?

   A. Start

   B. Event

   C. Stream

   D. Stop

2. What methods can be used to stream sound from a server (choose 2)?

   A. The Media Display component with MP3s

   B. The attachSound() method of the Sound class

   C. The loadSound() method of the Sound class

   D. The Media Controller component with MP3s

3. In what window can you adjust sound volume?

   A. In the Sound Properties dialog box

   B. In the Publish Settings dialog box

   C. In the Media Controller, under the Component inspector

   D. In the Edit Envelop, launched from the Property inspector

4. Which synch setting will play a new instance of a sound after shutting the previous one off, if it is already playing?

    A. Event

    B. Start

    C. Stop

    D. Stream

CHAPTER 25

Video

IN THIS CHAPTER

Importing Video   213

Adding Video to the Timeline   215

Using Media Components   216

Embedded Video Behaviors   218

Summary   219

Sample Questions   219

In Flash MX, video support was introduced. In Flash MX 2004, it was improved. Now, not only can video be imported, but it can be linked to externally without saving your Flash file as a QuickTime movie.

In this chapter, we review the use of video in Flash, and the use of media components to link to external video files.

Importing Video

Video can either be directly imported into Flash, or if it is in FLV format, it can be linked to externally. This first section we will review importing video and what to do with it once it's in.

Table 25.1 lists the video formats supported by Flash.

Table 25.1 Video Formats Supported by Flash

FORMAT	REQUIREMENT
AVI	QuickTime 4 or above; DirectX7 or above
DV	QuickTime 4 or above
MPG, MPEG	QuickTime 4 or above; DirectX7 or above
MOV	QuickTime 4 or above
WMV	DirectX7 or above
ASF	DirectX7 or above
FLV	Macromedia Flash Player

> **TIP**
>
> When you import video in Flash, you are doing so through the Sorensen Spark codec, which then compresses the video. The compression type is lossy; that is to say, it's like JPEG compression, and decreases output quality by kicking out data.

To import any of the above formats, select File > Import, and choose either Import to Stage, or Import to Library. As a best practice, import the video directly to your Library, then place the video in a Movie Clip. This way, you have more control over the video, and won't have to extend your main document timeline.

> **TIP**
>
> Video in Flash will attempt to extend the timeline that it's imported in or dragged to if the timeline doesn't have at least the same amount of frames as the video.

When the Video Import Wizard appears, you will be walked through several menu systems to assist you in your video import. The first screen will prompt you to either import the entire video, or edit the video first. Unless you want to edit, click the radio button for Import Entire Video.

> **TIP**
>
> If you choose to edit the video, when you click next, you will be sent to the Editing pane of the Video Import Wizard. The Editing pane allows you to set in and out points and rename a clip. You can also create multiple clips from a single file, which allows you to reorder the appearance of frames. This is great for quick edits, but for more fully featured editing options, you really should have the video edited in a tool like Final Cut Pro.

The next screen will prompt you to either embed the video in Flash, or link to an external MOV video file. If you link to an external MOV video file, you will have to export your Flash document as a QuickTime MOV rather than an SWF, so it's generally a better idea to embed.

The third screen allows you to select from a compression profile, or create your own. The compression profiles are:

- 56 kps Modem
- Corporate LAN 150 kps
- DSL/Cable 256 kps

- DSL/Cable 512 kps

- DSL/Cable 786 kps

- Create New Profile

> **TIP**
>
> These settings are optimized for bandwidth. They do have an effect on quality, but not quite the same effect as if you were to adjust the quality manually.

When you select Create New Profile, you will be placed in the Editing pane of the Video Import wizard. To the right is a preview of the video, and to the left is a series of optimization options. You can adjust settings for bandwidth as well as video quality, how often keyframes should be added, and whether or not the video should be synchronized with the Flash document's frame rate. Of course, every option you select will ultimately have an impact on document size and download speed.

> **TIP**
>
> In the third screen is also an advanced settings option. Use this to change things like hue, saturation, dimensions, and whether or not the video should be imported to a Movie Clip, Graphic Symbol, or to the main document timeline. Movie Clip is the best practice.

When you've selected a compression profile, click Finish. The video will be imported and stored in the document library with a digital video icon indicating what it is.

Adding Video to the Timeline

If you have not imported your video directly to the Stage, you will have to take your video out of the library and into a timeline. Instances of video need to live in a keyframe.

To add your video, drag it from the library and onto the Stage in the keyframe and layer you want the video to occupy. If the video's length exceeds the current length of the timeline, Flash will prompt you to extend the timeline.

> **TIP**
>
> Video on a timeline can accept an instance name, which means that it can be controlled programmatically. There are a number of behaviors that allow you to create simple video controls, and those are discussed in the Embedded Video Behaviors section later in this chapter.

> **NOTE**
>
> If you choose not to extend the timeline, the video will not play in its entirety.

For this reason, it's best to create a Movie Clip symbol that will have the video inside it, and then use that symbol out on the Stage. The benefits of this are:

- Movie clips have their own timeline, so nesting video in a movie clip allows you to create a more complex application.

- Digital video will inherit the properties of the Movie Clip instance that it is in, including opacity, rotation, and scale.

- Because the video is in a movie clip, you have more control over it using ActionScript.

> **TIP**
>
> There is one disadvantage to using digital video in a Movie Clip: Movie Clip symbols do not stream. They, and their contents, must fully download before they play.

Using Media Components

If you don't want to directly embed video in your Flash file, you can use the media components. As we saw in Chapter 24, "Sound," media components let you stream video and sound from the server, provided it's in the right format. In the case of Flash, that means FLV format.

> **TIP**
>
> FLV stands for Macromedia Flash Video. The format belongs to Macromedia, but most of the current digital video editors are capable of exporting to the FLV format. However, if you don't have a digital video editor like Final Cut Pro, you can download an FLV formatter for free from Macromedia's web site, or export video from Flash to the FLV format using the Library properties.

First, make sure your video is in FLV format. Second, drag a media component in the keyframe and layer that you want the video to appear in. You can use either the Media Display component or the Media Playback component.

> **TIP**
>
> The Media Display component will play back video, but does not have controllers, so your user cannot interact with it. Media Playback does have controllers, such as play, stop, and so on.

Select the instance of the media component on the Stage, and launch the Component Inspector by selecting Window > Development Panels > Component Inspector, or click the Launch Component Inspector button on the Property Inspector. Select the Parameters tab in the Component Inspector. Choose the FLV radio button.

The rest of the parameters are summarized below:

- **Video Length.** This determines the progress of the video as it is playing. The progress is reflected in the Playbar.

- **Milliseconds.** Sets the video length in milliseconds, instead of Frames.

- **FPS.** The frame rate for the video. If milliseconds is selected, this will be grayed out.

- **URL.** The location of your FLV on the server.

- **Automatically Play.** Plays the video as soon as the component is drawn on the Stage and enough frames have downloaded for the video to play.

- **Used Preferred Media Size.** When selected, uses the original size and aspect ratio of the FLV file. When deselected, uses the size set in the Component Inspector.

- **Respect Aspect Ratio.** Keeps the original aspect ratio of the FLV file, no matter whether or not it has been resized.

- **Control Placement.** Puts the playback controls at the top, bottom, left, or right of the FLV as it is playing in the component.

- **Control Visibility.** Determines whether or not the controls are collapsed, becoming visible when the user mouses over the video clip/component, or visible all the time.

To use the component, specify a URL (absolute or relative to the document), and set the other parameters as needed. You won't be able to see the video play in the FLA, but will have to test the movie for it to work.

The media components can also be set using ActionScript. For instance, you can use the `setMedia()`; method to simultaneously specify what file an instance of Media Playback or Media Display component should use. The general syntax is:

```
Media.setMedia(contentPath, mediaType);
```

Media would be the instance name of your component. The contentPath parameter is the location of your FLV or MP3 file. The second parameter, mediaType, is optional, and is used to set the media type to either FLV or MP3. The default is FLV. The following example illustrates what might be used in a real application:

```
flvBox.setMedia("videos/dogGrooming.flv","FLV");
```

> **TIP**
>
> You can also use the `Media.contentPath` property to specify an external FLV or MP3 file to play, but you cannot set the media type in that circumstance.

The Media Display and Media Playback components also have `stop()`, `play()`, and `pause()` methods which can be used to control playback. For more information on using ActionScript to control media components, see the Media class entry in your ActionScript Dictionary.

> **NOTE**
>
> The Media class is available for Flash MX Professional 2004 only.

Embedded Video Behaviors

When video in Flash is embedded, it can be controlled with pre-built behaviors from the Behaviors panel. Attach the behaviors to an object like a button.

> **TIP**
>
> Before you attach the behavior, you must make sure that the movie clip that contains the video has an instance name, and that the digital video instance inside the movie clip also has an instance name.

The behaviors are:

- **Play.** Plays the video instance.
- **Stop.** Stops the video instance and returns to the first frame.
- **Pause.** Pauses the video in its current frame, and resumes on play.
- **Fast Forward.** Fast forwards through the video.
- **Rewind.** Rewinds through the video.
- **Hide Video.** Makes the video invisible.
- **Show Video.** Makes the video visible.

> **TIP**
>
> These behaviors apply to the digital video instance itself, and not the movie clip that it resides in.

To use the behaviors, launch the Behaviors panel by selecting Window > Development Panels > Behaviors. Select a button instance and in the Behaviors panel, click the Add Behavior button (the Plus icon). From the Embedded Video category, choose the behavior you want. Each behavior will have a dialog box requesting specific parameters, such as the video instance to control. Fill out the appropriate parameters, and click OK to add the Behavior.

> **TIP**
>
> Make sure the triggering event is the one you want. The default event is Release. To change it, choose the pull-down menu, and select a different event.

To remove a behavior, select it in the panel and click the Remove Behavior button (the Minus icon).

➡ For more on Behaviors and the Behaviors panel, see Chapter 26, "The Behaviors Panel."

Summary

Flash MX 2004 can import video directly for inclusion in an SWF, or can link to QuickTime MOV's. Linking to any format other than an FLV requires that your Flash document be published as a QuickTime movie.

When you embed video, you can select a compression profile for bandwidth to keep file size at a minimum. When you add embedded video to a timeline, the timeline must have at least as many frames as the video in order for it to display. Flash will extend the timeline otherwise. In addition, there are a number of behaviors in the Behaviors panel that allow you to give an end user control over playback.

Flash Media components allow you to stream FLV formatted video through the Flash Player.

Sample Questions

1. Which component plays video without adding controllers for the end user to use?

   A. Media Display

   B. Media Controller

   C. Media Playback

   D. Video Display

2. Which of the following video types can be streamed from the server using Flash?

   A. AVI

   B. FLV

   C. MOV

   D. WMV

3. Why should you place digital video instances in a movie clip instead of the main timeline?

   A. Movie clips can stream the video.

   B. Movie clip timelines are independent and can have as many frames as the video without affecting the main timeline.

   C. Movie clip timelines are independent and need only one frame to display the video.

   D. Digital video cannot be placed in the main timeline.

4. Which behavior stops embedded video and returns it to its first frame?

   A. Stop

   B. Pause

   C. Fast Forward

   D. Rewind

PART 6

ActionScript and Behaviors

26   The Behaviors Panel

27   The Actions Panel

28   The Basics of ActionScript

CHAPTER 26

The Behaviors Panel

IN THIS CHAPTER

Behaviors   223

Behavior Categories   224

Adding and Removing Behaviors   225

Summary   226

Sample Questions   227

As of Flash MX 2004, Normal Mode in ActionScript is gone. But while one thing is gone, another has appeared, and that is behaviors and the Behaviors panel. The addition of the Behaviors panel brings Flash in line with most of Macromedia's other products, where some kind of pre-built script is stored and added by means of a Behaviors panel.

In this chapter, we review the Behaviors panel, what it does, and what behaviors can be added in Flash.

Behaviors

Behaviors are pre-built pieces of ActionScript that can be quickly and easily applied to something without having to write any script of your own. They're broken down into multiple categories, and each behavior has a special dialog box of its own that prompts you to add some additional information at the time of application so that the behavior can execute correctly.

The behaviors themselves have absorbed much of the most used aspects of Normal Mode in previous versions of Flash, and simplified them into easy to use and understand dialog boxes. When you add a behavior, the actual ActionScript is added to whatever was selected, and will show in the Actions Panel (see the next chapter for more on that).

Because the ActionScript that is written by the behavior is exposed, it's easy to go in and modify it, and this can be done without breaking the behavior.

TIP

Flash knows something is a behavior because of the comments added to the script. If you remove the comments from the ActionScript, Flash no longer recognizes it as a behavior.

Behaviors can be added either directly to Button symbols, Movie Clip Symbols, or Frames, although the types of behaviors that will be available will depend on what you actually have selected.

Behavior Categories

The Behaviors panel is broken down into the categories shown in table 26.1.

Table 26.1 Behavior Categories

CATEGORY	PURPOSE
Data	Used with Data components
Embedded Video	Used to control embedded digital video
Media	Used with Media components
Movie Clip	Used to control Movie Clip methods and properties
Sound	Used to add, play, and manipulate sound
Web	Used to navigate to Web pages

The Data category is used with Data components, such as the Web Services Connector and XML connector, instructing those components to go out and retrieve their data or to send data to some external source.

The Embedded Video category stops, plays, pauses, fast forwards, and rewinds digital video embedded in a Flash file. These behaviors work directly on instances of digital video.

➡ For more information on how these behaviors work, see Chapter 25, "Video."

The Media category is used to do things like link instances of the Media Display component to instances of the Media Controller component. It isn't used to directly control Media.

In the Movie Clip category are behaviors like Load External Movie Clip, and Go To and Stop at Frame or Label, which activate Movie Clip methods or control Movie Clips instances directly.

➡ We reviewed some of these behaviors in Chapter 18, "The Movie Clip Symbol."

The Sound category contains behaviors that attach sound instances from the library, start, and stop sounds.

➜ The more commonly used behaviors were reviewed in Chapter 24, "Sound."

In the Web category is one behavior, the Go To Web Page behavior, which sends people to new web pages. That behavior was used in Chapter 17, "Button Symbols."

Adding and Removing Behaviors

Behaviors can be added to keyframes in a timeline, or to Movie Clip and Button instances.

To add a behavior to a frame, select the frame that you want the behavior to execute in and launch the Behaviors panel. The panel is to some degree context sensitive, and will indicate the item selection. Make sure that it specifies the layer and the keyframe you want.

Click the Add Behavior button (the Plus icon) and select the behavior from the category you want. With a keyframe selected, you will have some limitations on what behaviors you can add. For instance, in the Movie Clip category, you will only see Go To and Stop at Frame or Label, Go To and Play at Frame or Label, Load External Graphic, and Load External Movie Clip. When a button is selected, you have nine more behaviors to choose from.

Fill out the behavior dialog box as prompted, then click OK. The behavior is added to the keyframe, and will execute when the playhead enters the frame.

> **TIP**
>
> When you add a behavior to a keyframe, you will not be able to change the event. The event will show None as the only event that is available is the playhead entering the frame.

To add a behavior to a Button or Movie Clip instance, select the object on the Stage, then in the Behaviors button, add the behavior from the category you want. When you have added the behavior, you will be able to change the triggering event. The default is Release. The other events available are: Key Press, Key Down, Release Outside, Press, Roll Over, Roll Out, Drag Over, and Drag Out.

Table 26.2 summarizes the events in the panel.

Table 26.2   Events in the Behaviors Panel

EVENT	WHEN IT'S TRIGGERED
Release	Executes when a user clicks and lets go of the mouse over top of an object.
Release Outside	Called when the user has pressed on an object, but lets go of the mouse off of the object.
Key Press	Executes when the user strikes a key on the keyboard.
Key Down	Executes when the user is holding down a key on the keyboard.
Roll Over	This event is called when the user rolls over an object.
Roll Out	Called when the user rolls off of an object.
Drag Over	Called when a user has pressed and is holding down the mouse, and then drags over an object.
Drag Out	Executes when the user has pressed and is still holding down on the mouse key, but drags off of an object.
Press	Executes when a user presses and holds down on the mouse over an object.

To remove a behavior, highlight it in the Behaviors panel, and click the Remove Behavior button (the Minus icon).

TIP

You can also remove the behavior by selecting the script that it writes in the Actions panel, and deleting it. If you delete the comments in the script, the script will remain, but the behavior will no longer appear in the Behaviors panel.

Summary

Flash MX 2004 has a number of pre-built actions that can be added to objects or keyframes from the Behaviors panel. The behaviors are organized by category, and can control sound, media, movie clips, data exchange, and navigation.

When you add a behavior, you fill out options in a dialog box, which in turn writes the ActionScript to execute the behavior on whatever it is you have selected.

Sample Questions

1. The Data category of the Behaviors panel controls which one of the following components?

   A. The Media Display component

   B. The Combo Box

   C. The XML Connector component

   D. The Text Area component

2. Which event responds to the cursor moving off an object?

   A. Drag Out

   B. Drag Over

   C. Roll Out

   D. Roll Over

3. Which behavior categories contain options that can be used for navigation (choose 2)?

   A. Data

   B. Web

   C. Movie clip

   D. Media

4. To which of the following can a behavior be applied (choose 2)?

   A. A frame

   B. A keyframe

   C. A component

   D. A movie clip

IN THIS CHAPTER

How the Panel is Organized   229

Using Panel Features   230

Using the Panel to Get Reference
   Information   232

Using the Panel to Set Preferences   233

Summary   234

Sample Questions   235

Even as a designer, you're going to find yourself using the Actions panel from time to time, whether you want to or not! Some people find it intimidating to use, but it's really just a matter of understanding how it's organized.

In this chapter, we review the panel itself, and how it's organized. We don't really discuss ActionScript until the next chapter, though.

How the Panel is Organized

The Actions panel is retrieved by selecting Window > Development Panels > Actions. Using this panel, you build very nearly all of your interactivity, even though the Behaviors panel gives you an automated way of doing some of the same things. But where the behaviors that you use are limited in scope, the Actions give you a much broader range of capability.

TIP

The behaviors that are written on an object or a frame are viewable in the Actions panel.

When it's launched, the Actions panel is separated into three different panes. Starting from the left and going counter-clockwise, those are:

- Categories pane. Contains all of the different Actions, Classes, Objects, and Components that come out of the box with Flash MX 2004.

- Code Inspector. Lists every item in your document that has ActionScript attached to it, and will jump you to that script when you select one of those objects in the inspector.

- Actions pane. This is where all the ActionScript is actually written.

> **TIP**
>
> The Actions pane, by default, does not show line numbers for the script you are writing. To turn on line numbers, select the Actions panel options, and choose View Line Numbers from the menu. Line numbers are critical for debugging.

The Actions pane itself is a tabbed interface. By default, when you select an object or a keyframe out on the Stage or timeline, the script in the Actions pane will automatically switch to show the scripts attached to that object. However, at the bottom of the Actions pane is a thumbtack icon, which allows you to "pin" a script in place. That way, when you select another object on the Stage, the pinned script remains in place, and the new script appears in a new tab.

> **TIP**
>
> You can also pin ActionScript from the Actions panel options menu. It's the very first item in the menu.

> **TIP**
>
> When ActionScript is attached to an object, the layer that the object is in must be unlocked for the ActionScript to appear in the Actions pane.

At the top of the Actions pane are a series of buttons, each of which accomplish a different task. We'll be looking at those in the next section.

Using Panel Features

In the old days of Flash, there was a mode called Normal Mode in the Actions panel, which gave a user a drag-and-drop type functionality. Normal mode is gone, but drag-and-drop functionality, still exists.

> **TIP**
>
> Dragging and dropping pieces of ActionScript into the script window isn't what it used to be. Flash assumes you know what you're doing, and that you've fleshed out your ActionScript on your own.

Say, for instance, you want to add a stop action to a keyframe. First, select the keyframe where you want the action. Next, in the Actions pane, verify that you have a frame selected. From the categories, select Global Functions > Timeline Control, and either double-click on `stop()` or drag and drop it to the Actions pane.

> **NOTE**
>
> In this example, the stop action takes no parameters, and nothing special has to happen for it to execute. In most circumstances, however, you would have to build the surrounding ActionScript to make the action useful.

Besides using drag-and-drop, you can actually use a series of pull-down and fly-over menus. At the top of the panel is a Plus icon, which is the Add New Item to Script button. When you click that button, pull-down and fly-over menus appear that reproduce the categories from the Categories pane. For instance, if you wanted to add the same stop action above using the Add New Item to Script button, you would select your keyframe, click the button, and select Global Functions > Timeline Control > Stop.

> **TIP**
>
> Don't forget, you can simply click in the Actions pane and type `stop();` just as easy!

Next to the Add New Item to Script button are the Find and Find and Replace buttons. These work just like traditional find and replace functions.

> **TIP**
>
> Find, and Find and Replace, only work in the current ActionScript showing in your Actions pane. They do not scan your entire document. However, if you use Find and Replace from the main edit menu, you'll be able to scan the whole document, and with regular expression support too!

The Insert Target Path icon is to the right of the Find and Replace buttons, and is used to point to objects with instance names out on the Stage that you are going to control with ActionScript. To use the feature, click the button, which will pull up the Insert Target Path dialog box. Select the object that you want to control with ActionScript, and click OK. This adds the path to the object in your Actions pane.

> **TIP**
>
> You must have an instance name for the path to be written correctly.

When you have written a block of ActionScript, you can easily check the syntax with the Check Syntax button. It's the icon at the top of the Actions pane that looks like a check mark. Any errors in your syntax will be caught, and the Output window will display the error and the approximate line number that it occurs on.

TIP

Check Syntax does not verify instance names or variables, just the "grammar" of your ActionScript. For more on syntax, see Chapter 28, "The Basics of ActionScript."

The AutoFormat button will clean up your ActionScript window to make things easier to read. If there is a problem with the syntax when you hit the button, the format operation will not be able to execute, and whatever the error is will be sent to the Output window for you to review.

The next button to the right is the Show Code Hint button. When you are writing ActionScript without the drag-and-drop features, depending on how you have named objects on the Stage and whether or not you have data typed them, you will get code hints. If for some reason, the code hinting doesn't pop up fast enough, you can click on this button to get hints. The hints give you a list of methods and properties of the object in question, which you can then select. When you select an item from the code hint window, it will add it to your ActionScript, and you can flesh it out from there.

NOTE

See Chapter 28, "The Basics of ActionScript," for more on data typing.

TIP

Code hinting preferences can be set in the general preferences of Flash. To open the general preferences on a PC, select Edit > Preferences. On a Mac, choose Flash MX 2004 > Preferences. In the dialog box, choose the ActionScript tab, and adjust the slider that determines how quickly code hints pop up. ActionScript preferences are also discussed below.

Using the Panel to Get Reference Information

One of the neat features of the Actions panel is that it allows you to quickly look up items in the ActionScript dictionary in two different ways.

First, you can select an item in the Categories pane, and either right- or Control-click it. From the Context menu, choose View Help. Flash will automatically open the Help window, and move to that item's entry in the ActionScript dictionary. This is really very useful when you're just learning, or when you need to look an item up that you've never used or heard of before.

You can also select the item in the categories, and select the View Reference button in the upper right of the Actions pane (it's the Book icon). The View Reference button will do the same thing as View Help.

Using the Panel to Set Preferences

Also in the panel are several options that set view preferences as well as general ActionScript preferences.

The View Options button is at the far right of the Actions pane, and has the following settings:

- **View Esc Shortcut Keys.** Escape shortcut keys add ActionScript through a series of keyboard commands. When you toggle this option on, the keyboard shortcuts show next to the ActionScript items in the categories.

- **View Line Numbers.** This toggles on and off the line numbers in the Actions pane. When line numbers are viewable, it makes it easier to find errors in the script, as the Output window will show errors by line number.

- **Word Wrap.** Turning on word wrap makes longer lines of ActionScript wrap in the Actions pane. By default, word wrap is not turned on, as it can make it difficult to read ActionScript.

> **TIP**
> These options can also be toggled on or off in the Actions panel Options menu.

Aside from the View Options, the ActionScript panel also contains preferences for how script is formatted as you're typing it. Auto-formatting is the default, and how that formatting occurs can be changed in the Auto Format options.

To change the options, select Auto Format from the Actions panel's Options menu. In the Auto Format Options dialog box, check the boxes that represent the formatting option you want. For instance, if you want "{" to be on a line after any function calls or "if" statements, select that option. The preview window in the dialog box will show you what it will look like when that option is selected. Click OK to set the option.

> **TIP**
> The Auto Format options will only apply when you click the Auto Format button on the Actions pane.

To set ActionScript preferences, select Preferences from the Actions panel Options menu. This opens the Preferences dialog box, and moves you directly to the ActionScript tab.

In the ActionScript tab, under the Editing Options category, you can toggle Automatic Indentation, and change the tab size for the indent, toggle Code Hinting and change the amount of time that it takes for the code hints to appear, and change your ActionScript encoding.

In the Text category, you can change the font used in the Actions pane, as well as its size. In addition, there is an option for syntax coloring, which changes the color of your ActionScript as you type it.

Alter your settings to your desired preferences, and click OK to set them.

TIP

You can also find the preferences by choosing Edit > Preferences on Windows, and Flash MX 2004 > Preferences on Mac.

Summary

The Actions panel in Flash is where script is written. It is broken down into three sections: Categories, Code Inspector, and the Actions pane. Categories contains the ActionScript elements that come out of the box with ActionScript, and can be used to drag and drop pieces of code into a broader framework. When you aren't sure what an ActionScript element in the Categories pane is, you can right- or Control-click it and choose View Help from the Context menu, or you can select the View Reference from the buttons at the top of the Actions pane.

The Code Inspector section shows all of the objects and keyframes that contain ActionScript in a document. Clicking on an item in the Code Inspector will move the Actions pane to the script on that selection.

The Actions pane is where the ActionScript is written. At the top of the Actions pane are buttons to add ActionScript, find and replace items in a script, check syntax, automatically format the script for easier reading, and to show hints to assist in writing ActionScript code.

ActionScript preferences can be set by selecting Preferences from the Actions panel's Options menu. The preferences include tab settings, code hint display, and syntax coloring.

Sample Questions

1. What view option shows keyboard shortcuts to add ActionScript?

   A. View > Show Shortcuts

   B. Select View Esc Shortcut Keys from the View Options button.

   C. Select Show Esc Shortcut Keys from the Actions panel's Options menu.

   D. Set Show Esc Shortcut Keys in the ActionScript preferences.

2. How do you prevent the Actions pane from changing when you select objects on the Stage (choose 2)?

   A. Click the Pin Script button at the bottom of the Actions pane.

   B. Click the Pin Script button at the top of the Actions pane.

   C. Choose Pin Script from the Actions panel's Options menu.

   D. Choose Pin Script from the ActionScript preferences.

3. How would you get more information about the setInterval Action from the Actions panel (choose 2)?

   A. Right- or Control-click the action, and choose View Help from the Context menu.

   B. Select the item in the Categories pane, and click the Check Syntax button.

   C. Select the Item in the Categories pane, and select Help > ActionScript Dictionary.

   D. Select the action and choose View Help from the Actions panel's Options menu.

4. How do you change Auto Formatting options in the Actions panel?

   A. Click the Auto Format button at the top of the Actions pane.

   B. Select Auto Formatting from the Actions panel's Options menu.

   C. Select Auto Formatting Options from the Action panel's Options menu.

   D. Set the Auto Format options in the ActionScript preferences section of the Preferences dialog box.

CHAPTER 28

The Basics of ActionScript

IN THIS CHAPTER

Object-Oriented Programming   237

Basic ActionScript Syntax   238

Variables   240

Functions   241

Attaching ActionScript to a
Timeline   242

Adding ActionScript to an Object   243

Summary   243

Sample Questions   244

ActionScript has continually evolved with each successive release of Flash, becoming more and more powerful. Without ActionScript, a Flash application would be lifeless.

In this chapter, we review the general syntax of ActionScript, and go over the fundamental concepts that are critical to developing a command of this powerful scripting language. This chapter is meant to be a review, and not an exhaustive treatment.

Object-Oriented Programming

ActionScript is now at version 2.0, and is more than ever an object oriented scripting language.

Object Oriented Programming (abbreviated OOP), is at its heart a simple concept. Prior to its invention, we were stuck with procedural languages (like BASIC), which worked by lines. When you wanted something special to happen, you sent it to a specific line in the code that contained the instructions you wanted to execute. Using procedural languages resulted in lots of lines of code that were no fun to fix (debug) should something not work right.

The idea of OOP is to take certain tasks and properties that a bunch of things might have in common and group them together in a thing called a "class." A class is more or less a template of functionality and identity for anything created from it.

In the class, you define methods, which is what something does, and properties, which is more or less things that items built from the class can have, such as width, color, position, and so on.

When you make an object from a class, you're creating an instance of the class. The object will inherit all of the methods and properties defined in the class, and because it is otherwise independent, those methods and properties can be controlled programmatically. When you need an object do look different, you can adjust its properties; when you need it to behave differently, you can adjust its methods, or attach new ones to it.

Basic ActionScript Syntax

ActionScript uses a number of OOP concepts. These core concepts give a developer a whole range of flexibility in how ActionScript is created. The core concepts of ActionScript are listed in Table 28.1.

Table 28.1 ActionScript Core Concepts

CONCEPT	DESCRIPTION
Classes	Define objects and their properties and functionality. Some classes do not actually create objects.
Objects	Instances of classes. Objects inherit the functionality described in a class.
Methods	Functions attached to objects and classes. They determine what objects do.
Arguments	Modify how methods execute.
Properties	Values that define an object's characteristics.
Dot Notation	Points to objects and calls methods or accesses properties.
Functions	Pieces of reusable script that execute repetitive tasks.
Variables	Hold values that can change or be changed with ActionScript.
Events	Broadcast when something happens in the application. Events can be either user- or system-driven.
Event Handlers	Methods or functions that execute when an event occurs.
Comments	Ignored by ActionScript. Comments are added by the programmer to provide information about the program to a person reading the script. Comments can also be used for debugging.

When you want to create an object, you have to instantiate it, which is the same thing as saying "build an instance of it from a class."

> **TIP**
>
> Not every class needs to have an object instance to work. The Accessibility, Capabilities, Key, Math, Mouse, Selection, Stage, and System classes work without the need for instances.

> **TIP**
>
> The Button class can only be instantiated visually, which means that you have to build it by converting an asset to a button symbol, or selecting Insert > New Symbol, and selecting button.

For example, to use the Sound class, you must first make a Sound object:

```
var mySound:Sound=new Sound();
```

mySound becomes the instance name, new is a keyword that explains to Flash that you're constructing an object, and Sound() indicates what class the object should be built from.

> **TIP**
>
> ActionScript 2.0 is absolutely 100 percent case-sensitive. mySound and MySound are not the same.

To access a property of an object, use dot notation, plus the property. The following example retrieves the x position of a movie clip on the Stage:

```
myMovieClip._x;
```

To assign a new value, use dot notation again:

```
myMovieClip._x=150;
```

Use a semicolon to tell the Flash player that the line of instruction is over. A semicolon "terminates" the statement.

To call an object's methods use dot notation. Some methods accept arguments, which change how the method executes. The example below uses the loadMovie method of a movie clip, and then uses the URL parameter of the method to retrieve an external SWF:

```
myMovieClip.loadMovie("mySpecial.swf");
```

All arguments are passed into the method using open and close parentheses.

> **TIP**
>
> All methods must have an open and close parentheses, even if they accept no arguments, or arguments are optional.

If you want something to execute when an event occurs, such as a mouse click, you have to specify the event that you want, then write an event handler, which will contain the instructions to execute when the event occurs. Event handlers are written differently depending on where you are writing the script.

All event handlers must have their instructions inside of curly braces. The following sections illustrate the use of curly braces in an event handler both on a timeline, and on an object.

Variables

Variables store values in Flash, and can be accessed or changed by anything that has access to it. Variables can also contain any type of data, but what kind of information any one kind of variable can hold should be specified.

To create a variable, use the var keyword to declare it. For example:

```
var myNumbers;
```

Next, you should data type the variable, which is specifying what kind of information it can hold:

```
var myNumbers:Number;
```

This tells Flash that the only kind of information this variable can hold is numeric information. It cannot hold strings (characters). If I store 42 in it, it will be happy. If I store "42" in it, the variable will cause a type mismatch error, because "42" is string information—literally one and two—while 42 is a number.

> **TIP**
> Variables do not have to be data typed, but it is a best practice. And yes, they are case-sensitive.

Where a variable can be used is called the variable's scope. When you use the var keyword, you make the variable usable only in that location. In the case of a keyframe, the variable can be used anywhere in the keyframe. If you use the var keyword within a function, the variable can only be used in that function. A variable with the same name outside the function would therefore be treated completely different. It's like having a person named Bob inside the living room, and a person named Bob in the TV. What happens to Bob on TV doesn't change the Bob in the living room.

If you want a variable to be used anywhere, by any script in any function, frame, or object, make it global. To create a global variable, use the _global keyword, as in the example below:

```
_global.myVariable="initial value"
```

When you want to make use of the variable in other locations, you can call it without using the _global prefix.

Functions

Functions are bits of reusable code that complete repetitive tasks. They come in several forms:

- **Built-in.** These are already defined in Flash, and can be used out of the box.

- **User-defined.** A named function created by a programmer that can be called in an application.

- **Anonymous.** A function with no name that is called on an object instance, usually from a frame script.

- **Methods.** Functions that are defined in classes, have names, and are otherwise attached to an object. Methods must be named.

A built-in function can be called without actually writing the code that makes it happen. For instance, to store my age in a variable, then send it to a text box, use the String function to convert the number 34 into character "34." For example:

```
var myAge:Number=34;
displayAge.text=String(myAge);
```

A user-defined function has a name, and instructions that do something. Generally, you'll write a function when a bunch of objects need to accomplish the same task, but only one or two things changes, such as names or position values.

To make a function, use the following general syntax:

```
functionName=function(parameter1:Data Type):Function Data type
{
    Instructions();
}
```

> **TIP**
>
> Functions do not have to be data typed, but it's a best practice. Function data types must match the kind of data they're returning. If they don't return information, data type the function as Void.

The following example creates a function that squares a number:

```
mySquareFunction=function(sqNum:Number):Number
{
    return sqNum*sqNum;
}
```

The following example calls the function and passes a number to it:

```
mySquareFunction(10);
```

Like variables, functions can be made global. To make a function global, add _global to the name:

```
_global.mySquareFunction=function(sqNum:Number):Number
{
    return sqNum*sqNum;
}
```

To call a global function, just call it as you normally would, without the _global.

Attaching ActionScript to a Timeline

When you attach ActionScript to a timeline, the ActionScript must be contained within a keyframe. It is considered a best practice to place ActionScript in a timeline and in a separate layer at the top of the layers panel so that it's easier to find.

To add ActionScript to the timeline, select the keyframe you want it in, or insert a keyframe in the position where you want the ActionScript to execute. In the Actions pane of the Actions panel, write the ActionScript you want. The following example sets the opacity of a Movie Clip to 70% when the Playhead enters the frame the ActionScript is in:

```
myMovieClip._alpha=70;
```

If you want to create an ActionScript in a keyframe that responds to a user event, you must write an event handler. The following example illustrates an event handler for a button that executes when a user clicked on the button.

```
myButton.onRelease=function()
{
    getURL("http://www.macromedia.com/");
}
```

The button must have an instance name so ActionScript knows what it should control or respond to. The function() is called an anonymous function, because it has no name and is associated with a single button instance. The instructions are enclosed in curly braces as required by the syntax.

Adding ActionScript to an Object

When you add ActionScript to an object, it must always be within an event handler, whether the ActionScript is on a button or a movie clip.

On a button, use the following general syntax:

```
on(event)
{
    instructions();
}
```

For example, if I wanted to redirect someone to a Web site, I would use:

```
on(release)
{
    getURL("http://www.macromedia.com/");
}
```

When you want to add ActionScript to a Movie Clip object, use the following syntax:

```
onClipEvent(event)
{
    instructions();
}
```

For instance, if I want to attach another movie clip from the Library to the Stage when a controller movie clip loads:

```
onClipEvent(load)
{
    this.attachMovie("badGuy",2);
}
```

> **TIP**
> Adding script directly to an object is not considered a best practice, because it makes it harder to find and harder to update.

Summary

ActionScript is an object oriented scripting language that comes with built-in classes and functions. The language can be used to build interactivity and control to a Flash application. Classes in Flash define the capabilities and general construction of objects built from them. Methods are what objects do, properties are what define the objects, and objects themselves are instances of a class.

Variables store values in Flash and can be local or global. Where a variable is used is referred to as its scope. Functions in Flash are pieces of reusable code that execute repetitive tasks. Like variables, functions can be global. Functions and variables are data typed to say what kind of information they can contain or hold, which is considered a best practice.

ActionScript can be added to keyframes or to objects. If ActionScript is added to an object, the instructions have to be contained within an event handler.

Sample Questions

1. How do you create a global variable?

   A. `_global.variableName:DataType;`

   B. `var _global.variableName;`

   C. `var global.variableName;`

   D. `_global.variableName;`

2. Dot syntax is used to (choose 2):

   A. Point to an object's location.

   B. Call a method.

   C. Alter a method's execution.

   D. Give a function a name.

3. What character terminates a line of ActionScript?

   A. }

   B. :

   C. ;

   D. .

4. A function attached to an object is:

   A. A method.

   B. An anonymous function.

   C. An event handler.

   D. Global.

PART 7

Optimization
and Publishing

29 Optimizing Your Flash
       Application

30 Publishing

CHAPTER 29

Optimizing Your Flash Application

IN THIS CHAPTER

The Bandwidth Profiler   247

Font Considerations   249

Sound Considerations   249

Video Considerations   251

Bitmap Images   251

Vector Shapes   252

Using Multiple SWFs   252

Using Shared Resources   252

Summary   253

Sample Questions   253

Flash MX 2004 applications are being delivered over an increasing variety of media, including CD-ROMs, commercial devices, and Local Area Networks. But the World Wide Web is still the primary vehicle for Flash content delivery, which poses a challenge for Flash designers. File size becomes, in these circumstances, a primary consideration.

In this chapter, we review some techniques to check your file size and to keep things as small as possible for faster delivery.

The Bandwidth Profiler

The Bandwidth profiler gives you information about the SWF as it would be published. This includes the final file size, how big individual frames are, and the capability of mimicking a modem speed. Prior to publication, it's a good idea to look at the bandwidth profiler and review the information it presents.

To view the bandwidth profiler, you first have to test the movie by selecting Control > Test Movie. In the test movie environment, select View > Bandwidth Profiler.

> **TIP**
> The Bandwidth Profiler will also be retrieved by selecting View > Streaming Graph

The Bandwidth Profiler sits on top of the SWF being test, and is separated into two panes. The pane on the left shows summary information, while the pane on the right is the Streaming Graph.

The summary pane shows:

- **Dim.** The dimensions of the published documents.

- **Fr rate.** The frame rate of the document.

- **Size.** The total file size of the document, in kilobytes.

- **Duration.** Total amount of time the document plays (if animated) in seconds.

- **Preload.** Preloaded frames in number of seconds.

- **Bandwidth.** Reflect the bandwidth settings when mimicking a modem speed.

- **State.** When simulating a modem speed, reflects the current number of frames loaded, kilobytes, and what percentage of the SWF has downloaded into the Flash player.

The Streaming Graph shows on the right. It displays the timeline, and has a number of vertical bars that represent the individual frames in the document. The size of the bar indicates how many kilobytes in size that particular frame holds.

The red line in the graph indicates which frames will stream when the SWF is playing. Any frame that extends above the red line will cause the SWF to pause at that point and wait until the frame has downloaded before it can move on.

> **TIP**
>
> In the View pull-down menu, you can toggle between the Streaming Graph and the Frame-by-Frame graph. They both essentially give you the same information; however, the Frame-by-Frame graph is more or less focused on the size of frames, whereas the streaming graph is meant to indicate potential problem frames when taking advantage of Flash streaming capabilities.

To use the Bandwidth Profiler to simulate download, first, select View > Download Settings, and select a modem speed from the fly-over menu. The default is 56K. Next, select View > Simulate Download.

> **TIP**
>
> Simulate Download assumes optimal conditions, such as low network traffic. It is estimation (and a good one at that).

Using the Bandwidth Profiler gives you a way to identify potential file size problems with your document that you can go back and fix when needed. Of course, you'll have designed with file size restrictions in mind, so you wont' really need to fix anything, right?

Font Considerations

Since Flash embeds font outlines in an SWF when you publish, simply using text can significantly increase file size for your published file. The more fonts you use for static text, the more file size you'll get.

One of the ways to keep file size down is to use device fonts. Device fonts are taken directly from the end user's computer, so Flash doesn't have to embed font outlines when you publish.

Dynamic text (and input text) use device fonts by default. You have to specifically embed font outlines in a field in order for them to not use device fonts. If you choose to do this, do so sparingly, if at all.

➡ For more information on fonts and text, see Chapter 14, "Using Text."

> **TIP**
>
> You can also use font symbols with runtime sharing to keep the file sizes low, sharing the symbols across multiple SWFs. That way, the font outline is only embedded in one file.

Sound Considerations

Sound has always been popular, and probably always will be. While some compression types are great for certain tasks, others may not be, so you must choose your sound compression profile carefully. What's more, limit your use of sound to only what's necessary.

When you import a sound in Flash, it is compressed as an MP3 at 16 kps by default. You can change the default compression to suit your needs, choose to use the imported file's compression instead.

The other compression types available are:

- **ADPCM.** Used mostly for short sounds, and is a compression type for 8 or 16 bit sounds.

- **Raw.** Raw is actually not compressed at all. However, you can control sample rates to decrease file size.

- **Speech.** The speech compression is optimized for sound files that contain voice-overs or spoken word.

Each one of these works by adjusting a kHz rate between 5 and 44. In general, 5kHz is acceptable for speech (except for ADPCM), 11 kHz is recommended for speech or sound qualities roughly at 1/4 CD quality. 22 kHz is the most common for web playback.

> **TIP**
>
> Individual sounds in Flash can have their own compression types and settings.

The MP3 compression uses bit rates, rather than kHz rates. When you import an MP3 file, the imported MP3 file's compression becomes the default for that particular sound.

MP3 bit rates can be between 8 and 160 kps. The higher the bit rate, the better quality sound you'll have; however, that will also create an increase in file size. MP3 compression also has the quality options of Fast, which lowers sound quality, Medium, which has a slightly better sound quality, and Best, which has the highest sound quality.

To change the compression type of an individual sound, select the sound in the Library, then click the Properties button at the bottom of the Library panel. In the Sound Properties dialog box, choose the compression type you want, and adjust its settings. The bottom of the dialog box will summarize the resulting file size. To hear the new sound quality, click the "Test" button. To set the properties and exit the dialog, click Ok.

> **TIP**
>
> You can also set default compression settings for all streaming and event sounds in Flash in the Publish settings dialog box, under the Flash tab. When you choose this option, it will compress all sounds at those settings, unless they've already been set in the library. Generally, it's best to set sound properties from the library.

Finally, you can store your sounds externally on the server as MP3 sounds, and load them into the interface as needed using the Sound object or Media components. Storing the MP3 files externally keeps your initial SWF download smaller, and you can take advantage of MP3 streaming in this fashion.

➜ See Chapter 24, "Sound," for more information on working with Sound.

Video Considerations

As popular as sound is, video is even more popular. Add video and sound together, and you have a behemoth of an SWF. But you can control in it a number of ways.

First, if you need to embed video in your document, it should be compressed before bringing it into Flash. Almost all digital video editors have some kind of compression utility available. During import, Flash will allow you to compress the video using the Sorensen Spark Codec, which is built into Flash.

The Sorensen codec uses lossy compression, which removes data from the file. The lower the quality, the smaller the file size.

You can also embed video into separate SWFs and call them when needed using loadMovie or loadMovieNum.

Finally, you can use the FLV format (Flash Live Video), and store it external to the SWF that you need it in. Using a media component, you can stream the FLV video through the Flash player. Storing a video file externally means that your initial SWF download time will be much smaller.

TIP

Restrict your use of video to what is absolutely necessary, and only if it adds value to your site. Just because you can use it doesn't mean you should.

➔ For more information on using video in Flash, see Chapter 25, "Video."

Bitmap Images

In general, bitmap images can pose two problems for a Flash application: bitmaps don't scale well, and they tend to be rather large.

First, optimize your bitmaps before you import them. You can optimize them in a utility such as Fireworks, and the general aim is to make the images as small as possible while maintaining a high image quality. When you publish in Flash, all bitmaps by default will be optimized with a JPG compression type, at 80 percent of their quality, which doesn't give you much in the way of control over individual image quality.

If an image needs some additional optimization, you can use the roundtrip-editing feature to open the bitmap in Fireworks and compress it a bit more. Select the image on the Stage and click Edit, or select it in the Library, and choose Edit with Fireworks in the Library's Options menu. Either way, the image will be opened in a special editing mode, where it can be reoptimized and updated.

Scaling is another matter altogether. It's usually best to bring an image in at the size that you want it to be, but if scaling is a concern, it's sometimes best to import your images at a slightly larger size, or to prevent scaling from happening to start with. We'll see how to shut scaling off in Flash later in this chapter.

➜ More information on scaling is detailed in Chapter 30, "Publishing." For more on working with Bitmaps, see Chapter 11, "Bitmap and Vector Artwork."

Vector Shapes

The two rules for vector art are: minimize the use of gradients and optimize shapes. The simpler a shape is, the smaller it will be in terms of file size.

Minimizing use of gradients is easy; just don't add so many. Optimizing a shape requires a few more steps.

To optimize a vector shape, select an editable shape on the Stage, and then Modify > Shape > Optimize. This will launch the Optimize Curves dialog box. The idea is to minimize the amount of curves in any shape, thereby reducing the amount of line segments needed to draw a shape.

➜ For more on working with vector art, see Chapter 12, "Working with Vector Art."

Using Multiple SWFs

As we saw in Chapter 15, splitting your Flash document has a number of benefits. First, it chops your Flash application into smaller content related pieces that can be called when needed, or when the user is interested in the content. Second, it keeps your file size smaller by removing content areas from the main document.

➜ For more information on using multiple SWFs in your project, see Chapter 15, Breaking Up a Project."

Using Shared Resources

Shared resources are symbols that are stored in an SWF on the server, and are retrieved from that location when a different SWF using one of those symbols is run.

Storing visual assets in a different library has much the same effect as using multiple SWFs, namely, it keeps the file size of your documents loading into the Flash Player down. It also has an advantage for updating. When a symbol changes in a shared library, everything that uses it reflects that change.

➜ For more information on shared libraries and symbols, see Chapter 9, "Organizational Tools and Where to Find Them."

Summary

Keeping file size at a minimum for web applications is critical in Flash. File size can be kept small by limiting the use of sound and video, as well as restricting the number of gradients used in vector artwork. It can also be controlled my making sure bitmap images are optimized prior to import, using device fonts instead of embedded fonts, using shared symbols, and splitting your application into multiple SWF files.

The Bandwidth Profiler provides information about the final SWF file size, and gives you the ability to mimic a download speed.

Sample Questions

1. What techniques can you use to minimize the impact of fonts on your file size (choose 2)?

    A. Alias static text fields.

    B. Use device fonts with static text fields.

    C. Embed character outlines in dynamic and input text fields.

    D. Use font symbols with runtime sharing to share font across SWFs.

2. How do you mimic a modem speed in the Bandwidth Profiler?

    A. Debug > Simulate Download

    B. View > Simulate Download

    C. File > Simulate Download

    D. Control > Simulate Download

3. Which compression type is the default in Flash?

    A. MP3

    B. ADPCM

    C. Raw

    D. Speech

4. How do you optimize an editable shape?

    A. Edit > Shape > Optimize

    B. Edit > Shape > Smooth Curves

    C. Modify > Shape > Optimize

    D. Modify > Shape > Smooth Curves

CHAPTER **30**
Publishing

IN THIS CHAPTER

Publish Settings   255

Flash Considerations   257

HTML Considerations   259

HTML Code   262

Flash Player Detection   263

Publish Profiles   264

Summary   264

Sample Questions   265

The final step in producing a Flash application is to publish your document in one of several formats. Without question, you will almost always produce a SWF, and use an HTML template from Flash to produce the code that embeds the file in an HTML document. There are, however, other formats to choose from for varying reasons.

In this chapter, we will review the publish settings in Flash, and the different options that the most commonly used settings have available.

Publish Settings

In Flash, there are a number of different formats that you can publish in, besides the SWF. They are all set in the Publish Settings dialog box, which can be retrieved from File > Publish Settings.

The different formats and their uses are detailed in the Table 30.1.

Table 30.1 Publish Formats

FORMAT	USE
Flash (.swf)	This format is interpreted by the Flash Player, and is required for web publication.
HTML (.html)	Produces the HTML file and tags that embed an SWF in a Web document. The tags generated are determined by the template you choose in the HTML tab of the Publish Settings dialog box.
GIF Image (.gif)	Produces an alternative GIF to show if for some reason a visitor to a Web site doesn't have the Flash player. By default, the image is produced from the first frame in the document and is static. However, an animated GIF can be set in the GIF tab of the Publish Settings dialog box.
JPEG Image (.jpg)	Produces a single JPG image from the first frame of the Flash document, to be used in a Web page if someone does not have the Flash Player.
PNG Image (.png)	Produces a single PNG image from the first frame of the Flash document, to be used in a Web page if someone does not have the Flash Player.
Windows Projector (.exe)	Publishes the document as an executable file that will run independently of the Flash Player. These files cannot be embedded in an HTML document.
Macintosh Projector	Publishes the document as an executable Mac file, usually with an .hqx extension. Macintosh platform does not require extensions.
QuickTime (.mov)	Publishes the document as a QuickTime movie.

TIP

When publishing in QuickTime format, the file produced is based on the version of QuickTime you've installed. Also, QuickTime currently only supports Flash 4 ActionScript and playback.

TIP

Remember, you can use the #static frame label to designate a single frame for publishing when you are using the PNG, JPEG, or GIF image options.

With the exception of the two projector types, selecting any of these options will produce a tab in the Publish Settings dialog box where you can further refine the settings for the formats that you've chosen. We will focus on Flash and HTML settings.

Flash Considerations

In the Flash tab of the Publish Settings dialog box are configuration settings for the SWF that's being produced. First and foremost is the version of the Flash Player that the SWF is being produced for, which can be anything from the current version to Flash version 1.0 (a blast from the past indeed).

> **TIP**
>
> Much of the Flash MX 2004 functionality is not useable with earlier versions of the Flash Player. To prevent serious headaches, this option should really be set when the file is first created, before any content or code is added. Every time you save the document from that point forward, Flash will let you know if what you're doing won't work in the player version you have.

> **TIP**
>
> Your player setting will affect your Flash Player Detection in the HTML tab.

Your layer load order is also determined here, and can be either top down or bottom up. The default is bottom up. If your users are accessing your Flash file over a slow modem or sluggish network, and your file is streaming, this will determine how your layers draw.

ActionScript Version is the next option down, and is either ActionScript 2.0 or ActionScript 1.0. ActionScript 2.0 can only be used by Flash Players 6 and 7. If you select a Flash Player version below 6, you will only be able to use ActionScript 1.0.

> **TIP**
>
> Flash Players 6 and 7 can interpret ActionScript version 1.0 just fine, if you are so inclined.

The Options section has the following choices, listed in Table 30.1:

Table 30.2   Flash Publish Options

OPTIONS	PURPOSE
Generate Size Report	When selected, produces a report that tells you how much data you have in a Flash file.
Omit Trace Actions	Trace actions are used to send information to the Output window for the purpose of debugging (usually). If you haven't deleted trace statements, selecting this option instructs the Flash Player to ignore any trace statements in encounters and remove them from the published file. Ignoring trace actions will keep the file size lower and improve performance.
Protect from Import	This prevents anyone from taking your SWF, importing it into Flash, and turning it back into an FLA file. When you choose this option, you can set a password.
Debugging Permitted	This is useful when developing applications. It allows remote debugging, and can be password-protected.
Compress Movie	This option is selected by default, and is certainly an option you want to use if you're publishing for Flash 6 or above. It compresses the SWF when it's published.
Optimize for Flash Player 6 r65	This is grayed out unless you are publishing for Flash Player 6. It is used for performance increase.

> **TIP**
> Compress Movie will not work with Flash Player 5 or below.

If you have selected either Protect from Import or Debugging Permitted in the Options section, you can set a password in the Password field. Otherwise, that option is not available.

Underneath the Password field is a JPEG Quality slider. When you publish a file in Flash, all bitmaps are compressed as JPEGs at a quality of 80 percent by default. You can adjust the quality setting with the slider, or by changing the value in the JPEG Quality input box. If you have already adjusted the quality of your bitmaps individually, or otherwise compressed them, set the quality to 100 percent.

Adjust sound settings either for Stream or Event sounds. The default is MP3 at 16 kps. If you have already adjusted settings for your sounds in the Library, these settings will not be applied. These apply only to sounds that have not already been modified. Selecting Override Sound Settings, though, *will* override anything you did in the Sound Properties dialog box.

> **TIP**
>
> These settings will apply globally to all sounds in the document if you check the Override Sound Settings box.

Export Device Sounds is used largely for mobile devices, and is only available in Flash Professional.

HTML Considerations

The HTML option creates the tags that embed the Flash SWF in an HTML document. There are a number of templates to use, depending on what it is you hope to accomplish. The HTML templates are summarized in Table 30.3.

Table 30.3   HTML Templates in Flash

TEMPLATE	PURPOSE
Flash for Pocket PC 2003	Used to display Flash content in Pocket PC devices.
Flash HTTPS	Runs Flash in an HTTPS server environment, and instructs the HTTPS client to get the Flash Player if the end user doesn't have it.
Flash Only	Builds the standard tags for HTML display.
Flash with AICC Tracking	Used in conjunction with learning applications. Builds AICC score tracking support into the tags.
Flash with FS Command	Publishes tags with support for FSCommand and JavaScript calls.
Flash with Named Anchors	Allows book marking for Flash Content. This only works with Flash Player 6 and above.
Flash with SCORM Tracking	Builds in support for the SCORM tracking standard in learning applications.
Image Map	Can only be used when the JPG, GIF, or PNG options are selected. Exports a bitmap with an image map in HTML.
QuickTime	Can only be used when the QuickTime options are selected from the Formats tab. Publishes the tags needed to embed QuickTime content in an HTML document.

If you select the Detect Flash Version button, the HTML will include JavaScript that looks to see if the user has at least the version of the player you are publishing for. Detect Flash Version has its own section later in this chapter.

The Dimensions section has three options in a pull-down menu. This option determines the size of the SWF, and can defeat scaling. The options are summarized below:

- **Match Movie.** This is the default, and it sets the width and height attributes in the HTML Tags to the same size as your Stage.

- **Pixels.** You determine the width and height attributes in the tags by entering your own values here.

- **Percent.** This allows the SWF to scale. It sets the width and height attributes to equal a fixed percent of the browser size. When the browser size changes, your Flash SWF will change to match the percent.

> **TIP**
>
> When you choose Match Movie or Pixels, your SWF will not resize with the browser.

The next section controls playback of the SWF when the HTML document first loads. The options are:

- **Paused at Start.** Prevents the SWF from playing until someone clicks on a button.

- **Loop.** Causes the SWF to play continuously unless there is an ActionScript to counter it. It is selected by default. Deselecting it will prevent an SWF from looping in the absence of a stop() action in the SWF itself.

- **Display Menu.** Deselecting the display menu will disable everything but the Settings and About Macromedia Flash Player items in the context menus in the Flash Player.

- **Device Font.** This option is available only on Windows platforms, and replaces fonts not installed on an end user's computer with anti-aliased system fonts.

The Quality pull-down menu allows you to alter quality settings for the Flash Player. The Quality setting doesn't really have any effect on file size, but it does affect the performance of the SWF during playback. The options are:

- **Low.** Doesn't anti-alias so that playback speed is optimal.

- **Auto Low.** Starts off by not anti-aliasing so that playback is optimal, but toggles anti-aliasing on when it can be used without sacrificing performance.

- **Medium.** Anti-aliases some items, but does not anti-alias bitmaps.

- **High.** Always anti-aliases most elements. Bitmaps are not smoothed, however, if the SWF contains any kind of animation.

- **Auto High.** Anti-aliases unless performance starts to degrade.

- **Best.** Anti-aliases everything.

> **TIP**
>
> The default is High.

The Window Mode option has to do with how Flash is displayed when embedded in a bounding box of some sort, or a "virtual window" like a DIV tag. The Window Modes are summarized below:

- **Window.** This is the default, and no special window attributes are included in the HTML. HTML cannot be rendered above or below the Flash content

- **Opaque Windowless.** Makes the background of your SWF opaque. Choosing this mode allows HTML content to be drawn above it, like menu systems.

- **Transparent Windowless.** Makes the SWF background transparent, so content underneath it is visible, and HTML can render above it at the same time.

> **TIP**
>
> Transparent windowless is supported by all current browsers, but may not work predictably in older browsers (prior to IE version 5.0).

The next section down is the HTML Alignment option. Choosing Default will center the application in the HTML window. Left, right, top, or bottom will align the SWF accordingly.

The Scale section has four options:

- **Default.** This shows the entire document and keeps the original proportions constrained.

- **No Border.** Fills the specified areas up to the border, but keeps the proportions of the SWF constrained.

- **Exact Fit.** Fills the entire SWF in an area without keeping the proportions of the SWF constrained. This can distort your SWF.

- **No Scale.** This will prevent the SWF from resizing should the Flash Player Window resize.

The Flash alignment section determines how the SWF is aligned within a browser window, and can be left, center, and right horizontally, and top, bottom, and center vertically.

Finally, the Show Warning Messages dialog box will display information during publishing if any of these settings conflict with tags used in one of the templates.

HTML Code

The following is an example of the HTML code produced when publishing:

```
<!DOCTYPE html PUBLIC "-//W3C//DTD XHTML 1.0 Transitional//EN"
    "http://www.w3.org/TR/xhtml1/DTD/xhtml1-transitional.dtd">
<html xmlns="http://www.w3.org/1999/xhtml" xml:lang="en" lang="en">
<head>
<meta http-equiv="Content-Type" content="text/html;
    charset=iso-8859-1" />
<title>bTest</title>
</head>
<body bgcolor="#ffffff">
<!—url's used in the movie—>
<!—text used in the movie—>
<object classid="clsid:d27cdb6e-ae6d-11cf-96b8-444553540000"
    codebase="http://fpdownload.macromedia.com/pub/shockwave/cabs/
    flash/swflash.cab#version=7,0,0,0" width="550" height="400"
    id="bTest" align="middle">
<param name="allowScriptAccess" value="sameDomain" />
<param name="movie" value="bTest.swf" />
<param name="quality" value="high" />
<param name="bgcolor" value="#ffffff" />
```

```
<embed src="bTest.swf" quality="high" bgcolor="#ffffff"
    width="550" height="400" name="bTest" align="middle"
    allowScriptAccess="sameDomain" type="application/x-shockwave-
    flash" pluginspage="http://www.macromedia.com/go/getflashplayer"
    />
</object>
</body>
</html>
```

Both the Object and Embed tags are required to view a Flash document in a Web page. The Object tag is used by any browser that requires ActiveX controls, and it instantiates the Flash Player, sets width and height attributes, and pulls the SWF into the player. Additional parameters, such as window mode and quality, are used within the object tag to provide additional information to the browser.

The embed tag does much the same thing, only it's there for browsers that do not support ActiveX. It is usually nested inside the Object tag, although it can be used outside of it. In that circumstance, all the additional settings are included in the embed tag as attributes, rather than as separate parameters.

Flash Player Detection

When you are publishing, you can automatically add Flash Player detection. Flash will write the JavaScript needed to perform the detection for you.

First, in the Publish Settings dialog box, select the Flash tab, and choose the version of the Flash Player you are publishing for. This will become the basis for the Player detection.

Next, click the HTML tab, and check the box that says Detect Flash Version, and click the Settings tab.

In the Version detection settings, the Flash version showing will be the version you selected to publish for. You have the option of adding a minor revision number, but it isn't required.

In the Filenames section, by default, the detection file is the HTML being produced by Flash. The content file is where the user will be directed if the Flash Player and correct version are detected (this would be the file containing your SWF). The Alternate file is where the user will be redirected if they don't have the Flash Player or the version you are trying to detect.

These are the defaults. If you have files that already exist, you can click the Use Existing radio button, and point to the appropriate files. Click OK to add the settings, and click Publish to create all the files.

Publish Profiles

After you have set all of your publishing preferences, you can save them as a profile, which you can use to publish from that point forward. In fact, you can also import and export publishing profiles to share with team members.

To save a publish profile, click the Add New Profile button at the top right of the Publish Settings dialog, enter a profile name in Create New Profile dialog box, and click OK.

> **TIP**
>
> This profile will remember all of the settings you set, including the settings in your Formats tab.

To export a profile to share with a team member, click the Import/Export Profile button in the Publish Settings, and choose Export from the Context menu. To import one, do the same thing, only choose Import.

> **TIP**
>
> All of your profile settings are stored in an XML file.

> **TIP**
>
> You can also delete and duplicate profiles by selecting the Duplicate Profile button and the Delete Profile button (the trash can icon) respectively.

To use a profile, choose it from the Current Profile pull-down menu at the top of the Publish Settings dialog box.

Summary

Flash MX 2004 can publish in a number of different formats to suit various needs. The two most widely used formats are the SWF format, which requires the Flash Player, and HTML, which creates the tags that allow an SWF file to be viewed in an HTML page.

Each file type that Flash can publish in can have more specific settings. HTML has a number of templates to choose from depending on the device a person is using or what the Flash application does, and can have Flash Player version detection included.

Once publish settings have been made, they can be saved in a profile. Profiles can be saved, exported, imported, duplicated, and deleted.

Sample Questions

1. Where do you set the Flash Player version that you want to detect?

   A. In the HTML tab of Publish Settings

   B. In the Flash tab of Publish Settings

   C. In the document properties

   D. On the Property Inspector

2. Which of the following formats do not have additional settings in the Publish Settings dialog box?

   A. JPEG

   B. PNG

   C. Macintosh Projector

   D. QuickTime

3. What tag is needed so that browsers using ActiveX controls can view Flash content?

   A. `<object>`

   B. `<body>`

   C. `<embed>`

   D. `<link>`

4. What Flash HTML template is used when you need to call external JavaScripts?

   A. Flash with HTTPS

   B. Flash with SCORM

   C. Flash with FSCOMMAND

   D. Flash with AICC

PART 8
Appendix

A Answers

Answers

Chapter 1

1. A and D   A site map is a flow chart of your SWF and how they relate to one another.

2. C   Monitor resolution determines the amount of screen space you have to work with.

3. A   Consistent, easy to understand navigation systems enhance your end user experience.

4. C   Since sound files tend to be large, using sound sparingly can keep your file size to a minimum.

Chapter 2

1. C   Since the content is stored outside of the SWF file, the SWF file is smaller and downloads quicker.

2. A and C   Static content is unable to be changed at runtime.

3. D   The `loadMovie()`; method of the MovieClip class is used to dynamically load JPEG and SWF files.

4. A   The LoadVars class is used to load variables in name-value pairs from text files on a server.

Chapter 3

1. C   The stacking order of grouped graphics and symbols in a
              layer is altered with Modify > Arrange. All graphics in a layer
              that are grouped with symbols occupy a stacking order.

2. D   The Property Inspector is used to change symbol instance
              properties, text properties, and editable graphic properties,
              to name a few items.

3. A   The Gripper is located on the title bar of panels in Flash,
              and looks like a series of faded out dots. Dragging on the
              gripper docks and undocks panels.

4. B and D   Fit in Window makes the entire Stage and its contents
              visible in the document window. The setting is found in the
              Edit Bar's zoom menu, as well as View > Magnification >
              Fit in Window.

Chapter 4

1. B and C   The Document Properties dialog box is retrieved using the
              Property Inspector, or by selecting Modify > Document.

2. D   The Button, Movie Clip, and Graphic symbols are most
              widely used to display graphics, among other things. The
              Font symbol is used to share fonts across SWFs.

3. A   Media Components come with Flash MX Professional 2004
              and are used to stream MP3 and FLV format files.

4. C   Stage width and height is set in the Document Properties
              dialog box.

Chapter 5

1. D   The Free Transform tool is used to control scale,
              skew, distort, and axis of rotation for visual assets. The
              Subselection tool is used to modify tangent handles.

2. A   Dragging tangent handles with the Subselection tool allows
              you to modify shapes.

3. B   Dragging with the Lasso tool draws freeform selection areas.

4. B   Using the Polystar tool, you can create polygon shapes or
              stars that have up to 32 sides.

Chapter 6

1. D   The Web 216 Color Palette is found in the Color Mixer panel, and is the default color palette used by Flash MX 2004.

2. A and B   ActionScript can be added to either objects or frames using the Behaviors panel, which has prebuilt scripts, or the Actions panel. You must write your own ActionScript using the Actions panel.

3. B   Alpha is a color option found in the Color Mixer panel, and can be modified to set transparency for editable objects.

4. C   The Components panel contains Version 2 components that come with Flash MX 2004 and Flash MX Professional 2004.

Chapter 7

1. B   The #p frame label designates individual frames and their contents as printable from the Flash Player.

2. C   ActionScript 2.0 is only supported by Flash Player Versions 6 and 7.

3. B   The Auto High quality setting disables anti-aliasing when SWF playback becomes slower than the frame rate for the SWF itself.

4. A and C   The printable area of the document is determined by the Stage size by default. However, a graphic can be placed in a frame labeled #b, and the size of the graphic in that frame will determine the printable area.

Chapter 8

1. A   The Grid is a layout tool in Flash. It is used to plan where items should be placed on the Stage.

2. A, C, and D   There is no option known as Don't Snap.

3. B and C   Guide layers do not publish with the SWF, and can contain graphics that assist in laying out a page.

4. B   Template categories are created in the Save as Template dialog box. Simply type a name for the category in the Category menu to create one.

Chapter 9

1. **B and D** The Info Panel and the Property Inspector both contain x and y boxes. Entering a new value in the boxes changes the position of a visual asset.

2. **C** The Linkage Properties dialog box contains the Export for Runtime Sharing option.

3. **A and B** The Insert New Layer button is located in the lower left corner of the Layers Pane in the Timeline. Right- or Control-clicking a layer name will pull up a context menu, where Insert New Layer is an option.

4. **B** The Select Unused Items option is available in the document library's Options menu.

Chapter 10

1. **A and C** Selecting the layer in the Timeline and clicking the Trashcan icon in the Layers pane deletes Layers. Layers can also be dragged into the Trashcan icon as well.

2. **B** Frame are used to display visual assets, and cannot be edited. In that way, frames act as placeholders for visual assets.

3. **B and C** Guide layers do not publish with the SWF file, and are largely used to trace or place graphics.

4. **A** Blank keyframes do not copy graphics from previous keyframes, and do not display visual information.

Chapter 11

1. **C** In vector art, the fewer corners a graphic has, the less file size it will occupy.

2. **C and D** When using `loadMovieNum()`, the upper left corners of the loaded JPEG and SWF files will always match the upper left corner of the first document loaded in the Flash Player.

3. B   Since vector artwork is defined using math, it doesn't lose resolution as it scales. Conversely, color information in a bitmap is affix to a grid, which expands as it scales up, causing resolution to be lost.

4. B and C   The target parameter of `MovieClipLoader.onLoad()` indicates the instance name of the Movie Clip that the external SWF or JPG image will load into.

Chapter 12

1. D   Changing an image's compression to "lossless" essentially converts it to a GIF or PNG image. This compression format only supports 256 colors, and therefore is not suited for images with complex color gradients or tonalities.

2. B   Macromedia Freehand MX supports multiple pages.

3. A and B   Switching bitmap images on the Stage with other images in the Library can be done using the Property Inspector by clicking on the Swap button. Likewise, you can use Modify > Bitmap > Swap Bitmap.

4. C   Open External Library allows you to open another FLA file's document library.

Chapter 13

1. A   The Color Swatches panel is where color palettes and swatches are added and managed.

2. A   The Subselection tool is used to move tangent handles to modify shapes.

3. B and C   Scale can be changed with the Transform panel, the Property Inspector, the Info Panel, or the Free Transform tool.

4. B   The Polystar tool requires at least 3 sides, and can have up to 32.

Chapter 14

1. **C**   Device fonts are retrieved from the end user's computer. If they don't have the font you've selected, it can be viewed, and the browser or system default will show.

2. **B**   The LoadVars class is used to retrieve variables from text files located on the server.

3. **C**   Toggling the Selectable button to its off position will prevent text from being copied and pasted from your application.

4. **B and C**   The text and htmlText properties of the TextField class can be used to assign input and dynamic textfields text using ActionScript.

Chapter 15

1. **C**   By default, SWF, XML, and text files can only be loaded into an SWF from the same domain that calls them.

2. **D**   By storing information in different external SWF files, file size for the main application is kept at a minimum.

3. **A**   The `loadMovie()` method of the MovieClip class loads SWF and JPEG images into Movie Clip instances.

4. **C**   A Movie Clip's depth is its stacking order in relation to other visual assets in an interface. Only one Movie Clip may occupy a depth at a time.

Chapter 16

1. **B**   The Alpha instance property of graphic symbols is found in the Color menu on the Property Inspector. Alpha controls transparency.

2. **A**   The Linkage Properties dialog box contains the Export for Runtime Sharing option.

3. **A and C**   The crosshair seen in symbol editing mode represents both the symbol's registration point and the absolute center of the symbol.

4. B and C   Assets can be converted to symbols using Modify > Convert to Symbol, dragging the assets into the library, using the keyboard shortcut F8, or right- or Control-clicking on the asset and choosing Convert to Symbol from the dialog box.

Chapter 17

1. B   Buttons instances must have instance names if they are to be controlled from an ActionScript located in a frame.

2. A   Event handlers contain instructions that must be executed when an event occurs.

3. D   Graphics in the Hit frame are not visible, and define the active area of a button. If a button only has a graphic in the Hit frame, it acts as a hotspot, since the button is invisible.

4. C   The Go to Web Page behavior is found in the Web category of the Behaviors panel. The behavior creates links from your document to a different Web page.

Chapter 18

1. D   The Load External Movieclip behavior is located in the Movie Clip category of the Behaviors panel. It's used to load external SWF files into target Movie Clips or levels of the Flash Player.

2. B and C   The _parent reference will always refer to the timeline that a movie clip instance is in. _root, on the other hand, always refers to the main document timeline.

3. B   Movie Clips have their own timeline which operates independently of the main document timeline.

4. C   The enterFrame event is broadcast continually based on the document's frame rate. If the frame rate is 12 frames per second, enterFrame events will occur roughly every 12th of a second.

Chapter 19

1. A   The Data property on the Property Inspector assigns data to a ComboBox. The Label property creates labels that the end user sees.

2. C   To change the appearance of all components in a document using the Styles API, use `_global.style.setStyle()`.

3. B   The `addItem()` method of the ComboBox adds information to the end of the ComboBox's pull-down list.

4. A   Restrict is a property of the TextArea component, not the Button component.

Chapter 20

1. B   Keyframes can be inserted using Insert > Timeline > Keyframe, the keyboard shortcut F6, or by right- or Control-clicking a frame and choosing Insert Keyframe from the Context menu.

2. C   Edit Multiple Frames is used to select entire animations across frames and move them to a different position.

3. B   Edit > Timeline > Remove Frames deletes a keyframe and all of its content.

4. A   To reverse the sequence of an animation, select Modify > Timeline > Reverse Frames with the frames selected.

Chapter 21

1. C   The instance property Alpha is in the Color pull-down menu on the Property Inspector. It can be used to fade symbols in and out in a motion tweened animation.

2. D   Buttons, Movie Clips, and Graphics symbols all can be motion tweened. Only symbols can be used with motion tweening.

3. B   Keyframes are used to set points in an animation where things like position or scale will change.

4. A   Edit > Timeline > Add Motion Guide is not an option in Flash.

Chapter 22

1. A and C   Only editable objects can be shape tweened. Grouped items and symbols cannot have shape tweens applied to them.

2. A   The Angular setting preserves sharp corners and straight lines during shape tweens.

3. D   Shape hints are used to control how shape tweens execute. Add them using Modify > Shape > Add Shape Hint.

4. C   Text must be converted to editable objects before being shape tweened. Breaking text apart twice converts fonts into shapes.

Chapter 23

1. C   All ActionScript written directly on a MovieClip instance must appear within an onClipEvent handler.

2. B   The onEnterFrame event will continue to execute whether or not a movie has stopped playing.

3. A   The functionName parameter is called every time the interval executes. The interval is the time in milliseconds between interval calls.

4. A   Intervals should be named so they can be cleared, since the intervals will continue to execute whether or not the movie stops playing. Intervals must be cleared using ActionScript.

Chapter 24

1. C   The "stream" sync setting forces your animation to keep up with the sound.

2. A and C   Media components are used to stream MP3 and FLV files from the server. Likewise, the loadSound() method of the Sound class can stream MP3s from the server.

3. D   The Edit Envelop contains edit handles that adjust the volume of a sound at key points in time.

4. B   The "start" sync setting will cause instances of the same sound to stop playing before the new one starts.

Chapter 25

1. A   The Media Display component does not have playback controls.

2. B   The FLV format is the only video format that can be streamed through the Flash player.

3. B   Instances of digital video require the timeline they are in to have at least as many frames as the video has in order for the video to play in its entirety.

4. A   The Stop behavior is found in the Embedded Video category of the Behaviors panel, and sends the playhead back to the first frame of the video after stopping playback.

Chapter 26

1. C   The Data category contains the Trigger behavior, which is used with the Data components that come with Flash MX Professional 2004.

2. C   The Roll Out event is triggered when the mouse cursor moves off of an object like a button.

3. B and C   The Web category is used to load Web pages into a browser. The Movieclip category contains options to control the position of the playhead in a Movie Clip's timeline.

4. B and D   Behaviors add ActionScript. ActionScript can be added to objects as well as keyframes.

Chapter 27

1. B   Keyboard shortcuts to add ActionScript are not shown by default. Selecting this option shows the keyboard shortcuts in the Categories pane.

2. A and C   Pinning the script will prevent your Actions pane from changing based on your selections on the Stage or in the Timeline.

3. A and D   Both of these options will open the ActionScript dictionary in the Help panel, and move you directly to the entry you've selected.

4. C   The Options menu of the Actions panel contains the Auto Formatting option.

Chapter 28

1. D   The _global keyword is used to create global variables and functions.

2. A and B   Dot syntax is used to refer to an object's location in the SWF, as well as access its methods and properties.

3. C   The ";" character instructs the Flash Player that the line of code it terminates is finished.

4. A   Methods are functions often defined in classes. Any function that has a name and is attached to an object is a method.

Chapter 29

1. B and D   When using device fonts with static text fields, the font is retrieved from the end user's computer, instead of being embedded in the SWF. Using a font symbol with runtime sharing embeds the font outline in one SWF, and then shares it across multiple SWFs.

2. C   When in the test mode of an SWF, View > Simulate download will mimic a modem speed. Modem speeds are set in View > Download Settings.

3. A   All sounds embedded in Flash are compressed as MP3 format unless otherwise specified.

4. C   Modify > Shape > Optimize contains settings that can smooth shapes to minimize file size.

Chapter 30

1. B   Flash detection is set in the HTML tab, but the version of the Flash Player the detection will use is set in the Flash tab.

2. C   Neither the Macintosh nor Windows projectors have any special settings in the Publish Settings dialog box, since they are compiled as executable applications.

3. A   The <object> tag is needed for browsers using ActiveX controllers to access plugins.

4. C   The FSCOMMAND template is used often to call JavaScripts embedded in a Web page.

INDEX

SYMBOLS

; (semicolon), 239
( ) (parentheses), 239

A

Accessibility panel, 49
Actions pane (Actions panel), 230, 234
Actions panel, 229–235
  about, 45
  adding Movie Clips from, 159–160
  looking up items in ActionScript
    dictionary, 232–233
  panes of, 229–230
  sample questions and answers, 235,
    278
  scripting interactivity for buttons,
    145, 147–149
  setting preferences in, 233–234
  using, 230–232
ActionScript animation, 195–200
  assets using, 195–196
  file size and, 196, 199
  onEnterFrame event, 196–197
  sample questions and answers,
    199–200, 277
  setInterval event, 198–199
ActionScripts, 237–244. *See also* Actions
  panel; ActionScript animation;
  behaviors
  adding Button symbol, 145–147, 150
  adding data to components,
    168–169, 171
  adding to object, 243, 244
  animating with, 195–200
  attaching to timeline, 242–243
  autoformatting, 233
  behaviors, 223–224
  changing movie clip properties, 156
  code hinting, 232

  concepts of, 238–240
  creating and adding Movie Clips,
    123, 158–160, 161
  dragging and dropping in script
    window, 230–231
  editing component appearance,
    169–170
  functions, 241–242, 244
  input text fields and, 113
  instance names in, 152
  linkage identifiers for sound, 204
  looking up items in dictionary,
    232–233
  nesting mouse events for
    buttons, 146
  Normal Mode, 223, 230
  object-oriented programming,
    237–238
  preferences for, 234
  preloader, 126–127
  printing frames from Flash
    Player, 54
  referring to main document and
    Movie Clip timelines in, 154
  sample questions and answers,
    244, 279
  scripting interactivity for buttons,
    147–149, 150
  setting media components from, 217
  syntax coloring, 234
  using with Flash Player, 53
  variables, 240–241, 244
Add New Profile button, 264
ADPCM compression, 249
AICC compliance, 51
Align panel, 41
animation, 175–180. *See also*
  ActionScript animation; motion
  tweening; shape tweening
  ActionScript, 195–200
  adding to Button symbols, 144

animation *(continued)*
determining frame rate, 178
fading in/out, 184
frame-by-frame, 175, 177
frames and keyframes, 176–178,
179–180
motion guides, 185–186, 187
motion tweening, 176, 179, 181–188
onion skin markers, 178–179
sample questions and answers,
180, 276
shape tweening, 176, 179, 189–194
sync setting for, 185
types of, 175–176, 179
answers. *See* sample questions and
answers
anti-aliasing text, 113, 118
applications. *See also* optimizing
applications; runtime sharing;
shared symbols
determining site dimensions, 5–6
optimal file size, 247–249, 253
optimizing with shared symbols, 252
structuring, 10–13
arrays, 169
assets
adding and deleting in Library,
71–72
animating with ActionScripts,
195–196
changing properties of in Info panel,
76–77
converting to symbols, 134
distinguishing editable, 189
Graphic symbols and, 133
motion tweening, 181
reusable, 133, 139
attachSound( ) method, 208–209
audience
end-user experience and
functionality, 4
web site design considerations
for, 3–4
author time sharing of symbols, 73–74
Auto Label option, 49
autoformatting ActionScripts, 233

B

bandwidth and compression profiles,
214–215
Bandwidth Profiler, 247–249, 253
behaviors
adding, 225–226
adding to Button symbol, 145–147
categories of, 224–225
comments in ActionScript, 224
defined, 223–224
embedded video, 218–219
removing, 219, 226
viewing in Actions panel, 229
Behaviors panel, 223–227. *See also*
behaviors
about, 45–46, 223, 226
adding behaviors, 225–226
adding Movie Clips from, 158–159
adding sounds to buttons, 205, 210
behaviors, 223–224
categories of behaviors, 224–225
embedded video behaviors, 218–219
events in, 226
loading JPG images from, 92, 93
removing behaviors, 219, 226
sample questions and answers,
227, 278
bitmap art. *See also* vector art
about, 87–88
breaking apart before using Lasso or
Magic Wand tools, 31
converting to vector art, 89
importing and editing, 97
optimizing, 251–252
roundtrip editing, 90, 251
sample questions and answers,
93–94, 272–273
selecting color from, 31
swapping bitmap images, 90, 93
blank keyframes, inserting, 176
breaking apart text, 111–112
breaking up projects, 121–129
dividing projects into multiple
SWFs, 121–122, 252
levels, 125–126
loading SWF into Movie Clips,
122–124, 128

breaking up projects *(continued)*
preloaders, 126–127, 128
runtime sharing, 127–128, 129
sample questions and answers,
129, 274
broadcaster/listener methodology for
event handlers, 171
browsers
loading sounds in cache, 12
options preventing resizing of SWF
files, 260
Brush tool, 34
built-in templates, 23–24
Button component, 166
Button symbols, 141–150. *See also*
buttons
about, 24, 141
ActionScripts for, 145–149, 150
adding behaviors to, 145–147
adding sound and animation to, 144
best practices for, 149
creating, 142–143
mouse events for buttons, 146
sample questions and answers,
150, 275
buttons. *See also* Button symbols
adding sound behavior to, 205, 210
enabling simple, 143
file size of complex, 144
mouse events for, 146
nesting mouse events for, 146
resizing, 166
scripting interactivity for, 145,
147–149

C

Categories pane (Actions panel),
229, 232–233, 234
Check Syntax button (Actions
pane), 232
child slides, 22
classes
function of in Flash, 237, 238, 243
MovieClipLoader, 92, 124, 127, 128
code hints for ActionScripts, 232
Code Inspector (Actions panel),
230, 234

color
assigning to vector art, 104–105, 107
creating custom, 42
custom color swatches, 106–107
finding RGB color percentages, 44
selecting in Color Swatches
panel, 43
text, 109
Color Mixer panel
assigning color to vector art with,
104–105, 107
setting stroke and fill color, 42
Color Picker, 32
Color Swatches panel, 42, 43
ComboBox component
adding data and labels to, 168
parameters for, 165–166
units of measurement for
parameters, 166
Commands pull-down menu, 50
Common Libraries, 51
Component Inspector
about, 46–47
adding data to components, 168–169
component parameters enabled
in, 168
editing components in, 165, 171
opening and using, 165
properties for video media
components, 217
components, 163–172. *See also specific*
components
about, 25–26, 163
adding data to, 168–169
changing appearance, 169–170
editing parameters, 165–168
handling events on, 170–171
sample questions and answers,
171–172, 276
types of, 163–164
Components panel, 46
compression
sound, 206, 249–250
video, 214–215, 251
configuring
documents for Flash Player version,
257–259
layer order, 257

configuring *(continued)*
  motion tweening, 182–183
constraining art, 104
content and structure in web design,
    9–14
  audience and web site content, 3
  dynamic content, 10, 13
  sample questions and answers,
      14, 269
  static content, 9–10, 13
  structuring applications, 10–13
Context menu, 53
control handles, 110
Convert to Symbol dialog box, 134
corner points, 30
createEmptyMovieClip action, 122
custom color swatches, 106–107

D

Data category, 224
data components, 163, 164, 171
Data Components panel, 46
data parameters, 166
data typing
  functions and, 242
  variables and, 240, 241
Debugger panel, 47
debugging files, 258
declaring variables, 240
default color palette, 104, 106
deleting
  frames and keyframes, 177
  motion guide layer, 186
  onEnterFrame event, 197
  profiles, 264
  shape hints, 192
  unused assets from Library, 72
depths of layers, 153
Design panels, 41–45
  Align panel, 41
  Color Mixer panel, 42, 104–105, 107
  Color Swatches panel, 43
  Info panel, 43–44, 76–77
  Scene panel, 44
  Transform panel, 45
Detect Flash Version button, 260

Development panels, 45–48. *See also*
    Actions panel; Behaviors panel
  Actions panel, 45
  Behaviors panel, 45–46
  Component Inspector, 46–47
  Components panel, 46
  Debugger panel, 47
  Output panel, 47–48
  Web Services panel, 48
device fonts, 249
Document Properties dialog box,
    about, 21
documents
  about, 21
  configuring for Flash Player version,
      257–259
  formats for publishing, 256–258
  organizing by scenes, 26
  saving as templates, 24
domains
  cross domain policies, 13
  loading SWFs to interface in
      same, 123
  locating text files and SWFs in
      same, 13
Down frames, 142, 149
downloading
  FLV formatter, 216
  simulating, 248
drawing tools, 32–34, 38
drawing vector art, 101–102, 107
duplicating profiles, 264
dynamic content, 10, 13
dynamic text
  device fonts with, 249
  using, 114–115, 119

E

Edit bar, features of, 19
Edit Envelop, 207
editing
  bitmap art, 97
  Graphic symbols, 136–137
  Movie Clips, 161
  multiple frames, 178
  roundtrip, 90, 251

editing *(continued)*
  templates, 64
  vector art, 102–104, 105–106, 107
Editing pane (Video Import
  Wizard), 214
embedding
  font outlines, 111, 114, 249
  video, 218–219, 251
enabled parameter, 168
enabling simple buttons, 143
enterFrame event, 160
EPS files, 99
Eraser tool, 37
event handlers
  adding ActionScripts to object with,
    243, 244
  broadcaster/listener methodology
    for, 171
  stopping sounds in, 209
  writing for components, 170–171
events
  behavior, 226
  button, 146
  enterFrame, 160
  Movie Clip, 157–158, 159
  onSoundComplete, 209, 210
  selecting video, 219
  setInterval, 198–199
  sound, 208
  synchronizing onEnterFrame and
    setInterval, 198
Eyedropper tool, 31

F

fading in/out, 184
file formats. *See also* SWF files
  bitmap, 97
  compatible import, 95–96
  FLA, 69, 73
  FLV, 163, 216, 219
  importing EPS and PDF, 99
  MOV, 214–215, 219
  PNG, 87, 88
  publish, 256–258
  sound, 203
  vector, 88
  video, 213

file size
  ActionScript animation, 196, 199
  application optimization and, 253
  complex button, 144
  component instance, 164
  dynamic content and, 10
  loading JPEG's dynamically and, 12
  scenes and, 44
  shape tweening and, 190
files. *See also* SWF files
  loading MP3, 12–13, 205–206,
    208–209
  loading text, 13
  protecting from importing, 258
  saving XML publish profiles, 264
  shared symbol, 72
fill
  changing, 105–106
  selecting color of, 43
Fill Transform tool, 105–106, 107
Find and Replace button (Actions
  pane), 231
Find button (Actions pane), 231
Fireworks. *See* Macromedia Fireworks
FLA files, 69, 73
Flash MX. *See* Macromedia Flash
  MX 2004
Flash Player, 53–59
  about, 19, 20, 53, 58–59
  Detect Flash Version button, 260
  detecting version of, 261, 263
  document compatibility with
    versions, 257–259
  magnification and playback, 58
  printing SWFs from, 54–56, 58
  quality settings for, 57, 59, 261
  sample questions and answers,
    59, 271
  settings, 53–54
  Window Modes for, 261
FLV (Flash Live Video) files, 163,
  216, 219
FLV formatter, 216
folders, layer, 81
Font symbols
  about, 25
  runtime sharing of, 249

Font symbols *(continued)*
    sample questions and answers,
        139–140, 274–275
    using, 138–139, 140
fonts
    appearance on Font menu, 139
    embedding font outlines, 111,
        114, 249
    optimizing, 249
    readable sizes of, 110
    scaling, 119
    selecting, 111
    working with, 118–119
form applications, 22–23
frame rates
    determining, 178
    enterFrame events and, 160
frame scripts, 171
frame-by-frame animation
    defined, 175
    inserting keyframes into, 177
frames. *See also* keyframes
    about, 180
    editing and deleting, 177
    frame rates, 160, 178
    function of, 177
    inserting keyframes, 83–84
    selecting for printing from
        timeline, 55
    stopping sounds in, 209
Free Transform tool, 35–36
functions, 241–242, 244

G

global variables, 241, 244
Grabber tool, 38
Graphic symbols
    about, 24, 133–134
    capabilities and limitations of,
        137–138
    creating, 134–135
    editing, 136–137
    instance properties of, 135
    sample questions and answers,
        139–140, 274–275
    using, 135–136

graphics. *See also* bitmap art; vector art
    Button symbol Hit state, 142
    file formats compatible with Flash,
        95–96
    images as static content, 9–10
    inherited with normal keyframes, 176
    positioning with rulers, 65, 68
    viewing only outlines of, 80
grids, 67, 68
guide layers, 66–67, 68, 81, 82–83
guides, 5–6, 66, 68

H

hiding
    all panels, 17
    layers, 80
    shape hints, 192
History panel, 50
Hit frames, 142, 149
HSB color mode, 42
HTML Alignment option, 262
HTML (Hypertext Markup Language)
    example of published code in,
        262–263
    publishing options in, 259–262, 264
    templates, 26, 259
HTML tab (Publish Settings dialog
    box), 57

I

images. *See* graphics
importing, 95–100
    about, 95–96, 99
    bitmap art, 97
    file formats compatible for, 95–96
    Fireworks PNGs, 98
    fonts without runtime sharing, 139
    options for artwork, 96
    PDF and EPS files, 99
    protecting files from, 258
    sample questions and answers,
        99–100, 271
    shared symbols, 73
    sounds, 203–204
    storyboard into guide layer, 67
    vector artwork, 88, 98

importing *(continued)*
  video, 213–215
Info panel
  about, 43–44
  changing properties of assets in, 76–77
Inkbottle tool, 37
input text, 112–113, 119
Insert Target Path dialog box, 231
inserting keyframes, 83–84, 176–177
instance names
  about, 152
  giving video, 215, 218
  paths and, 231
instances
  ActionScript animation of named, 197
  adding behaviors to, 225
isStreaming, loading sound with, 12

J

JPG images
  dynamically loading, 11–12
  progressive scan, 11, 91
  runtime, 91–92

K

keyboard shortcuts, 17, 233
keyframes
  about, 85, 179–180
  converting to normal frame, 177
  defined, 176
  editing and deleting, 177
  fading in/out, 184
  inserting, 83–84, 176–177
  onEnterFrame events for, 196
  removing, 84
  setting up shape tweening, 190–191
  shape hints in, 192
Kind column in Library, 164

L

Label component, 117–118
labels parameter, 166
Lasso tool, 31

layer folders, 81
Layer pane
  about, 18, 74–75, 77
  collapsing or closing, 75
layers, 79–86
  about, 79, 85
  adding and removing, 79–80
  adding from Layer pane, 75
  changing stacking order of, 18, 102
  configuring order of, 257
  depths, 153
  distributing letters to, 111
  drawing vector art in, 101–102
  loading SWF into Movie Clips, 123, 124
  locking and unlocking, 80, 186
  motion guide, 185–186, 187
  motion tweening and, 182
  organizing, 81
  renaming, 80
  sample questions and answers, 85–86, 272
  showing and hiding, 80
  timeline and, 83
  types of, 81–83
laying out projects, 63–69
  about, 68, 69
  creating templates, 63–64
  grids, 67, 68
  guide layers, 66–67, 68
  guides, 66, 68
  rulers, 65, 68
  sample questions and answers, 68–69, 271
leading, 110
levels, 125–126
Library
  adding assets to, 71–72
  art imported to, 96
  changing symbol properties on Stage and in, 137
  creating new symbols in, 72
  deleting unused assets from, 72
  Kind column in, 164
  sound imported to, 204
  symbol names on Stage and in, 152
  video imported to, 214
line numbering, 233

linkage identifiers for sound, 204
Load Sound from Library dialog
box, 205
loading
JPEG images dynamically, 11–12
sounds from MP3 files, 12–13,
205–206, 208–209
loadMovie() action, 7, 11, 91–92
loadMovieNum() action, 7, 11, 91–92
LoadVars object, 13
locking layers, 80, 186

M

Macromedia Fireworks
importing PNG files from, 98
roundtrip editing of bitmap art,
90, 251
Macromedia Flash MX 2004
ActionScript core concepts, 238–240
basic documents, 21
built-in templates, 23–24
components, 25–26
drawing vector art, 101–102, 107
editing bitmap using Fireworks, 90
form applications, 22–23
graphics file formats compatible
with, 95–96
HTML templates in, 26, 259
importing PNG files from
Fireworks, 98
PDF and EPS file imports, 99
Publish Settings dialog box, 26, 27
questions and answers on structure,
27–28, 270
saving documents as templates,
24, 27
scenes, 26, 27
slide presentations, 22
sound formats supported, 203
symbols of, 24, 27
tools, 29–39
versions of, 15
video file formats supported, 213
Magic Wand tool, 31
magnification and playback for Flash
Player, 58

Make Child Objects Accessible
option, 49
Make Movie Accessible option, 49
mask effects, 187
mask layers, 81, 82
master slides, 22
Media category, 224
media components
about, 163, 171
properties for video, 217
streaming MP3 files from server,
205–206
streaming video with, 216–218
Media Components panel, 46
Media.contentPath property, 218
Media Display component, 216, 218
Media Playback component, 205,
216, 218
menus
adding and removing commands on
Commands pull-down, 50
Context, 53
font appearance on Font, 139
navigating with tab-down, 7
pull-down, 16
Quality pull-down, 261
Synch pull-down, 208
methods
Flash, 237, 243
Movie Clip, 156–157
opening and closing with
parentheses, 239
minHeight parameter, 166, 168
minWidth parameter, 166, 167, 168
monitor resolution, 5
motion guides
dragging layers beneath, 82
using, 185–186, 187
motion tweening, 181–188
creating, 182–183
defined, 176, 179
mask effects, 187
motion guides, 185–186, 187
sample questions and answers,
188, 276
settings for, 185
symbols and, 181–182, 187
turning on, 183–184, 187

mouse events for buttons, 146
MOV video files, 214–215, 219
Movie Clip category, 224
Movie Clip symbol, 151–162. *See also*
    Movie Clips
    about, 24, 151, 161
    adding with ActionScripts,
        158–160, 161
    creating Movie Clips, 151–153
    editing, 153, 161
    events, 157–158
    importing video as, 215
    methods, 156–157
    Movie Clip timelines, 153–155
    properties, 155–156
    sample questions and answers,
        161–162, 275
    unable to stream, 216
Movie Clips. *See also* Movie Clip symbol
    about, 151
    adding behaviors to timelines, 159
    components, 25–26
    creating, 151–153
    editing, 153, 161
    events, 157–158, 159
    loading JPG into, 91–92
    loading SWFs into, 122–124, 128
    loading with `loadMovie()`
        action, 11
    `onEnterFrame` events for, 196–197
    progressive scan JPEGs replaced
        with contents of, 11
    timelines, 152, 153–155
Movie Explorer panel, 50–51, 76, 77
MovieClipLoader class, 92, 124,
    127, 128
MP3 files
    compressing, 250
    loading sounds from, 12–13,
        205–206, 208–209
    streaming from server, 205–206

N

`name-value` pairings for text, 115
naming. *See also* instance names
    form application screens, 23

naming *(continued)*
    Graphic symbols, 134
    instances, 152
    slides, 22
navigation design, 6–7
nested slides, 22
nested timelines, 85
nesting mouse events for buttons, 146
New Symbol dialog box, 73
normal keyframes, 176
Normal Mode, 223, 230
nudging art, 103

O

object-oriented programming (OOP),
    237–238
objects
    accessing properties, 239
    adding ActionScripts to, 243, 244
    controlling snapping, 30
    instantiating, 238–239
    shape tweening, 189–190
    Sound, 208–209, 210
`onEnterFrame` event, 196–197, 198
onion skin markers, 178–179
`onSoundComplete` method, 209, 210
OOP (object-oriented programming),
    237–238
Optimize Curves dialog box, 252
optimizing applications, 247–253
    Bandwidth Profiler, 247–249, 253
    bitmap images, 251–252
    fonts, 249
    loading SWFs, 7
    multiple SWFs, 252
    sample questions and answers,
        253, 279
    shared resources, 252
    sound, 249–250
    vector shapes, 252
    video, 251
organizational tools, 71–77. *See also*
        Library; tools
    Info panel, 43–44, 76–77
    Layer pane, 74–75
    Library, 71–72
    Movie Explorer, 50–51, 76, 77

organizational tools *(continued)*
    shared Libraries and symbols, 72–74
    Timeline, 75
organizing layers, 81
outlines
    embedding font, 111, 114, 249
    viewing graphics in layers as, 80
Output panel, 47–48
Over frames, 142, 149
Override Sound Settings dialog
    box, 259

P

page layout tools, 66, 68
Paint Bucket tool, 37
panels, 41–52. *See also* Actions panel;
    Behaviors panel; Component
    Inspector; Library; Property
    Inspector
    about, 16–17, 51
    Accessibility, 49
    Actions, 45
    Align, 41
    Behaviors, 45–46
    Color Mixer, 42, 104–105, 107
    Color Swatches, 42, 43
    Common Libraries, 51
    Component Inspector, 46–47
    Components, 46
    Data Components, 46
    Debugger, 47
    Design, 41–45
    Development, 45–48
    History, 50
    Info, 43–44, 76–77
    Library, 72, 77
    Movie Explorer, 50–51, 76, 77
    Output, 47–48
    sample questions and answers,
        52, 271
    saving layouts, 17
    Scene, 44
    showing and hiding all, 17
    Strings, 51
    Transform, 45
    Web Services, 48

parameters
    attachSound( ) method, 209
    Button component, 166
    ComboBox component, 165–166
    editing component, 171
    TextArea component, 167–168
_parent, 154
parentheses ( ), 239
password fields, 112
passwords
    adding for publishing options, 258
    setting for TextArea component, 167
paths
    converting text to, 111–112
    instance names required for, 231
PDF files, 99
Pen tool, 32–33
Pencil tool, 32
personalization and dynamic content, 10
playback in Flash Player, 58
playhead, 83, 204
PNG file format, 87, 88
points, 30
Polygon Lasso tool, 31
Polystar tool, 34
Preferences dialog box
    adjusting snap tolerance, 30
    turning on Start screen in, 16
preloaders, 126–127, 128
printing from Flash Player, 54–56, 58
progressive scan JPEGs, 11, 91
projects. *See* breaking up projects;
    laying out projects
properties
    accessing object, 239
    changing ActionScript movie
        clip, 156
    changing asset, 76–77
    editing symbol properties on Stage
        and in Library, 137
    Graphic symbol instance, 135
    settings for shape tweening,
        191, 193
    video media components, 217
Property Inspector
    about, 17
    adding data to components,
        168–169

Property Inspector *(continued)*
adjusting sound settings in, 206–207
changing component parameters in, 165, 171
Label component properties, 118
motion tween settings, 185
parameters not displayed for components, 166, 167
setting Movie Clip instance properties, 155–156
setting options for dynamic text, 114
sound events, 208
TextArea component properties, 116
TextInput component properties, 117
Publish Settings dialog box
about, 26, 27
file formats available in, 255–256
Flash tab of, 257
quality settings on HTML tab, 57
publishing, 255–265
configuring documents for Flash Player version, 257–259
example of published HTML code, 262–263
Flash Player detection, 261, 263
formats for document, 256–258
HTML options for, 259–262, 264
sample questions and answers, 265, 279
saving preferences in profile, 264

Q
Quality pull-down menu, 261
quality settings for Flash Player, 57, 59
QuickTime movies
compatiblity with Flash ActionScripts, 256
exporting Flash documents as, 214, 219
file formats compatible with, 96

R
raw compression, 249
Rectangle tool, 33
registration point on Stage, 135, 136

removing
behaviors, 219, 226
commands from menu, 50
frames or keyframes, 84
layers, 79–80
renaming layers, 80
resizing buttons, 166
reusable assets, 133, 139
reversing frames and keyframes, 178
RGB color mode, 42
rollovers, 7
_root, 154
roundtrip editing, 90, 251
rulers, 6, 65, 68
runtime sharing
Font symbols, 249
Font symbols in documents for, 138
runtime JPGs, 91–92
small project size with, 127–128, 129
symbols, 72–73, 137

S
sample questions and answers
Actions panel, 235, 278
ActionScript animation, 199–200, 277
ActionScripts, 244, 279
animation, 180, 276
Behaviors panel, 227, 278
bitmap art, 93–94, 272–273
breaking up projects, 129, 274
Button symbols, 150, 275
components, 171–172, 276
content and structure in web design, 14, 269
Flash MX 2004 structure, 27–28, 270
Flash Player, 59, 271
Graphic and Font symbols, 139–140, 274–275
on importing, 99–100, 271
layers, 85–86, 272
laying out projects, 68–69, 271
motion tweening, 188, 276
Movie Clip symbol, 161–162, 275
optimizing applications, 253, 279
organizational tools, 77–78, 272

sample questions and answers *(continued)*
  panels, 52, 271
  publishing, 265, 279
  sound, 210–211, 277
  text, 120, 274
  tools, 39, 270
  user interface, 20, 270
  vector art, 93–94, 108, 272–273
  video, 219–220, 278
  web site design, 8, 269
Sand Box rule, 123
Save as Template dialog box, 64
saving
  color swatches, 43
  grid settings, 67
  panel layouts, 17
  publish profiles, 264
scaling
  bitmap images, 252
  fonts, 119
Scene panel, 44
scenes, 26, 27
scope of variables, 240
SCORM compliance, 51
Screen inspector, 22
screens
  naming form applications, 23
  nesting, 23
scroll bars, 5, 6
scrubbing, 184
security and password fields, 112
selection tools, 29–31, 38
semicolon (;), 239
setInterval event, 198–199
settings for Flash Player, 53–54
setVolume() method, 209
shape hints, 192–193
shape tweening, 189–194
  defined, 176, 179
  editable objects for, 189–190
  property settings for, 191, 193
  sample questions and answers,
    193–194, 277
  setting up, 190–191
  shape hints, 192–193
shared symbols, 72–74
  author time sharing of symbols,
    73–74

shared symbols *(continued)*
  optimizing applications with, 252
  runtime sharing of symbols,
    72–73, 137
  using Font symbols in other
    documents, 138
Show Code Hint button, 232
showing
  all panels, 17
  layers, 80
Simulate Download, 248
site maps
  content of, 10–11
  making, 4–5
slide presentations, 22
slides
  master, child, and nested, 22
  naming, 22
snap ring, 29–30
Snap to Grid option, 67
Snap to Objects, 29–30, 186
Sorensen Spark codec, 214, 251
sound, 203–211
  adding to application, 203–206
  adding to Button symbols, 144
  adjusting sound settings,
    206–207
  compression types for, 249–250
  loading from MP3 files, 12–13,
    205–206, 208–209
  loading in browser cache, 12
  optimizing, 249–250
  sample questions and answers,
    210–211, 277
  setting for documents to be
    published, 259
  sound events, 208
  Sound object, 208–209, 210
  streaming MP3 files from server,
    205–206
Sound category, 225
Sound object, 208–209, 210
Sound Properties dialog box, 206
speech compression, 249, 250
stacking order
  depths and, 153
  layer, 18, 102

Stage
    about, 18
    determining print area by size of, 55
    finding X and Y positions on, 43–44
    importing art to, 96
    placing Button instance on, 143
    registration point on, 135, 136
    sound not visually represented
        on, 204
    swapping bitmap images on, 90, 93
    symbol names in Library and on, 152
    video imported to, 214
Start Dragging Movie Clip dialog
    box, 158
Start screen
    sections of, 15–16
    turning on, 16
static content
    defined, 9–10, 13
    dynamic vs., 10
#static frame label, 256
static text, 109–111, 119
status bars, 5, 6
Stop Dragging Movie Clip dialog
    box, 158
Streaming Graph (Bandwidth
    Profiler), 248
streaming MP3 files, 205–206
streaming video
    FLV format, 163, 216, 219
    media components for, 216–218
Strings panel, 51
stroke, 42, 43
Stroke color icon, 42
styles, 170
Subselection tool, 30
swapping bitmap images, 90, 93
SWF files
    checking file size of, 247–249, 253
    dividing projects into multiple,
        121–122
    dynamic content and, 13
    dynamic loading, 91–92
    loading into levels, 125–126
    loading into Movie Clips,
        122–124, 128
    loading performance of, 7

SWF files (continued)
    magnifying or controlling playback
        of, 58
    optimizing multiple, 252
    options preventing browser resizing
        of, 260
    page layout tools unpublished in
        final, 66, 68
    preventing embedded font outlines
        in, 111
    printing from Flash Player,
        54–56, 58
    quality settings for Flash Player,
        57, 59
    scenes vs., 44
    small content-based, 11
    specifying in Publish Settings dialog
        box, 26, 27
    viewing over web with Flash
        Player, 58
symbols
    Button, 24, 27, 141–150
    converting visual assets to, 72
    creating new symbols in Library
        panel, 72
    Font, 25, 138–140
    Graphic, 24, 27, 133–138
    motion tweening of, 181–182, 187
    Movie Clip, 24, 27, 151–162
    sharing, 72–74
sync setting for animation, 185
Synch pull-down menu (Property
    Inspector), 208
syntax coloring, 234

T

tab-down menus, 7
templates
    built-in, 23–24
    creating, 63–64
    editing, 64
    saving documents as, 24, 27, 64
text, 109–120
    breaking apart, 111–112
    color, 109
    dynamic, 114–115, 119
    fonts, 118–119

text *(continued)*
  input, 112–113, 119
  Label component, 117–118
  loading text files, 13
  name-value pairings for, 115
  sample questions and answers,
    120, 274
  static, 109–111, 119
  TextArea component, 116–117
  TextInput component, 117
  types of, 109
TextArea component
  adding data to, 168
  parameters of, 167–168
  properties of, 116–117
TextInput component, 117
theme organization, 26, 27
this keyword, 155
tick marks on rulers, 65
timelines
  about, 17–18, 75, 77, 83, 85
  adding behaviors to Movie Clip, 159
  adding video to, 215–216, 219
  attaching ActionScripts to, 242–243
  choosing frames to print from, 55
  frames and keyframes, 83–84
  Layer pane attached to, 75
  making movie clip timeline act like
    main document, 155
  Movie Clip, 152, 153–155
  movie clip inheritance of, 122
  nested, 85
  playhead, 83
toolbar design, 5, 6
tools, 29–39
  drawing, 32–34, 38
  Grabber, 38
  Info panel, 43–44, 76–77
  Layer pane, 74–75
  Library, 71–72
  Movie Explorer, 50–51, 76, 77
  organizational, 71–77
  page layout tools unpublished in
    final SWFs, 66, 68
  sample questions and answers, 39,
    77–78, 270, 272
  selection, 29–31, 38

tools *(continued)*
  shared Libraries and symbols, 72–74
  Timeline, 75
  transform, 35–37
  Zoom, 19, 38
Trace Bitmap dialog box, 89, 93
Transform panel, 45
transform tools, 35–37, 38
  Eraser tool, 37
  Free Transform tool, 35–36
  Inkbottle tool, 37
  Paint Bucket tool, 37
  types of, 35
Transparent Windowless mode, 261
turning on
  motion tweening, 183–184, 187
  Start screen, 16
tweening. *See* animation; motion
  tweening; shape tweening

U

UI (User Interface) components
  adding methods and properties to,
    169
  defined, 163
  reacting to events in event handlers,
    170–172
units of measurement
  ComboBox component
    parameter, 166
  grid and, 67
unlocking layers, 80
Up frames, 142, 143, 144, 149
usability, 4
user interface. *See also* Flash Player
  determining application site
    dimensions and, 5–6
  Edit bar, 19
  Flash Player, 19, 20
  Layer pane, 18
  panels and menus, 16–17
  Property Inspector, 17
  sample questions and answers,
    20, 270
  Stage, 18
  Start screen, 15–16

user interface *(continued)*
  timeline, 17–18
  versions of Flash MX 2004, 15
  Zoom tool, 19, 38
User Interface components. *See* UI
  (User Interface) components

V

Var field for dynamic text fields, 115
vector art, 101–108. *See also* bitmap art
  about, 88, 93
  assigning color with Color Mixer,
    104–105, 107
  changing appearance, 102–104
  converting bitmap art to, 89
  drawing in Flash, 101–102, 107
  importing, 88, 98
  making custom color swatches for,
    106–107
  modifying with Fill Transform tool,
    105–106, 107
  optimizing, 252
  sample questions and answers,
    93–94, 108, 272–273
  selecting with Lasso tool, 31
versions
  Detect Flash Version button, 260
  detecting Flash Player, 261, 263
  document compatibility with Flash
    Player, 257–259
  Flash MX 2004, 15
video, 213–220
  adding to timeline, 215–216, 219
  compression, 214–215, 251
  embedded behaviors, 218–219
  FLV format, 163, 216, 219
  giving instance names, 215, 218
  importing, 213–215
  media components for, 216–218

video *(continued)*
  optimizing, 251
  sample questions and answers,
    219–220, 278
Video Import Wizard, 214–215
View Layer as Outlines option (Layer
  Properties dialog box), 80
View Options button (Actions
  pane), 233

W

Wacom tablets, 34
Web 216 panel, 104, 106
Web category, 225
Web Services Connector component, 48
Web Services panel, 48
web site design
  considering audience in, 3–4
  content and structure in, 9–14
  designing navigation, 6–7, 8
  determining application site
    dimensions, 5–6, 8
  end-user experience and
    functionality, 4
  making site maps, 4–5, 8
  sample questions and answers, 8, 14,
    269
  usability, 4
Window Mode option, 261
word wrapping, 233

X

X and Y positions on Stage, 43–44

Z

Zoom tool, 19, 38
zooming in/out in Flash Player, 58

real world. real training. real results.

Get more done in less time with
Macromedia Training and Certification.

Two Types of Training

Roll up your sleeves and get right to work with authorized training
from Macromedia.

1. Classroom Training

   Learn from instructors thoroughly trained and certified by
   Macromedia. Courses are fast-paced and task-oriented to get
   you up and running quickly.

2. Online Training

   Get Macromedia training when you want with affordable, interactive online
   training from Macromedia University.

Stand Out from the Pack

Show your colleagues, employer, or prospective clients that you
have what it takes to effectively develop, deploy, and maintain dynamic
applications—become a Macromedia Certified Professional.

Learn More

For more information about authorized training or to find a class near you,
visit **www.macromedia.com/go/training1**